Symposium Series

PRIVATE AND PUBLIC ETHICS

PRIVATE AND PUBLIC ETHICS

TENSIONS BETWEEN
CONSCIENCE
AND
INSTITUTIONAL RESPONSIBILITY

DONALD G. JONES, EDITOR

THE EDWIN MELLEN PRESS
New York and Toronto

PRIVATE AND PUBLIC ETHICS
TENSIONS BETWEEN CONSCIENCE AND INSTITUTIONAL RESPONSIBILITY

Donald G. Jones, Editor

Cover design by

HISAYOSHI OTA

Library of Congress Cataloging Number 78-78184

ISBN 0-88946-993-8

CONTENTS

FOREWORD

This volume is designed as a classroom text and
as resource for scholars. It had its origins in the
annual Drew University Graduate Colloquium in 1977 where
new ground was broken in the exploration of issues cen-
tering around the theme, "Private and Public Ethics."
The effect of the three-day session was a re-casting
of traditional approaches to the problem from inter-
disciplinary perspectives including religious social
ethics, political science, history and sociology.

To give this collection focus and additional usefulness for teaching and scholarly research previously
published essays have been included.

The chapter by Reinhold Niebuhr, "Ethics and Power
Politics," is reprinted from *Reinhold Niebuhr on Politics,*
edited and compiled by Harry Davis and Robert Good by
permission of Charles Scribner's Sons. The chapter by
Ernest W. Lefever, "Morality Versus Moralism in Foreign
Policy," is reprinted from *Ethics and World Politics,*
edited by Ernest W. Lefever by permission of the author.
The chapter by Ernest W. Lefever, "The Trivialization of
Human Rights," is reprinted from the Winter 1978 issue
of *Policy Review* by permission of the author. The chapter by Charles Frankel, "Morality and U.S. Foreign Policy,"
is reprinted from the June 1975 issue of *Worldview* by
permission of *The Foreign Policy Association* where it was
originally published in Headline series #224. The chapter by Michael Walzer, "Political Action: The Problem
of Dirty Hands," is reprinted from the Winter 1973 issue
of *Philosophy and Public Affairs* by permission of Prince-

ton University Press.

This book is dedicated with profound respect to Dean Bard Thompson of the Drew Graduate School, whose scholarly concern, administrative professionalism, and personal generosity made possible the colloquium from whence came this book.

Donald G. Jones
The Drew Forest
Madison, New Jersey

1979

INTRODUCTION

THE TWO MORALITIES IN TENSION AND INTERACTION

DONALD G. JONES

I remember as a young boy hearing my father—a small businessman most of his life—teasingly ask the question of whether or not it is possible to be a morally upright person and at the same time be successful in business. Beneath my father's playful question—which I suspect was raised in part to needle my more innocent mother and in part to help a young son get prepared for the real world—was no doubt an acute awareness of the occasional difficulties in relating his private ideals to a commercial world of competing demands that sometimes strained his good conscience. Moreover, I now know it was a world in which one could not always count on the good will or moral integrity of certain venders, suppliers, buyers or lenders.

This book was engendered out of the kind of question my father once asked. Can one be utterly realistic about the way the world works; enter the worlds of business, politics, law, and various other institutional arrangements with the expectation of being successful and responsible; and at the same time be morally clean? It is an exceedingly practical question that conscientious people have struggled with for ages. And just because ordinary and extraordinary men and women of practical affairs have posed the question, scholars from the classical

Greek academy to the present have theorized and advised
regarding the problem: what ought to be the relation
between private and public ethics?

The authors of this volume respond to this question primarily as a problem of morality and politics in
recent American life and in the context of an ongoing
academic debate among political theorists, historians,
and ethicists. The point of departure for this book is
the well-known contention in Reinhold Niebuhr's introduction to *Moral Man and Immoral Society:*

> A sharp distinction must be drawn between the
> moral and social behavior of individuals and
> of social groups, national, racial, and econom-
> ic; and this distinction justifies and neces-
> sitates political policies which a purely indi-
> vidualistic ethic must always find embarrassing.

Niebuhr was not the first to draw a distinction between a purely private ethic and social ethics. Many
figures can be cited, but the most notable is Machiavelli
who, as we are reminded by Walzer in his essay, set out to
teach princes "how not to be good" in order to be good in
their calling. Machiavelli's problem is the problem of
any political leader who must consider techniques of
statecraft that do not always square with the barefoot
morality we learn as children in religious and family settings. For Machiavelli it is clear that responsible leaders must at times engage in deceit, use violence and break
promises. But the split between personal and social ethics
is not just a Machiavellian distinction. Martin Luther,
too, as noted by Edward Long in this volume, drew a sharp
distinction between what he called the earthly realm and
spiritual realm and specifically the coercive functions
of the state as opposed to expressions of love that are
possible and required between individuals. Max Weber
joins Machiavelli and Luther in affirming a legitimate

split between what is morally acceptable for individuals
and their private relations and what they must do in
their political commitments. From his essay, "Politics
as Vocation," we read:

> No ethics in the world can dodge the fact that
> in numerous instances the attainment of 'good'
> ends is bound to the fact that we must be will-
> ing to pay the price of using morally dubious
> means of at least dangerous ones—and facing
> the possibility of evil ramifications.

While a question may be raised as to why this statement is
not applicable to personal relations as well as to affairs
or state Weber, nevertheless, stands with those who
thought there was a distinction of importance.

In our day we are familiar with the political realist school identified with such names as Hans Morgenthau,
Arthur Schlesinger, George Kennan, Dean Acheson, Charles
Frankel and Earnest Lefever who affirm the clash between
personal morality and political reality. Kennan and Morgenthau are not sure that political behavior is even a
fit subject for moral judgment. Kennan warns against
asking too much of government:

> The process of government is a practical exercise,
> not a moral one. Primarily, it is a sorry chore,
> consisting of the application of restraint by man
> over man, a chore necessary because of man's ir-
> rational nature, his selfishness, his obstinacy,
> his tendency to violence.... A government is an
> agent, and no more than any agent may it attempt
> to be the conscience of its principles.

Morganthau in the same mode writes:

> The moral problem of politics is posed by the
> inescapable discrepancy between the commands of
> Christian teaching, of Christian ethics, and the
> requirements of political success. It is impos-
> sible, if I may put it in somewhat extreme and
> striking terms, to be a successful politician
> and a good Christian.

Others, such as Frankel and Lefever, want to apply

morality to politics, but in an indirect way. Frankel
contends that:

> The moral rules that apply to people performing
> complex social roles are not the same as those
> applying to people in their more intimate per-
> sonal or familial relations.

Schlesinger and Lefever are highly suspicious of politicians who apply personal moral criteria to the complexities
of foreign affairs and warn that such an approach can
easily degenerate into absolutism, intolerance and fanaticism.

   The problem of relating private and public ethics
has, however, not been just an academic matter for professors and former public officials to debate. It is an
issue of practical concern that has touched a nerve for
most Americans under the governance of President Nixon
and now Jimmy Carter. Watergate and post-Watergate morality as social facts of American life give to this book a
timely relevance.

   We are familiar with numerous statements from the
Nixon White House—many of them are pre-confessional—
that candidly admitted an approach to politics eschewing
the role of personal morality in favor of political realism.
The pursuit of national security, international stability
and the public good seemed to require a submergence of conventional moral standards in favor of political techniques
that ranged all the way from breaking and entering to tam-
pering with the Constitution. J. Fred Buzhardt, legal
counsel to Nixon, warned against excessive moralizing:
"Would you rather have a competent scoundrel or an honest
boob in the office?" Buzhardt, answering his own question
with unmistakeable emphasis, said: "You can make a strong
case that for a president in this day and this time you
don't want a babe in the woods. He's got to deal with

some pretty rough-and-tumble people." Many similar justifications were proffered by "Great Society" realists on behalf of Lyndon Johnson's approach to presidential leadership.

The question of whether a person can be a virtuous and at the same time, an effective president is not new to the American experience. Perry Leavell, in his fascinating case study of Theodore Roosevelt's approach to morality and politics quotes Amos Pinchot, who

> ...once advised Theodore Roosevelt that he would have to make a choice between two roles he wanted to perform. He could either be a great moral leader or he could be a great politician, but he could not be both.

Roosevelt disagreed because he clearly "enjoyed the role of moral authority" and also because he "believed that politics was a moral profession and that the presidency especially was a moral as well as political office." The presidency was, as he liked to put it, "a bully pulpit." Teddy Roosevelt's effort to conjoin personal morality with the "rough-and-tumble politics" of the progressive era is an interesting and cautionary story for contemporary Americans. Why? Because it touches a persistent antinomy in the American character. We have always thought of ourselves as being good in highly individualistic moral terms and at the same time prided ourselves on being pragmatic in knowing how to get things done.

But the story is more immediately relevant because Jimmy Carter is now our president. He is, of course, a pragmatic southern politician who came into the presidency with a record of "getting things done" and knowing how to get elected. On the other hand, Carter, perhaps more than any other president since Theodore Roosevelt and Woodrow Wilson, has tried to give moral leadership to the nation and make direct application of morality to international

politics. In the context of post-Watergate morality,
Carter has set himself apart from Watergate morality. He
does not accept as inevitable the choice between being
"a competent scoundrel" or "an honest boob." And like
Roosevelt, he has rejected the alternative of being
either a "great moral leader" or "a great politician."

On the campaign trail we were reminded time and
time again that he would not lie to us and that political
decision-making would be candid and open so that we, the
governed, might freely consent or dissent. The need to
restore decency, goodness, and compassion to our domestic
and foreign policy was a central theme of the campaign.
For Jimmy Carter, unlike the realists, there is no split
between absolute moral values and the necessities of
statecraft. In his Notre Dame address on May 22, 1977, he
expressed his desire to connect foreign policy formation
to "the essential character" and "historical vision of
America." The touchstone of his politics was expressed
straightforwardly: "Our policy is rooted in our moral
values, which never change.... Our policy is designed to
serve mankind."

Ernest Lefever in his essay, "The Trivialization of
Human Rights," pungently attacks the Carter approach to
international politics. Indeed, all of the essays in the
first section represent in one way or another a criticism
of the Carter approach in reconciling morality with politics. But other authors in this volume, while not dealing directly with Carter, are at least much more sympathetic with the effort to find points of interaction between private and public ethics. Hence, these revisionist
scholars lend theoretical support and concrete advice to
President Carter and other political practitioners who
seriously want to know how to relate basic moral values
to political reality.

Edward Long is convinced that such personal virtues as honesty, loyalty, and kindness can be profound resources for good governance and calls for recognizing and culti- vating the logical extension of these virtues into the public sphere of policy formation. His essay is a direct challenge to a "realist" tradition that denies the logic of the extension and looks for radically different virtues.

David Little, in his revisionist essay, rejects the sharp Niebuhrian distinctions between the morality of in- dividuals and groups and the either/or tension between conscience and institutional responsibility implied in the sub-title of this book. Treating the "functions and jurisdiction," the "content" and "procedures" of con- science, Little describes conscience as a kind of tribun- al within that functions to settle debates among a tangle of competing moral claims in both private and public spheres. As a court that selects priorities of value and assesses competing claims of interest, conscience then assigns blame or credit. Focusing on the procedures of conscience, which he calls "conscientiousness," he notes that the failure of Watergate was not so much a failure of conscience in terms of value content, but rather of conscientiousness, or the way values were related to pub- lic affairs.

Edward Weisband and Thomas Franck, in analyzing the role of ethical autonomy in Congress, believe that private morality can be a leaven and corrective on "the hill," but that certain institutional changes ought to be made so that the high personal cost of being conscientious is reduced. According to them, Watergate and other govern- mental misdeeds were primarily problems of institutional deficiencies.

Elizabeth Janeway and Karen Brown argue from femi- nist perspectives that in order to make comprehensive sense out of our topic we need greater clarity about the actual meaning of the terms private and public. They insist that perceptions of the private and public sectors are different for minorities; especially women in a male dominated society. Only by understanding this can there be a grasp of the issue that is relevant to minorities as well as the power elite.

Frank Wolf and Richard Rubenstein give us hard ethical cases in the context of bureaucratic systems. In a fashion similar to Weisband and Franck they illustrate the difficulties in being a moral hero where structures and conditioning for moral accountability are almost totally absent. With the exception of Rubenstein, they all point in the direction of structural strategies that would make ethical autonomy a greater possibility.

The authors in the last three sections of the book, for the most part, emphasize continuities between personal and social ethics. Their prescriptions for enhancing the social and political roles of personal ethics focus on procedures of ethical decision-making; institutional restructuring; and fresh assessments of what we mean when we use the term, "private and public ethics." The prophetic keynote in these reflections is struck by Professor Long, who proclaims:

> The essence of creative statesmanship in our time will be to conceive of more and more ways to institutionalize the link between public and private morality. The blueprint will come in the next fifty years.

The wisdom and feasibility of that pronouncement is given credence by the headway this volume makes in placing the issue of private and public ethics in interactional rather than antithetical terms.

PART I

PRIVATE AND PUBLIC ETHICS IN DISTINCTION

REALIST PERSPECTIVES

Ethics and Power Politics

ETHICS AND POWER POLITICS

REINHOLD NIEBUHR

I. MORAL MAN AND IMMORAL SOCIETY

A sharp distinction must be drawn between the moral
and social behavior of individuals and of social groups,
national, racial, and economic; and this distinction jus-
tifies and necessitates political policies which a purely
individualistic ethic must always find embarrassing. When
we speak of "moral man and immoral society" we state the
intended distinction too unqualifiedly, but it is nevertheless a fair indication of the argument to which the
following pages are devoted.

Individual men may be moral in the sense that they
are able to consider interests other than their own in
determining problems of conduct, and are capable, on occasion, of preferring the advantages of others to their
own. They are endowed by nature with a measure of sympathy and consideration for their kind, the breadth of
which may be extended by an astute social pedagogy. Their
rational faculty prompts them to a sense of justice which
educational discipline may refine and purge of egoistic
elements until they are able to view a social situation
in which their own interests are involved with a fair
measure of objectivity.

But all these achievements are more difficult, if
not impossible, for human societies and social groups.
In every human group there is less reason to guide and
check impulse, less capacity for self-transcendence, less

ability to comprehend the needs of others and therefore
more unrestrained egoism than the individuals who compose the group reveal in their personal relationships.

The inferiority of the morality of groups to that
of individuals is due in part to the difficulty of establishing a rational social force which is powerful
enough to cope with the natural impulses by which society achieves its cohesion; but in part it is merely the
revelation of a collective egoism, compounded of the
egoistic impulses of individuals, which achieve a more
vivid expression and a more cumulative effect when they
are united in a common impulse than when they express
themselves separately and discretely.[1]

Even when the individual is prompted to give himself in devotion to a cause or community, this egoism
may still be evidenced. In the family for instance, it
may express itself in part within the family circle and
in part through the family. Devotion to the family does
not exclude the possibility of an autocratic relationship toward it. The tyranny of the husband and father
in the family has yielded only very slowly to the principle of mutuality.

But even if perfect mutuality should be attained
within the family circle, the family may still remain a
means of self-aggrandizement. The solicitous father
wants his wife and children to have all possible advantages. His greater solicitude for them than for others
grows naturally out of the sympathy which intimate relations prompt. But it is also a projection of his own
ego. Families may, in fact, be used to advertise a husband's and father's success and prosperity. The truth
is that every immediate loyalty is a potential danger
to higher and more inclusive loyalties, and an oppor-

tunity for the expression of a sublimated egoism.

The larger social groups above the family, communities, classes, races and nations, all present men with
the same twofold opportunity for self-denial and self-
aggrandizement; and both possibilities are usually ex-
ploited. Patriotism is a high form of altruism, when
compared with lesser and more parochial loyalties; but
from an absolute perspective it is simply another form
of selfishness. The larger the group the more certainly will it express itself selfishly in the total human
community. It will be more powerful and therefore more
able to defy any social restraints which might be de-
vised. It will also be less subject to internal moral
restraints. The larger the group the more difficult it
is to achieve a common mind and purpose and the more inevitably will it be unified by momentary impulses and
immediate and unreflective purposes. The increasing
size of the group increases the difficulties of achieving a group   self-consciousness, except as it comes
in conflict with other groups and is unified by perils
and passions of war. It is a rather pathetic aspect of
human social life that conflict is a seemingly unavoidable prerequisite of group solidarity.

Furthermore the greater the strength and the wider
the dominion of a community, the more will it seem to
represent universal values from the perspective of the
individual. There is something to be said for Treitschke's logic, which made the nation the ultimate community of significant loyalty, on the ground that smaller
units were too small to deserve, and larger units too
vague and ephemeral to be able to exact, man's supreme
loyalty. Treitschke was wrong only in glorying in this
moral difficulty.

Thus, try as he will, man seems incapable of forming an international community with power and prestige
great enough to bring social restraint upon collective
egoism. He has not even succeeded in disciplining anti-
social group egoism within the nation. The very existence of human sympathies has therefore resulted in the
creation of larger units of conflict without abolishing
conflict. So civilization has become a device for dele-
gating the vices of individuals to larger and larger
communities. [2]

Unquestionably there is this alloy of projected
self-interest in patriotic altruism. The man in the
street, with his lust for power and prestige thwarted by
his own limitations and the necessities of social life,
projects his ego upon his nation and indulges his an-
archic lusts vicariously. So the nation is at one and
the same time a check upon, and a final vent for, the
expression of individual egoism.

The combination of unselfishness and vicarious
selfishness in the individual thus gives a tremendous
force to group egoism, which neither religious nor rational idealism can ever completely check. [3]

Our contemporary culture fails to realize the
power, extent and persistence of group egoism in human
relations. It may be possible, though it is never easy,
to establish just relations between individuals within a
group purely by moral and rational suasion and accommodation. In inter-group relations this is practically an
impossibility. The relations between groups must therefore always be predominantly political rather than ethical; that is, they will be determined by the proportion
of power which each group possesses at least as much as
by any rational and moral appraisal of the comparative

needs and claims of each group.[4]

II. THE PRIDE OF GROUPS AND NATIONS

Strictly speaking, only individuals are moral agents, and group pride is therefore merely an aspect of the pride and arrogance of individuals. It is the fruit of the undue claims which they make for their various social groups. Nevertheless, as we have seen, some distinctions must be made between the collective behavior of men and their individual attitudes. This is necessary in part because group pride, though having its source in individual attitudes, actually achieves a certain authority over the individual and results in unconditioned demands by the group upon the individual. Whenever the group develops organs of will, as in the apparatus of the state, it seems to the individual to have become an independent center of moral life. He will be inclined to bow to its pretensions and to acquiesce in its claims of authority, even when these do not coincide with his moral scruples or inclinations.

A distinction between group pride and the egoism of individuals is necessary, furthermore, because the pretensions and claims of a collective or social self exceed those of the individual ego. The group is more arrogant, hypocritical, self-centered and more ruthless in the pursuit of its ends than the individual.

The egoism of racial, national and socio-economic groups is most consistently expressed by the national state.[5] The modern nation is the human group of strongest social cohesion, of most undisputed central authority and of most clearly defined membership. The church may have challenged its pre-eminence in the Middle Ages, and the

economic class may compete with it for the loyalty of men
in our own day; yet it remains, as it has been since the
seventeenth century, the most absolute of all human associations.

What is the basis and reason for the cohesive power
and selfishness of nations? If we begin with what is
least important or least distinctive of national attitudes,
it must be noted that nations do not have the direct con-
tact with other national communities which is prerequisite
to the recognition of common interest. They know the problems of other peoples only indirectly and at second hand.
Since both sympathy and justice depend to a large degree
upon the perception of need, which makes sympathy flow,
and upon the understanding of competing interests which
must be resolved, it is obvious that human communities
have greater difficulty than individuals in achieving ethical relationships.[6]

More importantly, loyalty to the nation state is
strengthened by the fact that the state gives the nation-
alist sentiments and collective impulses of the nation
such instruments of power and presents the imagination of
individuals with such obvious symbols of its discrete collective identity that the national state is most able to
make absolute claims for itself, to enforce those claims
by power, and to give them plausibility and credibility
by the majesty and panoply of its apparatus. In the life
of every political group, whether nation or empire, which
articulates itself through the instrument of a state,
obedience is prompted by the fear of power on the one
hand and by reverence for majesty on the other. The temptation to idolatry is implicit in the state's majesty.
Rationalists, with their simple ideas of government rest-
ing purely upon the consent of the governed, have never

appreciated to what degree religious reverence for majesty is implicit in this consent.[7]

In other words the nation is a corporate unity,
held together much more by force and emotion than by mind.
Since there can be no ethical action without self-criticism, and no self-criticism without the rational capacity
of self-transcendence, it is natural that national attitudes can hardly approximate the ethical. Even those
tendencies toward self-criticism in a nation which do express themselves are usually thwarted by the governing
classes and by a certain instinct for unity in society
itself. For self-criticism is a kind of inner disunity,
which the feeble mind of a nation finds difficulty in
distinguishing from dangerous forms of inner conflict.
So nations crucify their moral rebels with their criminals
upon the same Golgotha, not being able to distinguish between the moral idealism which surpasses, and the anti-
social conduct which falls below that moral mediocrity on
the level of which every society unifies its life. While
critical loyalty toward a community is not impossible, it
is not easily achieved.[8]

Perhaps the most significant moral characteristic
of the nation is its hypocrisy. Self-deception and hypocrisy is an unvarying element in the moral life of all human beings. It is the tribute which immorality pays to
morality; or rather the device by which the lesser self
gains the consent of the larger self to indulge in impulses and ventures which the rational self can approve
only when they are disguised. One can never be quite certain whether the disguise is meant only for the eye of
the external observer or whether, as may usually be the
case, it deceives the self. Naturally this defect in individuals becomes more apparent in the less moral life of

nations. Yet it might be supposed that nations, of whom
so much less is expected, would not be under the necessity
of making moral pretensions for their actions. There was
probably a time when they were under no such necessity.
Their hypocrisy is both a tribute to the growing rationality of man and a proof of the ease with which rational demands may be circumvented. The dishonesty of nations is
a necessity of political policy if the nation is to gain
the full benefit of its double claim upon the loyalty and
devotion of the individual, as his own special and unique
community and as a community which embodies universal values and ideals.[9]

Sinful pride and idolatrous pretensions are thus an
inevitable concomitant of the cohesion of large political
groups. This is why it is impossible to regard the lower
morality of groups, in comparison with that of individuals,
as the consequence of the inertia of "nature" against the
higher demands of individual reason. It is true of course
that the group possesses only an inchoate "mind" and that
its organs of self-transcendence and self-criticism are
very unstable and ephemeral compared to its organs of will.
A shifting and unstable "prophetic minority" is the instrument of this self-transcendence, while the state is the
organ of the group's will.

Still, the egoism of nations must be understood as a
characteristic of the spiritual life, and not merely an expression of the natural impulse of survival. The most con-
clusive proof of this proposition is the fact that its most
typical expressions are the lust-for-power; pride (compris-
ing considerations of prestige and "honor"); contempt toward the other; hypocrisy (the inevitable pretension of
conforming to a higher norm than self-interest); and finally the claim of moral autonomy by which the self-deifica-
tion of the social group is made explicit by its presenta-

tion of itself as the source and end of existence.

It cannot be denied that the instinct of survival is involved in all these spiritual manifestations of egoism; but that is equally true of individual life. Every human self-assertion, whether individual or collective, is therefore involved in the inconsistency of claiming, on the one hand, that it is justified by the primary right of survival and, on the other hand, that it is the bearer of interests and values larger than its own and that these more inclusive values are the justification of its conflict with competing social wills. No modern nation can ever quite make up its mind whether to insist that its struggle is a fight for survival or a selfless effort to maintain transcendent and universal values.

The nation to which the individual belongs transcends the individual life to such a degree in power, majesty, and pseudo-immortality that the claim of unconditioned value can be made for it with a degree of plausibility. The significance of this claim is that through it human pride and self-assertion reach their ultimate form and seek to break all bounds of finiteness. The nation pretends to be God. A certain ambiguity which envelops this claim has already been noted. Collective egoism does indeed offer the individual an opportunity to lose himself in a larger whole; but it also offers him possibilities of self-aggrandizement beside which mere individual pretensions are implausible and incredible. Individuals "join to set up a god whom each of them then severally and tacitly identifies with himself, to swell the chorus of praise which each then severally and tacitly arrogates to himself."[10] [11]

Since nations constitute an extreme case of the sinful pride of groups, perhaps the best that can be expected

of them is that they should justify their hypocrisies by
a slight measure of real international achievement, and
learn how to do justice to wider interests than their own,
while they pursue their own.[12]

The special "immorality of groups" helps, incidentally, to explain the recalcitrance and stubbornness of the
man of power. This recalcitrance is not simply due to personal defects or self-deceptions. The real cause lies in
the representative character of the oligarch. He expresses not only his own impulses but those of a social group,
a class or a nation. He is the incarnation of a *raison
d'état*.[13]

It may be that group pride represents a particular
temptation to individuals who suffer from specific forms
of the sense of inferiority. The relation of modern fascist nationalism to the insecurity and sense of inferiority
of the lower middle classes is therefore significant. But
it hardly can be denied that extravagant forms of modern
nationalism only accentuate a general characteristic of
group life and collective egoism; and that specific forms
of inferiority feeling, for which this pride compensates,
only accentuate the general sense of inferiority from which
all men suffer.

Collective pride is thus man's last, and in some respects most pathetic, effort to deny the determinate and
contingent character of his existence. The very essence
of human sin is in it. It can hardly be surprising that
this form of human sin is also most fruitful of human guilt,
that is of objective social and historical evil. In its
whole range from pride of family to pride of nation, collective egoism and group pride are a more pregnant source
of injustice and conflict than purely individual pride.

The pride of nations is, of course, not wholly

spurious. Their claim to embody values which transcend
their mere existence has foundations in fact. It is the
very character of human life, whether individual or collective, that it incarnates values which transcend its immediate interests. A particular nation or group of nations
may actually be the bearers of a "democratic civilization"
or of a communist one. Men are not animals and never fight
merely for existence, because they do not have a mere animal existence.

But the real pride of nations consists in the tendency to make unconditioned claims for their conditioned values. The unconditioned character of these claims has two
aspects. The nation claims a more absolute devotion to
values which transcend its life than the facts warrant;
and it regards the values to which it is loyal as more absolute than they really are.

The fact that human pride insinuates itself into the
struggle of the Christian religion against the pride and
self-will of nations merely proves how easily the pride of
men can avail itself of the very instruments intended to
mitigate it. The church, as well as the state, can become
the vehicle of collective egoism. Every truth can be made
the servant of sinful arrogance, including the prophetic
truth that all men fall short of the truth. This particular truth can come to mean that, since all men fall short
of the truth and since the church is a repository of a revelation which transcends the finiteness and sinfulness of men,
it therefore has the absolute truth which other men lack.[14]

Human vitalities, then, express themselves from collective as well as individual centers, and both may be end-
lessly elaborated. Any premature definition of what the
limits of these elaborations ought to be inevitably destroys
and suppresses legitimate forms of life and culture. But

this capacity for human creativity also involves the destructive capacity of human vitality. Vitalities may be
developed inordinately. Various forms of vitality may
come in conflict with one another, or one form may illegi-
timately suppress another. The tension among the various
forms may threaten or destroy the harmony and peace of the
community.[15]

The limitations of the human imagination, the easy
subservience of reason to prejudice and passion, and the
consequent persistence of irrational egoism, particularly
in group behavior, make social conflict an inevitability
in human history to its very end.[16]

III. THE PERENNIAL STRUGGLE FOR POWER

All communal life represents a field of vitality,
elaborated in many forms which are related to each other
in terms of both mutual support and of potential conflict.[17]
Yet communal life is most accurately analyzed, not as Aristotle and Stoic rationalists analyze it—as merely an order of vitalities which is prevented from falling into chaos
by its conformity to particular structures which reason may
ascertain. It should be recognized rather as a vast series
of encounters among human selves and their interests. The
encounters are indeed regularized into patterns and stabilities, and the habit of conformity to these stabilities
mitigates the encounters. But these social patterns are
not "eternal laws" and they cannot hide the essential character of social life as an encounter between myself and
another, whether individually or collectively, and whether
the encounter is creative or destructive, cooperative or
competitive. Political life, that is, has to deal primarily with human selves and not with either mind, on the one

hand, or sub-rational vitalities, on the other.[18]

The perennial importance of power in social organization is based upon two characteristics of these selves.
The one is the unity of vitality and reason, of body and
soul. The other is the force of human sin, the persistent
tendency to regard ourselves as more important than anyone
else and to view a common problem from the standpoint of
our own interest. The second characteristic is so stubborn that mere moral or rational suasion does not suffice
to restrain one person from taking advantage of another.
Legal authority may be more sufficing; but there is no
legal authority which does not imply sanctions or the
threat of coercive action against recalcitrance. The first
characteristic, the unity of vitality and reason in human
nature, guarantees that egoistic purposes will be pursued
with all vital resources which an individual or collective
will may control.[19]

Consequently the perfect accord between life and life
is constantly spoiled by the inordinate concern of each
life for its own weal, especially as expressed in the corporate egoism of contending groups. Human society is full
of the friction of cross purposes.[20] Indeed it is in a per-
petual state of war.[21]

Disputes may of course be composed and conflicts arbitrated. The conflict of interest and passion among races,
classes, nations, and individuals can be arbitrated into a
tolerable harmony by wise statesmanship and astute methods
of adjudication.[22] Conscience may appeal to conscience and reason to
reason. There are in fact no conflicts in which these appeals are not made, even when the conflict has become physical. But in every conflict of interest the possibility
of marshalling every possible resource on either side is
implied. Most human conflicts are composed, or subdued,

by a superior authority and power, without an overt appeal
to force or without the actual use of force, either violent
or nonviolent. But the calculation of available resources
on either side is as determinative in settling the outcome
of the struggle as more purely rational or moral considerations.[23]

The contest of power, then, is the heart of political
life.[24] To understand politics is to recognize the elements
of power which underlie all social structures—the play of
power which may be obscured or submerged, but which cannot
be eliminated.[25] The peace of the world is always, as St.
Augustine observed, something of an armistice between op-
posing factions. There is no perfect harmony in history,
no peace within the limits of understanding.[26]

IV. TYPES OF POWER AND THEIR RELATIONSHIP

The spiritual and physical faculties of man are able,
in their unity and interrelation, to create an endless variety of types and combinations of power, from that of pure
reason to that of pure physical force. It is hardly necessary at this point to prove that reason may be the instrument of the ego in advancing its claims against another.
When it is so used it is a "power" which supports the
claims of one life against another. The shrewd do take
advantage of the simple. A rational solution of a conflict
may be a very unjust one, if the more robust has "over-
powered" the weaker intellect.

But there are other spiritual faculties which may
serve the same purpose. One man may keep another enslaved
purely by "soul" force. Such soul force may consist of
spiritual vitalities of various kinds, mental and emotional
energy, the possession or the pretension of virtue, the

prestige of an heroic life, or of a gentle birth. It follows that Gandhi's identification of "soul force" with non-
egoistic motives and "body force" with egoistic ones, is
almost completely mistaken. The type of power used by the
will to effect its purposes does not determine the quality
of the purpose or motive.

Pure physical force is always a last resort in individual relations. It is determinative in these relations
only on primitive levels. All civilized relations are
governed more by spiritual than by physical facets of power.
It is significant that they are not, for that reason, naturally more just.

The forms of power which are developed collectively
display an even wider variety of types. On the whole, social power rests upon differentiations of social function.
The soldier is the bearer of physical force in advanced societies, not because he is physically strong, but because
he has the instruments, and masters the techniques, of physical conflict. The priest has social power (especially po-
tent in the organization of early empires) because he medi-
ates the authority of some ultimate majesty and endows the
political authority of a given oligarchy with this sanctity.
The ownership and the control of property and economic process represents partly physical and partly spiritual power.
It is physical insofar as the wealth created by the economic
process is physical. It is spiritual insofar as the right
to use and control this physical force is derived from law,
custom, the prestige of function and other similar considerations.

The modern belief that economic power is the most
basic form, and that all other forms are derived from it,
is erroneous. The first landlords were soldiers and priests
who used military and religious forms of social power to

possess and to acquire land. Economic power, before the
modern period, was derivative rather than primary. It was
used to enhance the comforts of the oligarchs of society
and to insure the perpetuation of their social eminence
from generation to generation. But it did not give them
their initial eminence. In modern Germany, Nazi political
oligarchs transmuted political power into economic power.
In the bourgeois period economic power did tend to become
more fundamental and to bend other forms to its purposes.
In democratic societies it was, however, always under some
restraint from the more widely diffused political power of
the common man, inhering in the universal right of suffrage.

It has been an error in both liberal and Marxist social interpretations to identify ownership with economic
power. The control and manipulation of economic process
is also a form of economic power. It gives workers minimal
power resources to set against the power of ownership; and
the managers of economic process are acquiring an even
larger share of power. James Burnham's *The Managerial Revolution* is a one-sided correction of the error of identi-
fying ownership with economic power too simply. The error
contributes to the political miscalculations of Marxism.
For when it abolishes economic ownership it may merely
merge both economic and political power in the hands of an
oligarchy which controls both political and economic processes.

Political power deserves to be placed in a special
category, because it rests upon the ability to use and manipulate other forms of social power for the particular
purpose of organizing and dominating the community.[27] The
political power in any society is held by the group which
commands the most significant type of non-political power,
whether it be military prowess, priestly prestige, economic

ownership or the ability to manipulate the technical processes of the community.[28] The political oligarchy usually possesses at least two forms of significant social
power. In all early empires these two forms were the
priestly and the military power, which were either merged
in one class, or combined through intimate collaboration
between the military and the priestly classes.

Modern democracies tend toward a more equal justice
partly because they have divorced political power from
special social functions. They endowed all men with a
measure of it by giving them the right to review the policies of their leaders. This democratic principle does not
obviate the formation of oligarchies in society; but it
places a check upon their formation, and upon the exercise
of their power. It must be observed, however, that the
tyrannical oligarchy of fascism arrived at its eminence
by the primary use of political power (the demagogic manipulation of the masses) and then gradually acquired the
other forms of power: the control of economic process, the
pretension of religious sanctity, and the control of, or
collaboration with, military power.

The shifting interrelations of various types of power
in human society are determined by a wide variety of historical developments from the technical to the religious
level of social existence. Thus the development of modern
commerce gave the middle classes new economic power. They
used it to challenge the priestly-military oligarchy of
feudal society. They undermined the power of land-owner-
ship with the more dynamic economic power of the ownership
of bank stock. The development of modern technical industry had a twofold effect. It both enhanced the economic
power and wealth of the owners and manipulators of economic
process, and it gave industrial workers a form of power

(exercised for instance by their refusal to cooperate in
an interrelated economic process) which the common men of
agrarian societies did not have.

Sometimes a shift in power relations has a much more
spiritual origin. Who can deny that the development of
prophetic religion, which challenges rather than supports
political majesty in the name of the majesty of God, helps
to destroy priestly-military oligarchies and to create democratic societies? In this way the prophetic elements in
Christianity have contributed to the rise of modern democratic societies, just as conservative elements in the
Christian tradition have strengthened the pretensions of
oligarchies by their uncritical identification of political
power with the divine authority.

The complexity of the technical, rational and prophet-
ic-religious factors which contributed to the rise of modern
democracies illustrates the complex and intimate involvement
of all these factors in the whole historical process. The
interweaving of these various strands in the total fabric of
historical development refutes both vitalists and rationalists. No form of individual or social power exists without
a modicum of physical force, or without a narrow pinnacle
of "spirit" which transcends the conflict and tension of
vital forces. But the tension and balance of such forces
in any given social situation include vitalities and powers
which manifest the complex unity of spirit and nature, of
reason and force, in the whole of human existence.[29]

FOOTNOTES

[1] *Moral Man and Immoral Society*, pp. xi-xii.

[2] *Ibid.*, pp. 46-49.

[3] *Ibid.*, pp. 93-94.

[4] *Ibid.*, pp. xxii-xxiii.

[5] *Human Nature*, pp. 208-209.

[6] *Moral Man and Immoral Society*, pp. 83-85.

[7] *Human Nature*, p. 209.

[8] *Moral Man and Immoral Society*, pp. 88-89.

[9] *Ibid.*, p. 95.

[10] *Human Nature*, pp. 210-12.

[11] The quotation is from Philip Leon, *The Ethics of Power*.

[12] *Moral Man and Immoral Society*, p. 108.

[13] *Reflections on the End of an Era*, p. 43.

[14] *Human Nature*, pp. 212-13, 217.

[15] *The Children of Light and the Children of Darkness*, pp. 47-49.

[16] *Moral Man and Immoral Society*, p. xx.

[17] *Human Destiny*, p. 265.

[18] "Christian Faith and Social Action," in J. Hutchinson, *Christian Faith and Social Action*, pp. 240-41.

[19] *Human Destiny*, pp. 258-59.

[20] *Discerning the Signs of the Times*, pp. 186-187.

[21] *Moral Man and Immoral Society*, p. 19.

[22]*Discerning the Signs of the Times,*   p. 186-87.

[23]*Human Destiny,* p. 259.

[24]"Leaves from the Notebook of a War-bound American," *Christian Century,* Vol. 56 (November 15, 1939), p. 1405.

[25]*Christianity and Power Politics,* p. 123.

[26]*Discerning the Signs of the Times,* p. 187.

[27]*Human Destiny,* pp. 260-63.

[28]*Reflections on the End of an Era,* p. 151.

[29]*Human Destiny,* pp. 263-64.

* * *

This chapter is a compilation of quotes from various writings by Reinhold Niebuhr as indicated above. The edited essay was first put together by Harry R. Davis and Robert C. Good as Chapter VIII in their book, *Reinhold Niebuhr on Politics,* Charles Scribner's Sons, New York.

MORALITY VERSUS MORALISM
IN FOREIGN POLICY

ERNEST W. LEFEVER

The rising moral concern among Americans in the late 1960s about the conduct and consequences of their government's foreign policy has often been accompanied by increased moral confusion and impassioned rhetoric. Moral and political perplexity is not without merit, because the uncertainty it betokens can sometimes lead to greater understanding and more responsible behavior. The deterioration of moral discourse, not confined to critics or supporters of any particular foreign policy, is the product of recent external developments and a persistent philosophical ambiguity in the American character.

It is too simple to attribute the pervasive moral confusion to American involvement in Vietnam, though that protracted trauma doubtless has brought to a head the growing weariness with the burdens of our power and the disenchantment with what Denis Brogan once called "the illusion of American omnipotence." Even before Vietnam our earlier and more naive national self-confidence had been shattered by a series of disappointments and reverses—the "fall of China" in 1949, the inconclusive Korean war, the loss of Cuba to the Communist camp, and the divisiveness, conflict, and war that have followed in the wake of decolonization. With these bitter lessons, most Americans have finally learned that even the mighty United States cannot shape the destiny of peoples in the larger world, at least not without violating our profound moral inhibitions

21

against the exercise of unabashed force to aggrandize
our power or nourish our vanity. Few spokesmen since
Pearl Harbor, other than Henry Luce, have advocated that
we shed our cherished scruples in the quest for an American imperium.

Underlying the moral awakening and confusion has
been a continuing struggle between two different ways of
looking at history and politics, two streams of American
thought that have vied for ascendency, especially since
the mid-nineteenth century. I refer to what the late
Reinhold Niebuhr has called "rational idealism" and "historical realism," each manifesting itself in diverging political attitudes, expectations, and behavior.

Rational idealism in essence is the child of the Enlightenment and Social Darwinism, and in its pure form it
affirms the perfectability, or at least improvability, of
man and the possibility, if not inevitability, of progress
in history. The diverse schools within this approach are
united in their ultimate faith in the nobler nature of man.
The earlier idealists saw reason as the redemptive agent
that would save man and politics and eventually inaugurate
an era of universal peace and brotherhood—the socialist
paradise or the Kingdom of God on earth. The natural goodness of man, they believed, could be translated into the
structures of politics. Poverty, injustice, and war could
be eliminated. The rational idealists were supported by
the views of men such as Tom Paine, Walt Whitman, and Walter
Rauschenbusch, the articulate spokesman of the Protestant
Social Gospel movement. Wilsonian idealism, the manifestation of rationalism in the international sphere, reached
its zenith in 1928 with the signing of the Kellogg-Briand
Pact outlawing war as an "instrument of national policy."

Historical realism, in contrast, emphasizes the moral

limits of human nature and history and has its roots in
St. Augustine, John Calvin, Edmund Burke, James Madison,
and most other classical Western thinkers. Rejecting all
forms of religious and secular utopianism—including fascism and communism—the post-Versailles realists have included men as varied as Reinhold Niebuhr, Carl L. Becker,
Winston Churchill, and Dean Acheson. Noting that the extravagant expectations of the Wilsonians were not ratified
by subsequent events, the self-designated realists hold
that all political achievements are limited by man's dogged
resistance to drastic reconstruction. With this recognition of "original sin," they argue that perfect peace,
justice, security, and freedom are not possible in this
world, though approximations of these lofty goals are not
beyond man's grasp. To the rational idealist, the "impossible ideal" is achievable because it is rationally conceiv-
able. To the historical realist, the "impossible ideal" is
relevant because it lends humility without despair and hope
without illusion.

There are few wholly consistent adherents to either
approach. Were Jefferson and Lincoln rational idealists or
historical realists? Obviously they were a combination of
both: Jefferson leaning toward the idealistic view and
Lincoln toward the realistic. Like most Americans, they
tended to be optimistic about the more distant future and
at the same time practical and realistic about immediate
problems and possibilities.

Rational idealism and historical realism are not complete moral systems but two different perspectives coexist-
ing uneasily within the Western commitment to a political
order of justice and freedom. As approaches, they are subject to certain limitations and weaknesses. In one sense
each tends to balance and correct the other.

Most moral philosophers, political theorists, and statesmen tend toward one view or the other. On the practical
level, virtually all political leaders have been realists,
regardless of how idealistic their rhetoric may have been.
While I believe that the historical realist approach is a
more adequate reading of the deepest Judaeo-Christian tradition and a sounder guide to the art of politics than its
post-Enlightenment rival, I recognize that it, like rational idealism, is subject to corruption.

     Both of these respectable philosophical approaches
have in fact been demeaned and distorted by emphasizing
certain of their virtues to the neglect or exclusion of
other elements in the larger body of Western normative
thought. Each is vulnerable in its own way to the vices
of political aloofness, on the one hand, and crusading arrogance, on the other. Rational idealists, frustrated by
stubborn political realities, sometimes degenerate into
sentimentalists whose strident demand for perfection becomes a substitute for responsible behavior. When personal purity becomes more important than political effectiveness, the resulting aloofness is virtually indistinguishable from that of the Machiavellians who cynically insist
that might alone makes right. The historical realist becomes irresponsible when his preoccupation with man's
baser nature cuts the taproot of social concern and permits
him to become a defender of injustice or tyranny.

     A lopsided realist can come to hold that what is good
for America is good for the rest of the world and that it
is our "manifest destiny" to make other peoples over in
our own image, by force if necessary. An equally lopsided
idealist can support efforts to reshape other societies by
more subtle, but not necessarily less reprehensible, means.
Members of each approach can degenerate into cynical iso-

lationists or overbearing crusaders. Seen in this light,
the extremists in both groups really have more in common
with each other than with the mainstream of their own tradition.

The corruption of realism or idealism can be called
moralism—the most popular rival and imposter of genuine
morality. Morality or ethics (the Greek derivative with
the same meaning) has to do with right or wrong behavior
in all spheres. It is a discipline of ends and means.
However primitive or sophisticated, all moral systems define normative ends and acceptable rules for achieving
them. Moralism, on the other hand, is a sham morality,
a partial ethic. Often it is expressed in self-righteous
rhetoric or manipulative symbols designed to justify, enlist, condemn, or deceive rather than to inform, inspire,
or serve the cause of justice. The moralism of the naive
and well-intentioned may be sincere. The moralism of the
ambitious and sophisticated is likely to be dishonest.
Intellectually flabby and morally undisciplined, moralism
tends to focus on private interests rather than the public
good, on the immediate at the expense of the future, and
on sentiment rather than reason. It is often more concerned
with appearances than consequences. Morality is a synonym
for responsibility and moralism is a conscious or uncon-
scious escape from accountability.

The varieties of moralism flowing from the corruption
of the two approaches always subvert honest political dialogue and responsible behavior, but at the present point
in American history *soft moralism* of the sentimental
idealists is a greater threat than *hard moralism* of the
power realists. The views of the hard cynics—the Machia-
vellis and imperialists—find little hospitality in the university, the church, the mass press, or in the public gen-

erally. Few Americans call for the reconquest of the
Philippines or the "liberation" of Cuba or Eastern Europe.
The small voice of the hard moralists is barely audible.
In sharp contrast, the soft moralism of the rational idealists has had increasing appeal because many Americans are
wearied by the burdens of power—the cost of nuclear deterrence and the perplexities of helping to keep the peace in
distant places.

Today the rational idealistic approach—in its religious and secular versions—and the various corruptions
of this stance find wide acceptance in the church and university and are actively promoted by the mass media. Given
the high level of moral turbulence and uncertainty, it is
important to take critical note of this more pervasive
manifestation of American moralism, acknowledging that
some of its attributes are also similar to those of hard
moralism.

* * *

Moralism, soft or hard, tends toward a single-factor
approach to political problems, while mainstream Western
morality emphasizes multiple causation, multiple ends,
and multiple responsibilities. Many Americans have demanded peace (often simplistically defined as the absence
of war), with insufficient regard for the other two great
social ends—justice and freedom. Some have urged the
United States to withdraw immediately and totally from
Vietnam or to stop building nuclear arms without weighing
the probable impact of their advice on the prospects for
justice in Southeast Asia, freedom in Western Europe, or
global stability. Others have insisted that U.S. involvement in the Third World has thwarted the march toward justice. If one of several valued goals—peace, justice, or

freedom—becomes the supreme political end, the other two
are bound to suffer. Peace (order) without justice and
freedom is tyranny. Justice without freedom is another
form of tyranny.

The statesman has a multiple mandate to use the resources at his command to maintain a tolerable balance
among the competing claims of order, justice, and freedom,
though in grave crises he may be compelled to sacrifice
one temporarily to save the other two. Confronted with
the infamy of Pearl Harbor, the American people sacrificed
peace in the interests of security and were prepared to
accept limitations on their freedom for the same end. Any
political community must enjoy minimal security before it
can develop the discipline of justice and the safeguards
of freedom.

The preoccupation with one particular value, such as
"the right of self-determination (one expression of freedom), undercuts wise statesmanship and often has dire consequences. The single-minded emphasis on self-determination
insured the Balkanization of Eastern Europe after World War
I. In the 1960s when the Katanga and Biafra lobbies marched
under the same banner of self-determination the result was
prolonged conflict and suffering in the abortive secession-
ist attempts in the Congo (Zaire) and Nigeria. The pro-
Biafra crusade, a dramatic example of the moral flabbiness
of single-issue causes, was an improbable conglomeration of
the New Left and old right, humanitarians and hirelings,
churchmen and secularists, isolationists and intervention-
ists.

* * *

The soft moralistic view tends to distrust the state,
especially its coercive power, while Western ethical thought

affirms the necessity of the state and insists on the
responsible use of its power. Absolute power may corrupt
absolutely, as Lord Acton asserted, but less-than-absolute
power may or may not corrupt those who exercise it. There
is little evidence that Lincoln, Churchill, or Truman were
corrupted by power; they may even have been ennobled by it.
Hitler, Stalin, and Mao were doubtless corrupted before
they gained power. Power is amoral. It can be enlisted
to liberate or enslave, to guarantee security or take it
away. There is a vast difference between the Germany of
Adolf Hitler and the Germany of Willy Brandt.

The state government must possess a monopoly on the
legitimate use of violence within its domain. As the
sovereign authority over a given territory—whether city,
country, or empire—the government is the ultimate agency
for resolving internal conflicts of power and interest.
Were it not for the state, Saint Augustine said, men
would devour one another as fishes. Martin Luther said
the central task of the state was to protect the innocent
by restraining evil men. Of the modern democratic state,
Professor Niebuhr said: "Man's capacity for justice makes
democracy possible; but man's inclination to injustice
makes democracy necessary."[1]

The problem is not to eliminate the state, the professed goal of Marxists and anarchists alike, but to make
political power accountable to its citizens by a system
that permits them peaceably to give or withold concent
and if necessary to throw the rascals out. If a government becomes tyrannical and all peaceful means for redres-
sing grievances have been exhausted, the people, said

---

[1]Reinhold Niebuhr, *The Children of Light and the Children of Darkness* (New York: Charles Scribner's Sons, 1944),
p. xi.

Lincoln, have the right to rebel by violent means. The acceptance of Lincoln's view on the right of revolution does not negate the essential character of the responsible state. It is the fundamental agency for "insuring domestic tranquility, providing for the common defense, promoting the general welfare, and securing the blessings of liberty." In serving these central social objectives there is no substitute for the state—the sovereign political community.

* * *

Soft moralism is highly critical of the exercise of American military power, except in self-defense and this is often narrowly defined. America has been criticized for throwing its weight around, and even for repressive policies toward the Third World, though solid evidence is seldom adduced to buttress these charges. On the other hand, a few hard zealots have called for a stronger exercise of power to impose an American order in one part of the world or the other. Classical moralists reject both the arbitrary abstention from power and its unrestrained use and insist that the United States has a responsibility for international peace and order commensurate with its capacity to affect external events. Our military power—as a deterrent, a threat, or an active force—should be limited to dealing with real and present dangers to world peace. A workable international order can rest only on a propitious balance of forces with each of the two superpowers inescapably playing a vital role. U.S. military might, including its nuclear arsenal, is an essential factor in preventing a shift in the balance of forces that could lead to war or the capitulation of friendly states to nuclear blackmail.

The international security system led by the United
States—involving NATO, other mutual defense arrangements,
and military assistance—has gone a long way to protect
the weak against the ambitions of the strong. What would
have been the fate of Western Europe, Greece, Turkey,
Iran, Thailand, Taiwan, South Korea, and Japan if the United
States had not extended its protection? Since the balance
sheet on Southeast Asia is not yet completed, it is not
certain that U.S. involvement has set back the long-range
prospects for stability, order, and freedom. American
security assistance to some fifty Third World states in
the past two decades has helped to maintain in many of them
that minimal stability essential to constructive political
and economic development.

To affirm an indispensable American responsibility
for reinforcing the chance for peaceful change is not to
define the specific disciplines of that role. How, when,
and under what circumstances Washington should threaten or
use how much coercion—this perplexing political and moral
question—can be resolved only by statesmen who understand
both the limits and possibilities of American power in
situations where the United States has little control and
an uncertain moral mandate. Because of these complexities
and uncertainty about its own responsibilities, the United
States has on occasion used too little or too much power
or exercised it too early or too late. The Bay of Pigs
comes to mind.

* * *

Some adherents of the moralistic approach advocate
interventionist foreign policies designed to reshape the
internal customs and institutions of other states. At
the same time, they often downgrade or even deprecate the

primary security role of foreign policy. This strange
combination of reform-intervention and security-isolation
turns foreign policy on its head. In the classical view,
the first task of external policy is peace and security,
and the first task of domestic policy is order and justice.
The reform-interventionists, soft or hard, blur the sal-
ient distinction between what can and ought to be done by
a government for its own people, and what can and ought to
be done by a government in the vast external realm over
which it has no legal jurisdiction and where its moral and
political mandate is severely limited. The insistence that
the U.S. government employ extraordinary and sometimes coercive means to reshape the internal political, economic,
or social structures in other sovereign communities is
morally arrogant and flies in the face of the most basic
international law which, in the words of the U.N. Charter,
prohibits intervention "in matters which are essentially
within the domestic jurisdiction of any state."

Western morality respects the right of each political
community to develop in its own way at its own pace, as
long as it does not impinge coercively on other political
communities. President Nixon's words in Rumania in 1969
were a refreshing restatement of this principle: "We seek
normal relations with all countries, regardless of their
domestic system"; each state has the right to "preserve its
national institutions." His trip to China underscored his
words. Ignoring this self-constraint, moralistic voices
keep urging the U.S. government to withhold security or
economic aid to force domestic changes within Brazil,
Greece, and other friendly states whose structure or policies do not accord with the critic's preferences.

This peculiar American penchant to export our virtue
reached a high-water mark, at least in rhetoric, under

President Kennedy and found belated legislative sanction
in 1966 in Title IX of the Foreign Assistance Act which
declared that all U.S. Economic aid programs should encourage the development of "democratic private and local
governmental institutions" in the recipient countries by
using their "intellectual resources" to stimulate "economic and social progress" and by supporting "civic education
and training skills required for effective participation
in governmental and political processes essential to self-
government." This intrusive sally into other people's affairs, however naive or wrongheaded, does not compare to
to the breathtaking sweep or moral pretension of the Communist Manifesto with its strident call to the workers of
the world (read "self-appointed elect") to redeem societies
everywhere without regard to state frontiers. Arrogance
is the chief sin. Civilized human beings, said Leopold
Tyrmand, should "agree not to burden each other" with
their "excessive humanity."

Viewing U.S. foreign policy as an instrument for reform rather than of stability is not only arrogant; it
also ignores the severly limited capacity of any external
agency to influence and reshape alien cultures. As Gunnar
Myrdal pointed out in *Asian Drama: An Inquiry into the
Poverty of Nations* (1968), the economic and political development of low-income countries is determined largely
by internal forces—static and dynamic—though well-con-
sidered trade, investment, and aid from industrial states
may spur development. Any government has the right to
request American or Russian technical assistance. By the
same token, Washington and Moscow have the right to accept
or turn down the request. The provision of economic or
military aid that serves the interests of both parties
presents few problems. It is wrong, however, for the

donor government to give, withhold, or modify aid to force
significant domestic changes unacceptable to the recipient
regime and unrelated to the efficient use of the assistance.

The crusading impulse to reform should be clearly
distinguished from the humanitarian motive that has prompted the U.S. government over the years to do more for the
foreign victims of famine, earthquake, and war than any
other in history. Earthquake relief is not designed to
restructure institutions, overthrow regimes or promote
"free elections."

* * *

Soft moralism tends to associate virtue with weakness,
just as it associates vice with power. Western morality
affirms the fundamental worth of the poor and the weak and
recognizes that they are less able to defend their rights
than the rich and powerful. Further, under the rubric of
noblesse oblige men privileged by wealth or station are
duty-bound to protect and assist the lowly. But this does
not automatically endow the weak with innocence or virtue,
whether they are deprived by nature, sloth, exploitation,
or other circumstances.

The behavior of all states—great and small—must be
judged by the same moral yardstick, recognizing that the
degree of responsibility is commensurate with the capacity
to act. "He who has much given to him will have much required to him." Yet, there is a widespread tendency among
moralistic Americans to regard the fledgling new states
with a kind of perverse paternalism which excuses childish,
demanding, and otherwise irresponsible behavior, such as
that of the delegates who applauded the expulsion of Taiwan
from the United Nations in 1971 or those who charged

Washington and Brussels with "deliberate genocide" and
"massive canibalism" for rescuing more than 2,000 innocent foreign hostages of nineteen nationalities in the
Congo in 1964.

Neither the weak nor the strong are immune from error
or corruption. The celebrated and much confessed "arrogance of power" should not blind us to the arrogance of
weakness, which may express itself in simple claims of
virtue, insistence on unjustified "reparations," or demands for minority control, all calculated to exploit a
pervasive sense of guilt in the American character. As
Churchill pointed out, we Anglo-Saxons tend to feel guilty
because we possess power. Prime Minister Nehru and other
Third World spokesmen often assumed an air of moral su-
periority, insisting they were uncorrupted by power and
therefore possessed an innocence and humanity denied the
leaders of powerful, and hence guilty, states. In a U.N.
speech in 1960, Premier Saeb Salaam of Lebanon said: "We,
the small, uncommitted nations, can perhaps take a more
objective view of the world situation. We can judge international issues with comparatively greater detachment
and impartiality; in a sense, the small uncommitted nations
can be said to represent the unbiased conscience of humanity."[2]

Recent official Swedish statements reflect this moralistic tendency. Though espousing neutrality, Swedish
officials have been quick to condemn the behavior of the
big powers, particularly the United States, and to take
"moral" stands on a variety of international issues.
Stockholm has supported Hanoi and the Vietcong against
America and has given moral and material aid to the Com-

---

[2]*New York Times,* October 5, 1960.

munist-assisted guerrilla fighters seeking to overthrow
Western-oriented regimes in southern Africa. In November
1971, the Swedish government decided to prohibit arms
shipment to insurgent groups in Africa so as not to become directly involved and thus remain "neutral." It is
morally easy for politicians or religious leaders to cheer
and condemn from the sidelines when they have no responsibility and are unwilling to become committed. With studied hyperbole John P. Roche makes the point: "Power corrupts. And the absence of power corrupts absolutely."

The prevailing moralistic approach tends to be pre-
occupied with the present, neglectful of the past, and
nonchalant about the future. Impatient with imperfection,
the new romantics indulge in what Elton Trueblood has
called the "sin of contemporaneity." It may be argued
that enchantment with the chronological now represents
a positive contribution from the existential emphasis on
the present-tense imperative, but evidence suggests it is
usually an escape from the eternal now which binds the
past and future in an endless chain of responsibility.

According to classical morality, man is not an isolated actor suddenly thrust onto an alien stage and expected to respond to the strange sights and sounds around
him. Man is born and nurtured in an ongoing community, a
continuous web of cause and effect, a tapestry of gifts
and expectations. Man is a creature of history, a product
of the past, an actor in the present, and an influence for
the future. To reject the past, as so many radicals do,
is to reject the fabric of human continuity that gives
moral meaning to the present.

The widespread and strangely indiscriminate view that
the status quo is bad and change is good suggests that
history is "a tale told by an idiot," a story without mean-

ing. Western morality insists that history, like man, is
morally ambiguous and that the task of the present generation is to accept the best of the past and reject the worst.
This selective dependence on history is not possible if
there is no understanding of the major ideas, events, and
forces that have shaped the present. Many students today
show no interest in the developments that had the most dramatic impact on the political outlook of their parents.
If events like Pearl Harbor, Korea, and the Budapest Up-
rising are not known or have no common meaning, how can
the two generations communicate? The understanding of recent history is vital, even if earlier eras must be short
changed. This suggests the advisability of teaching history backward, starting with today's newspaper and covering
the past decade before moving to the more distant past.

* * *

In their disdain for history, ancient and recent, and
their insistence on achieving quick solutions, many romantic idealists sell the future short by neglecting the disciplines of moral and political calculation. The principal
practical test of any political decision is not the intention of the actor or the means he uses, but the immediate
and long-range consequences of his decision. These consequences are also essential in making a moral assessment of
the decision.

Moral choice demands calculation—an assessment of
multiple causes, multiple alternatives, and multiple consequences. Seemingly good courses often have disastrous results. Many critics of U.S. defense policy condemned the
announced underground nuclear test which was carried out
in Alaska in November 1971. Some said it would trigger

a devastating earhtquake on tidal wave or otherwise damage the natural environment. Other critics insisted that
the test was a giant step in accelerating the strategic
arms race. After careful calculation President Nixon decided to go ahead, convinced that the natural risks had
been exaggerated and that the probable consequences were
on balance good for U.S. security and world peace. After
the test there was no indication of a radioactive leak,
and the damage to the environment appeared to be slight.
The test did demonstrate the feasibility of the Spartan
warhead, an essential component in any viable ABM system
designed to protect America's land-based Minuteman missiles. These missiles in turn are designed to deter a
nuclear attack against this country and thus avoid a con-
flagration. Further, the test may well have strengthened
the U.S. position at the Strategic Arms Limitation Talks
with the Russians, which are seeking to control offensive
and defensive nuclear weapons on both sides. These and
many other factors were considered in the calculus preceding the president's decision. Unlike the president, the
critics do not bear the burden of decision, but are they
not obligated to consider all the major issues at stake
before they pronounce final moral judgments?

                        * * *

     Some of the more extreme American moralists, baffled
by complexity and impatient with the untidy state of the
world, sometimes adopt what amounts to a devil-theory of
politics, and ever-popular version of the single-issue
approach. They attempt to identify the central flaw, the
fatal error, the demonic force underlying our present
plight.
     The earlier rational idealists discovered a series of

plausible devils that, separately or in combination, were
held responsible for war, injustice, poverty, and many
other afflictions of mankind. Each was fatally vulnerable
to its rational and righteous counterpart. The prince of
darkness, capitalism, could be slain by socialism. The
confusion of tongues, the cause of international misunder-
standing and conflict, could be cured by education and
Esperanto. Nationalism could be exorcised by internationalism and world government. The military and the "merchants
of death" could be abolished by the renunciation of war.
The winding road from Versailles to Pearl Harbor and beyond is cluttered with the debris of well-intentioned cru-
sades—the League of Nations, the Kellogg-Briand Pact, and
compulsory arbitration of interstate disputes, to name a
few. The idealists and their ideal solutions failed. The
Wilsonians, it has been said, reached for utopia and gave
us hell.

The targets of present-day devil-theorists bear a
striking resemblance to those of earlier decades. Now it
is the military-industrial complex, the establishment, the
system, the corporate structure, technology, or greed. For
many of the radical dissenters, the chief demon is "deca-
dent liberalism" a menacing Mephistopheles embracing all
the vices of gradualism, reform, due process, and peaceful
evolution—benign bourgeois beautitudes that blur the
necessity to "destroy the system" and thus subvert revolutionary zeal. Some zealots prefer more personal devils,
such as Lyndon Johnson, Dean Rusk, or Richard Nixon. By
the same token, they have personal messiahs such as Mao,
Ho, and Che.

The devil-theory approach lends itself to an apocalyp-
tic interpretation of the political situation. The whole
world is polarized and the golden mean, the vital center,

and orderly change are thrown to the winds. The forces
of good (read progressive or revolutionary) at home and
abroad are arrayed against the forces of evil (read status
quo or reactionary) and there is no compromise. The "establishment" will be crushed and "the people" will prevail
It is only a matter of time and dedication. Here one sees
the rhetoric of the Maoists and Marxists being used loose-
ly and without discipline by the soft romantics.

* * *

Most American moralists have an inadequate understanding of the limits and possibilities of logic, rationality,
and calculation. According to classical Western norms,
moral reasoning is a possibility, indeed a necessity. Man
is a reasoning creature. Within the limits of circumstance,
he can plan, devise, calculate, though he can rarely control or determine events. Circumstances are too complex
and intractable and human emotions too unpredictable to
come up with solutions. Precise prediction is impossible
and risk is never absent. Tolstoy dramatizes the human situation by describing the dilemma of a military commander who

> ...is always in the midst of a series of shifting events
> and so he never can at any moment consider the whole im-
> port of an event that is occurring. Moment by moment
> the event is imperceptibly shaping itself, and at every
> moment of this continuous, uninterrupted shaping of events
> the commander in chief is in the midst of a most complex
> play of intrigues, worries, contingencies, authorities,
> projects, counsels, threats, and deceptions and is con-
> tinually obliged to reply to innumerable questions ad-
> dressed to him, which constantly conflict with one
> another.[3]

To acknowledge the serious limits of rational calcu-

---

[3]Leo Tolstoy, *War and Peace* (New York: Simon and
Schuster, 1942).

lation in politics is not to deprecate reason, or the necessity to marshal relevant facts, or the desirability of
projecting the probable consequences of competing lines of
action.   Politics is more an art than a science, but the
scientific discipline of weighing evidence is a compelling
moral obligation.   To ignore evidence, to disdain logic,
or to overlook empirical data is to retreat into blind
emotion which spawns illusions.   If the romantics fail to
discipline their desires with data or their passions with
power and persist in their illusions, they become almost
indistinguishable from cynics or nihilistic trouble makers.

    Just as the contemporary sentimentalists expect too
little of reason, the earlier rational idealists expected
too much.   Reason provides the capacity to conceive of
noble ends and to comprehend the barriers to their fulfillment.

THE TRIVIALIZATION OF HUMAN RIGHTS

ERNEST W. LEFEVER

Human rights are what politics is all about. Fifteen
centuries ago Saint Augustine said that were it not for government,
men would devour one another as fishes. He was, of course,
referring to good government, but governments often become
corrupt, cruel, or tyrannical. When this happens, they
are the most monstrous fish of all. Depending on its
character, government can be the most effective protector
of human rights or the most vicious violator of them.
Hence, the struggle for viable and humane government is
the heart of politics.

It is important to distinguish between two frequently confused concepts of human rights.[1] One has more immediate universal application because it is rooted in the
religion and ethics of virtually all cultures and calls
for sanctions against political authorities and others
guilty of genocide, brutalizing innocent people and similar
atrocities. The second and more precise concept of human
rights is the fruit of the recent Western democratic experience and embraces a variety of substantive and procedural
rights and safeguards that are enforced in perhaps fewer
than a score of states. These rights include freedom of
speech, assembly, press, and religion; equality before the
law; periodic elections; the concept of being innocent

---

[1]This distinction is elaborated in Peter L. Berger's
"Are Human Rights Universal?", *Commentary,* September, 1977.

until proved guilty; a judicial system independent from
executive authority; and a range of safeguards for accused
persons. Many of these Western democratic rights are unknown and unattainable in large parts of the world where
both history and culture preclude the development of full-
fledged democratic institutions. Nevertheless, there are
significant differences in the extent to which human
rights, more generally defined, are honored in undemocrat-
ic states. And some of these states have introduced a few
of the specific Western safeguards.

The never-ending battle to maintain and enlarge the
areas of proximate liberty and justice must be fought
against external and internal forces which seek to impose
authority without freedom, often by brutal means. Human
rights as we know them in the United States and other democratic countries can be eroded or even obliterated from
within by acquiescing to willful men who seek to capture
the reins of power for their own narrow ends or from without by totalitarian regimes determined to extend their dominion.

Our Founding Fathers wrestled with the problem of
creating a free and independent country ruled by a government with sufficient authority to overcome domestic and
alien threats and with sufficient openness to respond to
the will of the people. Their formula was the judicious
balance between authority and freedom embraced in the Declaration of Independence and elaborated in the Constitution. The former asserted that "governments are instituted
among men, deriving their just powers from the consent of
the governed" to secure certain fundamental rights, among
them "life, liberty, and the pursuit of happiness." The
Constitution was promulgated to "establish justice, insure
domestic tranquility, provide for the common defense,

promote the general welfare, and secure the blessings of
liberty."

   This audacious experiment prospered in an inauspic-
ious world. In the face of new challenges, the American
system provided for increasingly broader political participation and other specific rights spelled out or implied
in the Constitution and its amendments. Our history is
not without blemish, but compared to other political communities past and present, the American record is a beacon
of freedom and justice in a world bedeviled by chaos, authoritarian rule, and messianic tyranny.

THE CURRENT HUMAN RIGHTS CAMPAIGN

   The current wave of concern for human rights around
the world was foreshadowed by several developments, not-
ably Woodrow Wilson's crusade for "self-determination" and
the Universal Declaration of Human Rights adopted by the
United Nations in 1948. The U.S. campaign to make the advancement of human rights abroad an objective of foreign
policy is more recent, but it did not start with President
Jimmy Carter. He simply built on the lively interest developed in Congress during the past several years which has
been expressed largely in foreign aid legislation designed
to prohibit or restrict economic or military assistance to
any government "which engages in a consistent pattern of
gross violations of internationally recognized human rights,
including torture or cruel, inhumane, or degrading treatment or punishment, prolonged detention without charges, or
other flagrant denial of the right to life, liberty, and
the security of person" (Foreign Assistance Act, Section
502B, adopted in 1974). Most of the congressional human
rights activists have limited their advocacy of punitive
measures to Chile, South Korea, and Iran. In practice,

the restrictions have had little effect on limiting aid,
loans, or military sales, even to these countries.

Human rights was a natural cause for President Carter. As a born-again Baptist and a latter-day Wilsonian,
he repeatedly stated his intention to restore integrity
and compassion to American domestic and foreign policy.
In his address at Notre Dame University on March 22, 1977,
Mr. Carter looked back to the immediate past and deplored
our "intellectual and moral poverty," illustrated by our
Vietnam policy, and our "inordinate fear of Communism
which once led us to embrace any dictator who joined us
in that fear." He called for a "new" American foreign
policy, "based on constant decency in its values and an
optimism in its historical vision." The most conspicuous
manifestation of his new policy is the effort to promote
human rights in other countries by means of U.S. statecraft, including private diplomacy, public preaching, and
measures to deny or threaten to deny economic, military
or nuclear assistance. Mr. Carter's campaign has been
given bureaucratic visibility by establishing a new post,
Assistant Secretary of State for Human Rights and Humanitarian Affairs, currently filled by Patricia Derian, who
sometimes discusses her assignment in moralistic rhetoric
alien to traditional diplomatic discourse.

The human rights campaign has received mixed reviews
at home and abroad. Last July in a *New Yorker* article
friendly to the effort, Elizabeth Drew reported that Mr.
Carter's people "are pleased, and some even a bit awe-
struck, at the impact that the human-rights campaign has
had thus far. 'I think' says one, 'that the mulish world
has noticed the two-by-four.'"

There is no doubt that the threatening plank has
been noticed, and probably in isolated cases it has accom-

plished some good. But it should be recorded that some un-mulish elements in the world, including friendly and allied governments, have also seen the two-by-four and are not convinced that its whack, however well-intended, has always been redemptive. There is no doubt that it has harmed relations with some allies and has both irri- tated and comforted adversaries.

It is by no means clear that the campaign has re- sulted in any significant relaxation of Soviet restric- tions against emigration or political dissent. There is evidence that the opposite may be the case. On December 30, 1977, a *New York Times* page-one story reported: "The small Soviet human rights movement...is at its lowest point in years after a campaign of arrests, threats, and forced exile."

It is clear, however, that a score of allies has been unhappy with a policy they regard as arrogant and unfairly applied. Brazil, Argentina, Uruguay, and Guate- mala have been alienated to the point where they have re- fused military assistance from Washington. And Brazil has served notice that it wishes to withdraw from its Security Assistance Agreement of 25 years standing. This aliena- tion of allies gives aid and comfort to Moscow which more than offsets the minor embarrassment it suffers from Mr. Carter's conspicuous "intervention" on behalf of Soviet dissidents.

SIX FLAWS IN THE HUMAN RIGHTS POLICY

Far more serious, however, the Carter campaign has confused our foreign policy goals and trivialized the con- cept of human rights. It both reflects and reinforces serious conceptual flaws in the worldview of its most ar- ticulate spokesmen. These flaws, if permitted to instruct foreign policy, or even influence it unduly, could have catastrophic consequences for the security of the United States and the cause of freedom in the world. Six inter-related flaws deserve brief mention:

1. UNDERESTIMATING THE TOTALITARIAN THREAT

Human dignity and freedom are under siege around the world. It has been ever so. The islands of community protected by humane law have been contracting ever since postwar decolonization began. The citizens of most of the newly independent states in Asia and Africa now experience less freedom and fewer guaranteed rights than they did under Western colonial rule.

But the greatest threat to human rights comes from messianic totalitarian regimes whose brutal grip brooks no opposition. Their self-anointed and self-perpetuating elites have become the arbiters of orthodoxy in every sphere—politics, economics, education, the arts, and family life. The ruling party even usurps the place of God. In totalitarian states like the U.S.S.R., Cuba, Cambodia, and Vietnam, there are no countervailing forces to challenge the power, will, or policies of the entrenched elite.

In spite of notable exceptions, the general political situation in the Third World is characterized by chaos and authoritarian regimes. Democratic and anti-democratic ideas and institutions are competing for acceptance. In this struggle, we should not underestimate the attraction of the totalitarian temptation to leaders who are grappling with the perplexing problems of moving traditional societies into modern, welfare states.

The human rights activists tend to underestimate the totalitarian threat to the West and the totalitarian temptation in the Third World. Hence, they neglect or trivialize the fundamental political and moral struggle

of our time—the protracted conflict between forces of
total government based on coercion and the proponents of
limited government based on popular consent and humane
law. In their preoccupation with the minor abridgment of
certain rights in authoritarian states, they often overlook the massive threat to the liberty of millions. They
attack the limitation of civil rights in South Korea and
at the same time call for the United States to withdraw
its ground forces, an act that may invite aggression from
North Korea. It would be a great irony if Washington in
the name of human rights were to adopt a policy that would
deliver 35,000,000 largely free South Koreans into virtual
slavery.

2.   *CONFUSING TOTALITARIANISM WITH AUTHORITARIANISM*

In terms of political rights, moral freedom, and
cultural vitality, there is a profound difference between
authoritarian and totalitarian regimes. Most Asian, African, and Latin American countries are ruled by small
elites supported by varying degrees of popular consent.
Some are run by brutal tyrants like General Idi Amin of
Uganda, others by one-party cliques, military juntas, or
civilian-military committees. Almost all authoritarian
regimes permit a significantly greater degree of freedom
and diversity than the totalitarian ones in all spheres—
political, cultural, economic, and religious. Authoritarian rulers often allow opposition parties to operate and
a restrained press to publish. Foreign correspondents
usually can move about freely and send out uncensored dis-
patches. They often permit and sometimes encourage relatively free economic activity and freedom of movement for
their citizens. The quality of life possible under such
rule, of course, depends not only on the character of
central control, but on the cultural and economic level

of the population as well.

There is, for example, far more freedom of choice,
diversity of opinion and activity, and respect for human
rights in authoritarian South Korea than in totalitarian
North Korea. There is also far more freedom and cultural
vitality in Chile—even under its present state of siege—
than in Cuba. There have been political prisoners in
Chile and there may be a handful now, but there are an
estimated 15,000 to 60,000 political detainees in Cuba.
These facts are noted, not to praise Chile or condemn
Cuba, but to emphasize the consequential difference of
human rights in the two kinds of regimes.

Another crucial difference is the capacity of authoritarian rule to evolve into democratic rule. This has happened recently in Spain, Portugal, Greece, and India. In
sharp contrast, a Communist dictatorship has never made a
peaceful transition to more representative and responsive
rule.

3. OVERESTIMATING AMERICA'S INCLUENCE ABROAD

If the human rights zealots do not indulge in what
Denis Brogan once called "the illusion of American omnipotence," they tend to overestimate our capacity, or the
capacity of our government, to influence the external
world, particularly domestic developments in other countries. America is powerful, but it is not all-powerful.
Our considerable leverage of the 1950s and even our diminished leverage of the 1960s has been seriously eroded by
OPEC, the great leap forward in Soviet military might,
and our abandonment of Vietnam.

Quite apart from our limited capacity to influence
intractable realities abroad, there is and should be a
profound moral constraint on efforts designed to alter
domestic practices, institutions, and policies within

other states. Neo-Wilsonian attempts to make the world
safe for human rights seem to be rooted in what Professor
Ronald Berman has called "a planned confusion between domestic and foreign policy. The rest of the world is de-
picted as if it were an American constituency, driven by
our own motives, vulnerable to our own rhetoric."[2] To be
sure, the extravagant rhetoric of a Carter or a Wilson,
with its crusading and paternalistic overtones, draws upon
a persistent idealistic stream in the American character.
But there is another and quieter stream equally honorable,
but less pushy and perhaps more persuasive—symbolized by
the Biblical parable of a candle upon a candlestick or a
city set upon a hill, an example to the "lesser breeds
without the law," as it was put in a more candid era.

John Quincy Adams expressed this more modest understanding of America's external responsibility: "We are
the friends of liberty everywhere, but the custodians
only of our own." Thirty years later, Abraham Lincoln
spoke of "liberty as the heritage of all men, in all lands
everywhere," but he did not claim that the United States
was the chosen instrument for fulfilling this heritage.

4. *CONFUSING DOMESTIC AND FOREIGN POLICY*

Elaborating on Professor Berman's point, many human
rights crusaders confuse the fundamental distinctions between domestic and foreign policy which are rooted in age-
old practice, international law, the U.N. Charter, and
common sense. They do not take seriously the distinctions
in authority and responsibility that flow from the concept
of sovereignty which underlies the modern state system.
Our President and all other heads of state have authority

---

[2] See footnote 3.

to act only in their own states, within the territory of
their legal jurisdiction. They are responsible only for
the security and welfare of their own people, including
their citizens living or traveling abroad.

There are, of course, multiple modes of interaction
and cooperation between states based on mutual interest,
ranging from trade, investment, and cultural exchange to
military assistance and alliance ties. These activities
are consistent with the concept of sovereign equality and
non-interference in internal affairs. But short of a
victorious war, no government has a right to impose its
preference on another sovereign state. The mode and quality of life, the character and structure of institutions
within a state should be determined by its own people, not
by outsiders, however well-intentioned. The same is true
for the pace and direction of social, political or economic change.

U.S. foreign policy toward another state should be
determined largely by the foreign policy of that state.
Domestic factors and forces are significant determinants
only if they bear on external realities. Washington is
allied with Iran, Taiwan, Thailand, and South Korea, not
because their governments are authoritarian, but because
they are regarded as vital in the struggle against the expansion of Soviet or Chinese power. It is therefore, appropriate to provide economic or military assistance to
them, even if they do not hold regular elections. In sum,
U.S. aid can properly be given to encourage a friend or
ally to pursue constructive external policies, but not to
promote internal reforms opposed by the assisted government. This leads to the next point.

5. *IGNORING THE PERILS OF REFORM INTERVENTION*

The impulse to impose our standards or practices on

other societies, supported by policies of reward and punishment, leads inevitably to a kind of reform intervention. We Americans have no moral mandate to transform
other societies, and we rightly resent such efforts on
the part of the totalitarians. There is more than a touch
of arrogance in our efforts to alter the domestic behavior
of allies, or even of adversaries.

As noted above, the Foreign Assistance Act states
that a principal goal of U.S. policy is to promote internationally recognized human rights abroad. Further, Title
IX of the Act says that U.S. aid should be used to encourage "democratic private and local government institutions"
within the recipient states. The implications of this
seemingly innocent phrase are disquieting. Should U.S.
assistance be used to alter domestic institutions? Should
we insist on an ideological or reform test before providing
economic or military aid? Is this not a form of uninvited
interference in domestic matters? If we take sovereign
equality seriously, we will recognize that the people of
every state should determine their own system of justice
and how they want to defend themselves against domestic or
foreign dangers.

Other states may request assistance from friendly
governments on mutually agreed terms. But external forces,
however nobly motivated, cannot impose justice, human
rights, or freedom on other states without resorting to
conquest. It may be possible to "export revolution"—as
the phrase goes—but we cannot export human rights or respect for the rule of law. Freedom and justice are the
fruit of long organic growth nurtured by religious values,
personal courage, social restraint, and respect for law.
The majesty of law is little understood in traditional societies where ethnic identity tends to supersede all other

claims on loyalty and obedience.

6. *DISTORTING FOREIGN POLICY OBJECTIVES*

A consistent and single-minded invocation of a human
rights standard in making U.S. foreign policy decisions
would subordinate, blur, or distort other essential considerations. After all, our foreign policy has vital but
limited goals—national security and international peace—
both of which have a great impact on human rights. Aggressive war and tyranny are the two chief enemies of freedom
and justice. Our efforts to deter nuclear war and nuclear
blackmail are calculated to protect the culture and free
institutions of Western Europe and North America. In the
Third World we seek to maintain a regional stability conducive to responsible political development and mutually
beneficial economic intercourse among states. Economic
productivity alleviates stark poverty and thus broadens
the range of cultural and political choice.

Therefore, our policies of nuclear deterrence should
be determined by our understanding of the Soviet nuclear
threat and our trade policies toward Moscow should be determined by our economic and security interests. Neither
should be influenced, much less determined, by the extent
of human rights violations in the Soviet Union. Likewise,
in dealing with Third World countries, their foreign policy
behavior should be the determining factor, not their domestic practices. Even though South Korea has an authoritarian government, we should continue our security support because it is a faithful ally under siege from a totalitarian
neighbor and because its independence is vital to the defense of Japan and Japan's independence is vital to the
U.S. position in the Western Pacific and the world.

THE PITFALLS OF SELECTIVE APPLICATION

These six conceptual flaws which underlie the human
rights crusade have already led to unwise policies and if
carried to their logical conclusion, could end in disaster. Perhaps the most widely criticized and resented aspect of the campaign thus far has been its capricious and
selective application to both Communist states and American allies.

During his visit to Poland last December, President
Carter raised the human rights issue several times in
public. On the one hand, he criticized his hosts for not
permitting a handful of dissident journalists to attend
his press conference. On the other, he praised Poland's
rights record (compared to that of other Eastern European
states) and said: "Our concept of human rights is preserved in Poland," to which a Polish writer replied: "The
words are the same," but they "mean different things in
the United States." The impropriety, not to say irony,
of raising the sensitive rights issue in a Communist state
whose fragile and problematic autonomy is precariously
maintained at the sufferance of a totalitarian superpower,
did not seem to concern Mr. Carter. Nor did the fact that
Poland is forced to imitate many of the repressive measures
of its master. By focusing on the absence of a handful of
dissenting journalists at his press conference when the
entire Polish people are held in bondage by the Soviet
Union, President Carter distorted and trivialized the real
meaning of human rights.

The policy of the Administration and the Congress
toward the Soviet Union has also been vacillating and confused, seemingly more intent on scoring merchandisable
victories than on grappling with the fundamental problem.
Were it not for the Jewish emigration issue, Moscow would

probably be receiving less critical attention than it is.
How else can one explain the almost complete neglect of
the massive violation of civil and political rights in
Communist China, North Korea, Vietnam, and Cambodia?

Cambodia provides a particularly poignant example
of this double standard toward totalitarian countries.
Since the Communists took over on April 17, 1975, reliable
studies estimate that 800,000 to 1.5 million Cambodians
have died by execution or from starvation and disease
caused by the forced evacuations from cities. This means
that one in every six or seven has perished in the ruthless Communist bloodbath. Yet, where is the outcry from
the advocates of human rights? Why this strange silence
about what may well be the most brutal atrocity of our
century? Measured by relative population, the Communist
purge in Cambodia has destroyed more lives than Hitler's
concentration camps or Stalin's Gulag Archipelago.

The great silence can be explained in part by racial
and ideological factors. To certain rights advocates it
somehow seems more reprehensible if violations or brutal-
ity are directed toward members of a different race. A
white South African regime denying blacks the vote seems
more morally repugnant than black regimes denying all
citizens the vote (which is the case in most other African
states). Filtered through a racist lens, it does not seem
as bad for Cambodian Communists to murder thousands of innocent Cambodians—men, women, and children—as for a much
smaller number of Cambodian soldiers to die in a war in
which the United States was involved.

This suggests that an ideological factor is also
present. A recent *Wall Street Journal* editorial pointed to
the frequent alliance between liberal moral outrage and
revolutionary causes: the "crimes of the Khmer Rouge, even

though they dwarf some other state crimes of our times
...have attracted less attention because they are in-
flicted in the name of revolution." One can only wonder
what the reaction would be if the new government had employed "conservative" rhetoric and announced that it was
going to cleanse the country of all socialist or Marxist
influences.

Turning to American allies, some of the most articulate rights advocates concentrate their outrage on the
very regimes that are under the most severe pressure from
the totalitarians—South Korea, Taiwan, Iran, and Chile.
The first three are geographically and militarily exposed
to Communist power. Chile under Allende was the target
of a massive internal and external assault by Marxist
forces seeking to transform it into a Cuban-style dictatorship. All four of these states have authoritarian regimes, primarily in response to their present or recently
endangered position, but in each the range of rights permitted or guaranteed by the regime is far greater than
that of the Communist governments that seek to subvert or
replace them. This suggests that the human rights standard is sometimes used, not to advance freedom, but as a
cloak to attack anti-totalitarian allies.

Some rights advocates have simultaneously urged
punitive policies against Chile and measures to normalize
relations with Cuba. This is a double irony. Human
rights are more honored in Chile than in Cuba and Chile
is pursuing a more peaceful foreign policy than Cuba.
Havana is a mischief maker on a grand scale, acting as a
cat's-paw for Moscow. Castro, in addition to shoring up
a minority regime in Angola with 19,000 Cuban troops, has
sent Cuban soldiers to support the Marxist military junta
in Ethiopia and to assist "revolutionary" regimes and

other groups in a dozen other African states.

   This double standard is often promoted by the media.
According to a tabulation of news stories, editorials,
and signed opinion for 1976, the prestige media's big
five—*New York Times, Washington Post,* and the TV evening
news shows of ABC, CBS, and NBC—carried 227 items about
rights violations in two allied countries, Chile and South
Korea, in contrast to only 24 stories about violations in
three Communist countries, North Korea, Cuba, and Cambodia.   The tabulation drawn up by Accuracy in Media follows:

	Chile	South Korea	North Korea	Cuba	Cambodia
New York Times	66	61	0	3	4
Washington Post	58	24	1	4	9
ABC-TV	5	2	0	0	1
CBS-TV	5	3	0	0	2
NBC-TV	3	0	0	0	0
Totals:	137	90	1	7	16

The content of the items was not examined, but the bias
was clearly revealed by the inordinate attention given the
small human rights sins of two loyal allies compared to
the massive sins of three totalitarian adversaries—a
ratio of almost ten to one.

   Admittedly, it is far easier to get reliable information about the imperfections of authoritarian societies
than those of closed, totalitarian states, but this is
hardly an excuse for the media which pride themselves on
vigorous investigative reporting.   Certainly a little effort could have yielded considerably more data on violations in Cambodia, North Korea, and Cuba, to say nothing
of China where both blunt and subtle forms of repression
have been developed into an exquisite craft.

   The lopsided application of human rights criteria

is justified by White House and State Department spokesmen on pragmatic grounds. They frankly admit that they
give more critical attention to allies than to adversaries because they have more leverage over the former—we
can withhold or threaten to withhold aid from our friends,
so why not strike a blow for freedom where we can, or, if
one prefers, why not administer the two-by-four to a mulish friend?

WHAT IS AMERICA'S RESPONSIBILITY?

In a formal and legal sense, the U.S. Government
has no responsibility—and certainly no authority—to promote human rights in other sovereign states. But this is
hardly the whole story. Because of our heritage, our dedication to humane government, our power, and our wealth,
we Americans have a moral responsibility, albeit ill-
defined, in the larger world consistent with our primary
obligations at home and commensurate with our capacity to
influence external events. We are almost universally regarded as a humanitarian power and as the champion of
freedom and decency. We should be proud of our humane occupation policies in Germany and Japan. But we enjoy no
occupation rights now, and the role of our government
abroad is less clear. Saying this, the American people
and their government can make two major contributions to
the cause of human rights in other countries.

First, in the spirit of John Quincy Adams and Lincoln, we can be worthy custodians of the freedom bequeathed
us by the Founding Fathers and thus continue to give heart
to the aspirations of peoples everywhere. We can give hope
to those in bondage by illustrating what the late Reinhold
Niebuhr has called "the relevance of the impossible ideal."
We can never fully realize our own ideals. And in most

other cultural settings, full respect for human rights
cannot be expected in the foreseeable future. A quick
change in government will not enshrine liberty of justice.
The message of our example is subdued, but not without
hope—the struggle for a bit more freedom of choice or a
better chance for justice is a never-ending one and after
small gains have been made, eternal vigilance is vital to
avoid sliding back into bondage. Serving as an example
of decency, then, is our most effective way to nudge forward the cause of human dignity.

     Second, our government can advance human rights by
strengthening our resolve and our resources to defend our
allies who are threatened by totalitarian aggression or
subversion. This requires security guarantees, military
assistance, and in some cases the presence of U.S. troops
on foreign soil. Our combined effort to maintain a fa-
vorable balance of power has succeeded in preserving the
independence of Western Europe, Japan, and South Korea.
But because of our half-hearted commitment, we failed in
Vietnam, Cambodia, and Laos, and in a different sense, in
Angola.

     We have a domestic consensus for continued support
of our North Atlantic allies and Japan, but some of our
commitments elsewhere have been eroded by confusion over
the nature of the threat. We are being severely tested
in Taiwan, South Korea, and southern Africa. In each
case, the totalitarians are pressing relentlessly by military, economic, political, and subversive means to destroy
and replace Western influence. The struggle in these
areas is hardly one of pure freedom against totalitarian-
ism, but human rights (as well as peace) are clearly at
stake. Any regime installed or sponsored by Moscow or
Peking in Seoul, Taipei, or Pretoria will certainly pro-

provide less justice and freedom than the imperfect regime it displaced.

Beyond serving as a good example and maintaining our
security commitments, there is little the U.S. Government
can or should do to advance human rights, other than using
quiet diplomatic channels at appropriate times and places.
Moscow and other governments should be reminded of their
pledges in the United Nations Charter and the Helsinki
Agreement. Public preaching to friend or foe has limited
utility. As we have already seen, it is both embarrassing
and contra-productive to threaten punitive measures against
friendly, but less than democratic, regimes which are at-
tempting to achieve a reasonable balance between authority
and freedom at home, often under severely trying circumstances, and are pursuing constructive policies abroad.

THE IRONY OF VIRTUE

The Carter Administration is not of one mind on the
significance, purpose, or effects of the human rights crusade. The administration is even less united in the implementation of the program in specific cases. During his
visit to Iran last December, President Carter gave his
final approval for the sale of six to eight nuclear re-
actors to that country whose government has been the target
of human rights activists as well as of Marxist groups.
Alleged rights violations by the Shah's government have
apparently had little effect on U.S. arms sales there.
The same appears to be true of South Korea. In fact, some
observers believe that the entire campaign so far has been
more rhetoric than reality, and some suggest that it was
launched more to satisfy the impulses of U.S. domestic
groups than to effect real changes in the external world.

In any event, there appears to be a growing recogni-

tion of the moral and political limitations of a foreign
policy crusade which, to repeat Mr. Carter, is based on
"constant decency" and "optimism." While defending the
campaign in principle, Secretary of State Cyrus Vance
notes some of the reservations and flaws developed above.
In a Law Day address, April 30, 1977, Mr. Vance warned
against a "self-righteous and strident" posture and said
"we must always keep in mind the limits of our power and
of our wisdom." He added that "a doctrinaire plan of
action" to advance human rights "would be as damaging as
indifference."

The tone of Mr. Vance's address stands in sharp contrast to President Carter's Notre Dame speech, which has
been criticized as arrogant, self-righteous, and naive by
Senator Daniel Moynihan and eight other foreign policy
observers in a monograph published last December.[3] Among
other things, these critics took exception to Mr. Carter's
view that there have been "dramatic worldwide advances in
the protection of the individual from the arbitrary power
of the state." In his pragmatic response to the security
and other political realities, however, the President is
far closer to Mr. Vance's words than to his own rhetoric.
In the interests of reasonable consistency, the President
has two choices—he can alter his rhetoric or alter his
actual policies. Politically and morally, reality is more
compelling than rhetoric.

---

[3]See *Morality and Foreign Policy: A Symposium on Pres-
ident Carter's Stance,* ed., Ernest W. Lefever, published by
Ethics and Public Policy Center, Georgetown University,
December 1977. The other critics are Robert L. Bartley,
Ronald L. Berman, Jeane Kirkpatrick, Charles Burton Mar-
shall, Michael Novak, John P. Roche, Eugene V. Rostow, and
Roger L. Shinn.

The canons of prudence, statesmanship, and accountability all suggest that the President tone down his
rhetoric. He should quietly recognize the political and
moral limits of promoting particular reforms in other
societies. He should recognize that a policy rooted in
a presumption of American righteousness and in our capacity to sponsor virtue in other states often leads to
the opposite effect. In some circumstances, the invocation of a rigid standard could undercut our security ties
and invite a disaster in which millions of persons would
move from partial freedom to tyranny.

Mr. Carter's policy is full of irony, precisely because his good intentions may lead to dire consequences.
Irony is not the result of evil intention or malice, but
rather of a hidden defect in virtue. In Mr. Carter's
case, at least in rhetoric, the defect is a kind of vague,
romantic optimism with an excessive confidence in the
power of reason and goodwill. This comforting view of
human nature, the child of the Enlightenment and social
Darwinism, differs sharply with the more sober Biblical
understanding of the nature and destiny of man. Be that
as it may, the President should not be judged on his
philosophical consistency, but rather by the actual policies he pursues. Since there is some relation between
how one thinks and feels and what one does, it is not inappropriate to recall the words of columnist Michael Novak: "One of the best ways to create an immoral foreign
policy is to try too hard for a moral one."

MORALITY AND U.S. FOREIGN POLICY

CHARLES FRANKEL

The United States was never an isolationist country except in a Pickwickian sense of the term. It went through no period of excluding the outside world, as the Japanese did for two hundred years. On the contrary, the United States, in consequence of its openness to immigration, linked itself, between 1790 and 1920, ever more closely by ties of culture and blood to the various countries of Europe. It engaged in trade with them, allowed and invited their economic support in the task of settling and exploiting the American continent, and sent its upper-class children and its best writers, artists, and scientists on mandatory tours of Europe for the good of their souls. Culturally, ethnically, in its historical affinities, the United States has been perhaps the least isolated of nations. It is, indeed, as has often been remarked, *Europe*—reestablished on this continent, not in its separate national units, but as a single new unit and new breed. The isolationism of the United States insofar as it has existed has been specifically political and military, and even in these areas it has been sporadic and highly selective.

Thus, the United States declared itself, early in the nineteenth century, through the Monroe Doctrine, the military guarantor of the Western Hemisphere against further European infiltration. In the course of the nineteenth century the United States assured itself a secure hand and

ample room in moving across the continent by conducting
a war against Mexico. It bought Florida from Spain, vast
territories from France, and Alaska from Russia. It became increasingly involved, through its traders, mission-
aries, and naval activities, with China. Its warships
off Edo Bay forced the opening of Japan. And it ended
the nineteenth century, like any nonisolationist country,
by securing its distant Western flank through the occupation of the Philippines. This is not a record of quiescence, of keeping clear of foreign governments, or of
failure to use American power affirmatively to advance
practical American interests or to extend the nation's
economic and military room for maneuver.

What then is meant by the common belief that, roughly between the times of Thomas Jefferson and Woodrow Wilson, the United States followed a policy of isolationism,
and that it reverted to this policy in the period between
the two world wars? Isolationism, it may be suggested,
refers essentially to three aspects of American relations
to the external world:

1. *Refusal to be a regular member of the European
diplomatic bargaining system and to take part as a normal
matter in its coalitions, negotiations, wars, and settle-
ments.* To put this positively, isolationism is the putting into practice of Hegel's dictum, pronounced in 1828,
that "America...is an ideal country for all those who are
weary of the bric-a-brac of Old Europe."

2. *Unilateral acquisition and maintenance of secure
borders and spheres of influence, using the prevailing
system of international understandings as the framework
and justification for this policy and relying, though
without saying so, essentially on Britain, particularly
its navy, to police those arrangements.* The symbolic act

is James Monroe's, who declined to join with the British
in a joint statement, as the British cabinet had suggested, but issued what came to be known as the Monroe
Doctrine in the form of a unilateral declaration in 1823.
If the only sanction behind this statement of protective
responsibility for two continents, addressed to the powerful nations of the Holy Alliance, had been the armed
force that the small and scattered American Republic could
put together, it would have been an act of laughable pre-
sumptuousness.   The statement had teeth because it could
be realistically assumed both by Americans and by the
members of the Holy Alliance that the British, though they
were not cosignatories of the statement, were nevertheless
prepared to enforce it.

   3.   *A settled rationale for this policy of collect-
ing the benefits of the international system while not
paying the taxes to support it.*   This rationale consisted
in the doctrine that the interstate system of alliances,
treaties, and negotiations was a European game, that the
governments engaged in it were not people's governments
based on consent or committed to the elevation of the free
individual, and that the object of the entire system was
not genuinely to abolish the evils of the international
scene like war and lawlessness, but only to conduct a
continuing political game of negotiation and balancing of
powers.   The United States, separated by an ocean and by
a Constitution guaranteeing the rights of man, should not
contribute, the doctrine maintained, to the perpetuation of
such a system.   The posture has a striking resemblance to
Thoreau's rationale for secession from the American body
politic: "I simply wish to refuse allegiance to the state,
to withdraw and stand aloof from its effectually...though
I will make what use and get what advantage of her I can,

as is usual in such cases."

Unlike Thoreau, however, who was only a private citizen, the United States Government could in fact half secede from the international system, particularly with the conveniently placed British navy to provide a feeling of security. Its isolationism did not prevent it from engaging in commercial relations or entering into inter-governmental understandings when it was expedient to do so. It consisted simply in the disposition—one-third conscious policy, one-third consecrated habit, one-third mere forgetfulness—to avoid anything but ad hoc and tem-porary involvement with the European diplomatic system of continuing negotiation, balancing and rebalancing of powers. It was not an imprudent way for the American na-tion to proceed from the point of view of its own self-interest. It thereby gained the advantages of the inter-national peace-keeping system and suffered few of the costs. And it had a rationale for its own continental expansion and for its activities in the Caribbean and Latin America—the protection and spreading of free gov-ernment; at the same time it also had a rationale for op-posing European imperialism—opposition to the spreading of unfree government. One may call this doctrine "moral-ism" if one will. Yet the large service it performed to the cause of American interests, realistically construed, should not be overlooked.

While there are many explanations of the entrance of the United States into World War I, and the arguments still continue, indeed, as to whether it was a wise de-cision, it is reasonably plain that when America abandoned its traditional military isolationism in 1917 the percep-tion had grown on our leaders that the British shield was not so impregnable as had been supposed. Confronted with

this situation, Woodrow Wilson envisaged our entry into
the war as more than a makeshift operation. It was a
step in earning the right and power to participate in
the postwar settlement. And the function of that settlement was to install a new interstate system to replace
the one whose failure was proved by the Great War. Britain could no longer, by itself, make balance-of-power
politics work in Europe, nor could it protect the United
States zones of economic and political autonomy. Accordingly, the United States would have to be a permanent part
of the new system.

But it was to be a new system. Speaking extempor-
aneously in Colorado in 1919——it was the last speech he
made before his disabling stroke——Wilson spoke of Gold
Star mothers he had seen:

> Why should they weep upon my head and call down the
> blessings of God upon me? Because they...believe,
> and they rightly believe, their sons saved the lib-
> erty of the world. They believe that wrapped up
> with that liberty is the continuous protection of
> that liberty by the concerted powers of all civi-
> lized people.... These men were crusaders...and
> all the world accepted them as crusaders, and their
> transcendent achievement has made all the world
> believe in America as it believes in no other
> nation organized in the modern world.... I wish
> sane men in public life who are now opposing the
> settlement for which these men died...could feel
> the moral obligation that rests upon us not to go
> back on those boys, but to see the thing through,
> to see it through to the end and make good their
> redemption of the world. For nothing less depends
> upon this decision, nothing less than the libera-
> tion and salvation of the world.

Reading these words fifty years later, with our own
disappointments and not Wilson's lying in our minds, they
may seem the words not of a statesman but of a Presbyter-
ian divine in an inflamed spiritual condition. But one
must see Wilson's problem as he saw it. The old interna-

tional system was dead, a new one was needed, and America
had to be part of that system. But it could not be unless
it was a redeemed system. For one who is not a Wilson
scholar speculation as to the "real beliefs" in Wilson's
mind would be fruitless. But if we look at the situation
he faced, the external rationale for the stance he took
is reasonably plain. America had to abandon a traditional position. The nation could be brought to do so only
by invoking its traditional sense of itself, by appealing
to its founding ideals and their universal meaning. Nor
did Wilson have to contrive such an approach to the problem consciously. He did not choose to imitate the cadences of the biblical prophet. They were his cadences,
the cadences of the culture that made him.

   And, almost as important, his American opponents
shared, by and large, that same way of perceiving international affairs. They believed, too, that an unredeemed
international system was not one in which the United
States could participate. "The little group of willful
men" around the first Senator Henry Cabot Lodge believed
that only the old worn and wicked system was being re-
stored. They thought the United States should stay out
of it, just as, on the other hand, Wilson thought that
there was no alternative to a radically reformed system
and no way of creating an effective one without United
States participation. The terms of the debate on both
sides were the same, and they were continuous with the
classic American tradition in foreign policy: scorn for
mere balance-of-power politics and for the selfish nationalism and imperialism perceived to characterize the
behavior of other nations; conviction that America's role
must be uniquely that of protecting liberty, law, and
moral principle.

It is in this context that the emergence of that
approach to American foreign policy known as realism
must be understood. The realists, chastened by the consequences of the combination of isolationism and high
pronunciamento that characterized American policy during
the long armistice of 1918-39, wanted the United States
to become a member, permanent, dues-paying, active, of
the interstate system of continuous negotiations. But
they did not believe that this system would be or could
be a redeemed system. They were internationalists who
agreed, philosophically, with Henry Cabot Lodge's jaun-
diced estimate of the diplomatic world. They needed to
put American participation in the international system,
therefore, on a new basis. The outcome was realism. It
was an effort to put American thinking about foreign affairs in a frame compatible with the country's conducting
a long, unremitting diplomatic enterprise, lit occasionally by successes, darkened much more often by disappointments and frustrations, possibly keeping the planet from
another holocaust, but never to be conceived as terminating
in a final victory of Light over Darkness.

                          * * *

The most influential spokesmen for the realists have
been extraordinary men: George Kennan, Hans Morgenthau,
and Reinhold Niebuhr. Gifted scholars and courageous public men, their realism is anything but the tired view that
moral principles are for children and that nothing counts
in foreign affairs but success. Indeed, what has given
their positions much of their attractiveness is the depth
of their *moral* conviction that in foreign affairs we deal
with the corruptions of human nature and must accept less
than the ideal.

Kennan, an historian, a professional diplomat, a man of unusual sensitivities to cultural climates different from his own, has not been repelled merely on practical grounds by the American tendency to lecture others on the moralities. The tendency—so, at least, it seems to this observer—has cut him to the moral quick: He has seen it as a breach of basic principles of tolerance and respect for others. In his view it is not merely naiveté; it is contempt for human diversity, for the profusion of God's creation, to fail to see that the world cannot be governed in accordance with any particular nation's conception of right and wrong. Morgenthau, more the systematizer than Kennan, is explicit in his concern for rationality in foreign policy. He regards it as a moral norm, not simply a technical imperative, as an instrument for reducing human pain, and not only for achieving tactical victories. Finally, Niebuhr was to the realists, in Kennan's words, "the father of us all." No one who knew him or his writings could fail to see that he was animated by both an acute moral sensibility and a passion for justice.

Whatever one's judgment as to the soundness of the position they have taken, these realists opened the windows and let in air. They have put the pontificators on the defensive and made it more difficult to discuss every national choice as though it were one between Heaven and Hell. In clarity, candor; humility, and compassion for impalpable and deceptive abstractions, they have raised the moral level of discussion by a considerable measure. That is one reason, perhaps the main reason, why they have won a following.

Yet the realists in foreign affairs, rather like their counterparts, "the legal realists" in jurisprudence,

represent not a tight doctrine but an approach, a conver-
gence of attitudes. They represent indeed the feeling
that the realities of international relations are too
complex and elusive to be caught by any doctrine. Nevertheless, seven major themes and guiding principles can
be discerned in their writings and statements, which allow us to indicate the main drift of their position.

   1. *All general principles, not only moral principles, are suspect in foreign policy.* This is particularly the emphasis in George Kennan's case. Aghast at the
overextended interpretation of the containment doctrine
as he had formulated it in his classic "Mr. X" article,
he has come, over the years, to make a principle of the
danger of abstract principles.

   2. *Moral principles are the worst kind of general
principles, for they add to the considerable dangers of
universalism the aggravated dangers of zealotry and utopianism.* Hoist on the banner of ultimate right and wrong,
the foreign policy maker is unable to compromise. He will
have a tendency to interpret every practical problem as an
illustration of a basic moral choice. And thus he will
drift into the interpretation of problems in outsize symbolic terms far outrunning any interpretation of their
significance by concrete and practical standards. The
symbols of eternal and ubiquitous confrontation, of a
trial by combat in which the whole world was the scene of
action and what was won by "them" was lost by "us," came
to take precedence over considerations of mere money, ge-
ography, culture, or identifiable military or political
challenge. Living this life of its own, like a cancer,
the containment doctrine, universalized, moralized, took
us by inexorable steps into Vietnam.

   3. *Beyond their suspicion of universalism and moral*

*zealotry the realists express a general skepticism about
the flashier aspects of foreign affairs—the signing of
treaties, the proclamation of peace by verbal agreement,
the theatrical international meetings at which old adversaries embrace.* Again like the legal realists, who led
a similar housecleaning expedition in the law, the foreign affairs realists think that what counts over the
long run is not the law in the books—the treaties on
the parchment pages—but the law in action—the day-to-
day progress of professional negotiators in understanding
one another, in ironing out issues under contention, and
in rendering competing national interests less mutually
threatening.

4. *As may have begun to emerge, the realists, to
a not inconsiderable extent, have been spokesmen for the
professionals in foreign policy.* Their approach, prag-
matically viewed, means that greater freedom, more room
for decision and maneuver, ought to be given to the non-
political, nonideological, permanent diplomatic corps.
This facet of the realist approach is more pronounced in
George Kennan and Walter Lippmann, who in many respects
belonged to the realist movement, than it is in Charles
Bohlen or Morgenthau or Niebuhr. Lippmann, in *The Political Philosophy,* spoke of the "malady" from which liberal
democracies were suffering, the mistaken distribution of
roles which assigned the electorate too much direct influence over foreign policy and prevented those who were best
informed from exercising effective leadership.

5. *Realists have insisted on the dichotomy between
morals and politics.* The principles by which men and women judge themselves in their private lives and personal
relations are not applicable to the behavior of states or
the conduct of people performing governmental roles. Hans

Morgenthau has put the matter starkly: "Neither science
nor ethics nor politics can resolve the conflict between
politics and ethics into harmony.... To act successfully,
that is, according to the rules of the political art, is
political wisdom. To know with despair that the political
act is inevitably evil, and to act nevertheless, is moral
courage."

6. *Realists have insisted that foreign policy
should be based on man as he is, not on man as a theoretic-
ian might desire him to be.* Niebuhr used the Christian
doctrines of history and human nature to make this point,
stressing the incurable seed of corruption in all things
human and the peculiar character of sin, which masks ego-
tistical drives behind universalist creeds. Foreign policy
realism, and particularly that of Niebuhr, must be seen
against the background of the failed political faiths of
the present century. It offered a framework for the belief that if people scaled down their moral demands, they
might develop a foreign policy capable of accomplishing
modest but decent purposes and of avoiding major disasters.

7. *Finally, the realists have stood for the reaffir-
mation of a picture of the interstate system that goes back
in its essentials to Hobbes's notion that war is the natural state of man.* Peace, in sum, is essentially a negative condition—the interval between wars—and while it
can, by arts of diplomacy, be indefinitely extended, the
process of doing so is like the process of extending the
length of human life: At the end one can only know that
one has conducted a successful delaying operation. Professor Morgenthau has been the most systematic in codify-
ing this approach to the theory and practice of international relations. He calls for the treatment of international politics rigorously in terms of "the concept of

interest defined in terms of power," and asserts that in
these terms international politics may be seen "as an independent sphere of action and understanding apart from
other spheres, such as economics, ethics, aesthetics or
religion."

                            * * *

     Let us consider the principal tenets of the realist
position one by one.
     1. *The suspect character, in foreign policy, of all*
general principles. Taken as a warning against overgener-
alization and overcommitment, this is sound and necessary
advice. Taken as a positive recommendation for conducting
the foreign affairs of a powerful modern state, it fails
on grounds of its unrealism.
     First, in the interest of creating a climate of psy-
chological security, other nations have to know, within
reasonable limits, what to expect of the United States.
If we do not give a hint as to our general intentions and
standards of behavior, they will make these up for themselves, constructing them from what they percieve to be
our behavior. If only to signal the nuances and qualifications that it wishes to have understood, a modern nation
particularly one from whose actions and inactions every
other nation takes cues, cannot afford not to make its
own general statements of purpose. The imperatives may
have been different when governments took their cues with
regard to one another from the exchanges and understandings of professional diplomats meeting and talking inti-
mately every day. But these professionals are no longer
the *in erlocuteurs valables* they once were; something more
is needed to discern the effective policy of a democratic
government than a daily conversation with its ambassador.

The centrality of this consideration in the mount-
ing of an effective foreign policy for a world now moving
pell-mell into the twenty-first century can hardly be
overemphasized. The United States declared war on Spain
in 1898 two days after Spain had acceded to the basic
American demand that it correct its relations with Cuba.
A primary reason, historians generally agree, was that
William Randolph Hearst's *New York Journal* and its con-
frères in the yellow press had built up so much public
hostility toward Spain that President McKinley's peaceful
options had been narrowed if not foreclosed. Seventy-
five years after that episode the world's nerve ends lie
even more exposed to the media of communication. Decis-
ion-makers lose control of policy because powerful public
reactions take over and divert the course of events into
unforeseen or unwanted channels, and foreign governments
find it difficult or impossible to read an ally's or adversary's intentions when they have to be discerned
through the thick smoke screen erected by the press and
television. In these conditions it becomes an indispensable prerequisite of stable relations with other governments that they know what our own government thinks are
its guiding principles.

Second, what is true for the foreign audience is at
least as true for the domestic audience. For better or
worse, a foreign policy will not be effective over the
long run if public opinion does not support it; and since
public opinion cannot be expected to have an informed
judgment on each specific decision taken day-by-day, its
assent has to be the general tendency and direction of
the policy—to its guiding principles. This is a prudential principle, but it is also one that goes to the
integrity and vitality of a democratic system. When for-

eign military-political policy was not a major concern
of citizens, it may have been possible to reserve a large
area of discretion for foreign affairs professionals and
say little or nothing to the public about the broad considerations of policy underlying their decisions. But
the American citizen today is immediately affected in
his everyday life by the price of oil, airplane hijack-
ings in political causes, military appropriations and
manpower demands, international monetary affairs, foreign
aid programs, and the Turkish attitude toward poppies.
Further, the press and television see to it that the citizen is also called upon to react, day after day, to matters whose practical bearing on his life may be somewhat
more remote, such as the Cyprus controversy of the terror-
ism in Ulster.

None of these matters can be dealt with rationally
if specialized knowledge and the professional skills of
diplomacy are not brought to bear on them. But the professionals acquire authority to make decisions for a democracy only insofar as they make them within a broader
consultative framework. This is a requirement of democracy *de jure and de facto*. The principles of democracy are
denied when this doesn't happen, and the practical capacity of a government to make decisions that the country
will accept and pay for is also diminished. But since
consultation, of course, cannot be on the day-to-day decisions, it must be on the framework of policy. The
framework, therefore, has to be made explicit.

Third, the agents of the policy themselves need
some general principles. Foreign policy is sustained
these days by large bureaucratic organizations. Consistency of action, proper preparation for contingencies,
the critique or reevaluation of what is being done—all

require more explicitness with regard to principles and
purposes than the realist formulas condemning general
formulas suggest. Indeed, do not the makers of policy
at the very top also need principles? How else are they
to articulate to themselves the reasons for their decisions? To be sure, they are likely to realize, if they
are experienced men and women, that no single principle,
not even two or three, will be adequate for navigating in
international waters. In making decisions, principles
have to be defined, limited, balanced against others, and
put in some order of priority appropriate for the case
at hand. But if decisions are to be made rationally,
reasons have to be given that apply to more than the case
at hand. Logically there is no way away from principles.

Realism, in sum, reaffirms the traditional wisdom
of lawyers and diplomatists that holds it is a mistake to
make a decision on broader grounds than are needed, because one will live to regret the straitjacket one has
made for oneself. But it overstates the case. If we
took some of its extreme statements literally, foreign
policy would be turned into the cult of a secret guild.

2. *The enunciation of moral principles in foreign
policy contexts encourages zealotry and utopianism.* Perhaps the greatest appeal of the realists lies in their
spirit of toleration and moderation. They are men of
peaceful and conciliatory intent, not doctrinaire, not
prigs. Like Thomas Hobbes, they detest most of all the
morally illuminated, the people who know the answer to
every problem and believe it consists in resurrecting
some moral platitude. In an age of rampaging political
ideologies they speak for the utility of a dispassionate
tone and a straightforward factual analysis in the formulation and conduct of foreign policy.

Once again they have their finger on an important truth, but their statement of it turns it into a dangerous half-truth. What makes moral principles irresponsible is their enunciation without regard to putting them into practice, or to their consequences if acted upon, or to their coherence with other moral principles to which attention also has to be given. In other words, what makes moral principles dangerous is their treatment as absolutes, their immunization from criticism in the light of facts and possibilities. But it is no solution to this problem to suggest, "Look only at the facts; moral principles are distractions." Shorn of their aura of mystery and sanctimony, moral principles are simply guidelines to action. They help us to decide what to do. They are *moral,* not merely technical or pragmatic, because they help us to decide what to do not about evanescent or intermediate matters but about dearly prized values in which our civilization has deep investments and our own sense of identity and self-respect is involved. It is hard to believe that the realists have counseled the extrusion of moral considerations in this sense of the term. What they have wished to extrude, it may be assumed, is moral absolutism. It is not helpful to pursue this absolutism. It is not helpful to pursue this objective by what can be too easily construed as a general denigration of the value of moral principles to foreign policy.

It might be said, of course, that the difference between the realists' view and that expressed in the present essay is merely a matter of emphasis. This, in his trenchantly reasoned book *In Defense of the National Interes:,* which warned effectively against the dangers of the cold war missionary spirit, Professor Morgenthau distinguished between three types of American foreign policy:

"the realistic—thinking and acting in terms of power—
represented by Alexander Hamilton; the ideological—
thinking in terms of moral principles but acting in terms
of power—represented by Thomas Jefferson and John Quincy
Adams; and the moralistic—thinking and acting in terms
of moral principles—represented by Woodrow Wilson." Perhaps only a question of degree separates this view from
one which maintains, as the present essay does, that for
a long period in the nineteenth century the American commitment to liberty, popular government, and disengagement
from the evildoing of the Old World was compatible with
an aggressive and power-oriented foreign policy, and indeed, for better or worse, helped explain and justify
that policy.

Nevertheless, it is hard to avoid the impression
that the realists' emphasis on power is more than merely
a warning against utopianism. Professor Morgenthau's
threefold distinction between realism, ideology, and
moralism rests on the unexamined assumption that thinking
in terms of morals and thinking in terms of power are inevitably two different things. It leaves out a fourth
possibility—that thinking about morals and thinking
about power may interact on each other so that the uses
of power are guided by moral considerations even while
moral principles are corrected and criticized in terms of
their applicability to the realistic possibilities of life.
Lacking this fourth possibility, Professor Morgenthau's
argument has to cross a logical vacuum. He argues that
the concept of national interest has moral dignity because,
in the absence of an integrated international society, the
hope for an attainment of a minimum of moral values is
"predicated upon the existence of national communities
capable of preserving order and realizing moral values

within the limits of their power." Accordingly, when a
national community struggles for self-preservation, this
has moral consequences. But this apparently tough-minded
position contains a nest of unanswered questions. *Which*
national communities shall be permitted to struggle for
self-preservation? The Biafrans or federal Nigeria, the
Scots or the United Kingdom? Are there reasonable limits
to what may be done in the name of national self-preservation? Is there a point at which a struggle for the national interest—defined as self-preservation—destroys
crucial moral values not only externally but internally?
Indeed, what is a national community, and what does its
self-preservation mean?

In the case of societies survival is a slippery
term to define. In terms of blood lines the Mayans survive in Mexico. In terms of philosophy, drama, and a
conception of citizenship the ancient Greeks survive. In
terms of vigorous communal life the Basques, Bretons,
Welsh, and Zulus survive, but not one has political sovereignty. After the Nazi conquest France retained a version
of sovereignty, but in the eyes of many of its own people
it had sacrificed what was most worth preserving in the
country. In sum, the definition of the national interest
that is the be-all and end-all of policy is radically in-
complete unless a deliberate choice is made of the characteristics that are held to be definitive of the society
and worth preserving.

This requires a moral judgment. Not even the pres-
ervation of national sovereignty is a self-sufficient
goal. Would an America that retained its sovereignty
only by rejecting constitutional government, practicing
apartheid, and turning loose a secret police be prefera-
ble to an America that was a province of a foreign land,

but one which protected traditional American rights?
Obviously this is an extreme case. But it shows that
the problem, logically, is one of the relation of means
to ends, and that we can take no end so much for granted that
we do not ask what is done in its name. People have been
known to ruin a country in the name, after all, of defending it. A man who would stand for anything his government does can be charged not with love of his country
but with contempt for it.

     3. *The preference for genuine working understand-
ings over dramatic agreements on paper.* No stronger
point, in my estimation, has been made by the realists.
It would benefit, however, from two qualifications.

     The first is that the working understandings must
be spelled out, in the contemporary world, not only in
the day-to-day cooperation of professional diplomats but
in the far broader patterns of conduct worked out in international business and trade, in philanthropies and
technical assistance, and in scientific, cultural, and
artistic partnerships. With the exception of the higher
orders of the Church and the very top of the international
intelligentsia, professional diplomats were once the only
effective transnational community. That is not true now,
and an effective "structure of peace" cannot be built by
them alone.

     The second qualification follows. The evolution
of working understandings along a broad spectrum of transnational activities is indeed the substance of progress
in foreign affairs. Spectacular agreements by chiefs of
state or their principal ministers on forms of words are
superficial in comparison. However, progress in effective
transnational cooperation is facilitated by government
actions that signal new opportunities and alter the legal

and psychological settings. Summitry can easily be over-
done, to the point, indeed, of being little more than an
expensive form of theatre. But the writers of treaties
and the participants in publicized conferences still
have indispensable work to do. Symbolic gestures are
messages. The international arena requires them.

4. *The emphasis on professionalism in foreign policy.* The professionals in foreign policy have indeed had
in the United States much less than the respect to which
they are entitled. Perhaps no group in the country has
had to put up with more vicious and ignorant abuse than
the Foreign Service, and it has come from every side—
left, center, and right. Nevertheless, the idea of increasing the power of the professional corps of foreign
service officers, as against the power of the committees
of Congress or of the President and his appointees, does
not recommend itself as having a practical political future. Nor does it fit the conventional canons of elective government. And beyond these difficulties it contends with two others.

The first is that professional diplomats often know
foreign countries better than their own and lack the powers
of communication to touch base effectively with the citizenry at home. They must lean on politicians if only to
receive help in transmitting their professional judgments,
and politicians are unlikely to perform this service while
refraining from exercising influence over those judgments.
As Charles Bohlen, the professionals' professional, observed: "The most carefully thought-out plans of the ex-
perts, even though one hundred per cent correct in theory,
will fail without broad public support. The good leader
in foreign affairs formulates his policy on expert advice
and creates a climate of public opinion to support it."

It is others who create and maintain this climate of
support for the professional. He remains, therefore,
essentially an advisor and an executor of other people's
wills. His room for maneuver and his power of trans-
lating policy into practice may be considerable, but he
is not a legislator, not even a judge, and his authority
is mainly derivative from that of his patron. The patron
will, in the end, call the tune.

The second difficulty in the translation of respect
for professionalism into an operative governmental policy
is that the professionals do not themselves perform as a
unified group with a common judgment. The failure to
note the significance of this fact is one of the basic
gaps in the argument by Walter Lippmann in his influential
The Public Philosophy. He there complains that the foreign policy élite, the people capable of making knowledge-
able decisions, are not permitted to make them. But, as
it happens, they are not of one mind. The sticky practical problem is to decide whose counsel to follow. How
shall that be done? And by whom? And shall it be done
without checking with those responsible for the orchestra-
tion of tax policies, economic programs, conservation,
education, and all the other matters with which a government deals? An old political dream, as old as Plato, is
to get rid of politics itself, to do away with pressures,
accommodations, bargains, and the entire messy problem of
deciding intractable issues by imprecise standards, and
to substitute the cool authoritative judgment of those
who know the "true" and the "good" and have no motive but
to serve them. Oddly, something that looks a little bit
like that utopian dream lurks in the realist desire to
give the professionals more elbow room.

5. *The dichotomy between morals and politics.* The

realist states a general truth which applies to far more
than foreign policy. That truth is that the moral rules
that apply to people performing complex social roles are
not the same as those applying to people in their more
intimate personal or familial relations.

There are at least three reasons why the morality
appropriate to the performance of a formalized social
role and the morality of small-scale, face-to-face relations are different. First, the role is usually specialized; second, it is fiduciary—the decision-maker is
acting for others; third, large numbers of people, usually unknown to the decision-maker, are likely to be affected. Rules for behavior in such a domain are properly
different from those for settings in which the actor is
acting for himself, in which he can directly observe the
consequences, and in which the primary people affected
are people he knows personally and lives with in a variety of situations. In stressing that there are differences
between the morality of large-scale social relations and
the morality of the home and neighborhood, political realism has had a valid point. Building peace in the world
is not the same sort of process as organizing a community
picnic.

But this truth is obscured when it is stated as a
conflict between the realm of morals and the nonmoral
realm of politics. What is involved is a collision between different sets of moral rules, not the extrusion of
morality from one domain. A major source of this confusion is the unstated presupposition that morality or ethics stand only for the traditional maxims of face-to-face
relations. Professor Morgenthau, for example, defines
morality in terms of the classic Kantian precept that
every person should be treated as an end and never as a

means. It is an opaque maxim at best, which cannot be
applied, except by tortuous casuistry, to contemporary
conditions of work, exchange, or social regulation. The
unintended but unavoidable consequence of using such a
precept is to imprison the moral outlook of society within a perspective attuned to conditions long since changed,
and to cut off large areas of human life from the control
of reasoned moral standards. In this way morality is condemned *a priori* and by definition to be ineffective.

This habit of restricting the meaning of morality
to a narrow and traditional frame is a major obstacle to
the humane improvement of complex social institutions.
For example, the habit, derived from codes designed for
face-to-face relations, of thinking that liability for
injuries done to others must require specific fault, long
impeded the adoption of legal reforms like strict liability and no-fault insurance. Similarly, the traditional
notion that one owes family and friends special loyalty
is today an obstacle, in many countries, to the establishment of competent civil services. More broadly still, the
habit of insisting that the norms applicable to intimate
relations are the only moral norms is a principal reason
why large areas of social life in our rapidly changing
world are normatively unregulated. This fallacy is implicit in Professor Morgenthau's separation of ethics
from politics. International affairs are simply a particularly pertinent and poignant illustration of the problem of resolving conflicts of moral standards. They are
not a domain where people have no choice but to be immoral.

What are we to make of statements like Professor
Morgenthau's to the effect that "the political act is
inevitably evil"? In the ordinary use of the word evil

the statement is false: political acts aren't *inevitably* evil. A successful negotiation staving off a bloody war, a nuclear test-ban treaty, an international agreement to combat malaria are none of them evil in the everyday language of everyday people. The only explanation for this otherwise puzzling statement is that Professor Morgenthau is using the word in an esoteric way. He means, one must presume, that in negotiating an end to a war or arriving at international agreements some people's interests will be adversely affected, that forms of bargaining will probably take place which would not be appropriate in a roomful of old friends, and that some moral values will be treated as less important than others. In sum, choosing, weighing, balancing, and blending take place. But to call this "evil" is to reserve the word "good" for only those kinds of behavior where we know exactly what the right thing to do is, and don't need to think about the matter at all. It saves the word "good" for the behavior of gods.

Yet the author does not believe he states merely an inference from what Professor Morgenthau says. The following passage from his writing, one of many that might be offered, indicates that he takes this position explicitly:

> The very act of acting destroys our moral integrity.... Why is this so with respect to all actions and particularly so with respect to political actions? First of all...the human intellect is unable to calculate and to control completely the results of human action....[Second], the demands which life in society makes on our good intentions surpass our faculty to satisfy them all. While satisfying one, we must neglect others, and the satisfaction of one may even imply the positive violation of another.... Whatever choice we make, we must do evil while we try to do good, for we must abandon one moral end in favor of another.

> While trying to render to Caesar what is Caesar's
> and to God what is God's, we will at best strike
> a precarious balance which will ever waver between
> both, never completely satisfying either. In the
> extreme, we will abandon one completely in order
> fully to satisfy the other. The typical solution,
> however, will be a compromise which puts the strug-
> gle at rest without putting conscience at ease
> (*Scientific Man Versus Power Politics*).

This must regretably be called not political realism but moral melodramatics. Professor Morgenthau is
pointing only to the fact that man cannot have or do
everything he wants, that he must choose, and that he
must do so though inadequately informed and equipped.
To turn these not entirely recondite facts into evidence
for the proposition that politics is no place for ethics
is a resounding *non sequitur.* Human fallibility and
choice are not evil. They are the conditions that make
the moral life, and therefore both good and evil, possible.

In sum, the utopianism in realism keeps rearing its
head. Realism takes a standard of good applicable to immortal and omniscient beings, and then, because it does
not find this standard attainable in the international
arena, pronounces action in that arena inevitably evil.
But is there not something wrong with a standard which,
in relation to the arena where the most fateful decisions
about life, death, pride, liberty, justice, and the distribution of wealth are taken, yields the result that
considerations of right and wrong are somehow out of
bounds? The desideratum is not tough-sounding statements
about "immoral society." It is the evolution of moral
standards appropriate to the limits and possibilities of
international relations.

6. *Foreign policy should be based on man as he is
and not as the policy-maker would like him to be.* Again

it would seem, realism has pushed a sound point too far.
There are, no doubt, people who think that peace can be
achieved if only the Good or Enlightened take over from
he Wicked or Unenlightened. Others, though not so naive,
appear to hope that mankind can achieve in the international arena what it has not yet achieved, with some
scattered exceptions, in smaller forms of social organizations, e.g., a secure system of law and order equitably
administered, religious and racial tolerance, and a division of the world's goods to which no significant group
makes objection. Excessive hopes, which people around
the world have entertained, and which have been repeatedly shattered in this century, have often caused great
damage. It is a distortion of historical perspective, a
kind of preoccupation with the American case alone, to
identify such vaulting idealism with Wilsonianism alone,
but it is understandable that the realists should take
some of Wilson's rhetoric as a symbol of such hopes and
that they should warn against them.

However, the inverted utopianism in the realist vision has pushed this valid insight astray. The words
Niebuhr employed to explain the intractable facts of the
international scene are words like sin and human corruption, belonging to an otherworldly morality. It is perhaps natural to revert to such words given to us by the
religious tradition, but their use tends to do precisely
what the realists condemn. Statements about foreign policy are absorbed into a framework designed to deal with
the religious alternatives of damnation and redemption.
Reading Woodrow Wilson and then reading Niebuhr, one recognizes the same language and preoccupations. Wilson
often talked as though he believed that God had given His
people a progressive mission on earth. In reaction,

Niebuhr warned that the essence of sin was to mistake an
earthly perspective or possibility for a divine one. But
the disagreement was between two profoundly religious men
speaking on a religious theme. If we wish to break foreign policy thinking free from evangelical horizons, the
desirable strategy is to use a language without such religious overtones and less conducive to the fallacy of
supposing that since heaven is unattainable we must put
up forever with hell or purgatory. The language of Niebuhr, and even of Morgenthau, when he speaks of "the very
act of acting" as destroying "our moral integrity," belongs to the tradition of evangelicalism; it is merely
its brokenhearted version.

     A classic example of an alternative language is
Spinoza's entirely naturalistic discussion of the goodness and evil of mankind in the political arena. He
wrote in his *Political Treatise:*

> I have labored carefully not to mock, lament, or exe-
> crate, but to understand human actions; and to this
> end I have looked upon passions such as love, hatred,
> anger, envy, ambition, pity, and the other perturba-
> tions of the mind not in the light of vices of human
> nature, but as properties just as pertinent to it as
> are heat, cold, storm, thunder, and the like to the
> nature of the atmosphere, which phenomena, though in-
> convenient, are yet necessary, and have fixed causes.

Spinoza's description of political man was unillusioned. But he did not use transcendental standards,
applicable to a world before the Fall, in order to condemn men and political institutions for being what they
are. Spinoza, though he believed that "vices will exist
as long as men do," and though he understood that statesmen must be practical and said they have a duty to be so,
did not conclude that this reduced ethics to a subordinate role. The object of a good ordering of public

affairs was to insure that those who administered these affairs, "whether guided by reason or passion, cannot be led to act treacherously or basely." These are moral concerns.

It should be noted, too, that although man has vices, it is also man who makes the judgment that he has vices. The "reality" of human affairs, surely the "reality" of international politics, is not constituted only by the presence of fear, cupidity, greed, and envy. Aspiration is present and a glimmering of reason, mutual comprehension, and human fraternity. Only a passion can conquer a passion. Spinoza remarked, *That* is realism. It is passion—other people's passion and his own—that destroys the foreign policy technician's plan and predictions, and reveals him, in the end, to be a closet thinker. If the fiercer and more unregenerate passions that lead to the greatest disasters in international affairs are to be controlled, a foreign policy needs animating ideals; it needs hopes which though not unrealistic, are generous. The realists in international affairs, with their emphasis on limits, not possibilities, do not meet this need. A nation's foreign policy requires an animating idea behind it. A nation like the United States requires an idea that the future is not condemned to repeat the past.

7. *The emphasis on international relations as rivalry-relations, and on the object of foreign policy as the pursuit of the national interest.* It is superfluous to say that rivalry is a constant of foreign affairs. But in reviewing the picture of international politics to which the realist approach tends, one is reminded of David Hume's response to philosophers whose desire to be unillusioned led them to portray human nature as overwhelmingly selfish:

"The descriptions which certain philosophers delight so
much to form of mankind in this particular are as wide
of nature as any accounts of monsters which we meet with
in fables and romance." As Hume pointed out, though
self-love is perhaps the strongest single emotion in
most people, the combination of their other feelings—
for example, their love of their families, their desire
for the respect of their fellows, their concern, in consequence of communal traditions and education, for the
institutions and aspirations of their society—is often
sufficient to override self-love. The ultimate problem
of education and social arrangements is to create conditions in which this desirable balance among the emotions
is normal.

May not international relations be approached from
a similar point of view? It would not be less realistic
than the realistic view; it would only be more open to
the variety of relationships across the borders that actually exist, and to the possibilities of cultivating
the more desirable of them. For it is not the case that
the international scene is only a system of competing
national sovereignties. International business, the arts,
cinema, and sciences, ideologies, philanthropies, cultures and countercultures, medicine, religion, social
ideals like liberty and equality—all cross borders.
Transnational communities, formal and informal, active or
latent, have been formed around all these interests and
activities. In relation to such communities frontiers
are anachronisms and give misleading notions of the
facts. And the sovereign state is relatively ineffective
in shutting off this transnational and many-sided exchange
and cooperation. Not even the homeopathic measures
adopted by the Soviet Union have been entirely successful.

Nor are common interests, occupations, and ideas
the only things that interrupt the play of national rivalries. The common problems of the nations do so as
well. The oil crisis, the world food shortage, the indifference of pollutants in the air and water to national boundaries, the international character of in-
flation, the "North-South" difficulties in tariffs, trade,
and movements of population are all problems which no
nation can solve by itself. If realism represents an
interest in survival, then it is unrealistic to suppose
that twentieth-century affairs are susceptible to being
managed by outworn national policies and institutions
created to take care of rivalry and little else.

The narrow terms of national self-interest made
more sense, at least *prima facie,* in the nineteenth century, when military power was less hideous, nations were
less interdependent, and the status quo better established
and accepted.   In such conditions foreign policies exclusively concerned with maintaining the balance of power
among major sovereign states—an essentially status quo
enterprise—were intelligible. Today, when powers of
destruction are almost unlimited, when change is constant
and accelerating, and when the fates of so many are inevitably interwoven, new conditions for international cooperation need to be constructed. This requires more
clearly formulated basic principles than when the desideratum was simply to maintain a status quo.

The degree to which common dangers can today force
otherwise hostile nations together is illustrated by the
two-sided effect of nuclear armaments on the world scene.
On the one side we have what Herbert Butterfield, the
noted British historian, has called "the predicament of
Hobbesian fear": "If you imagine yourself locked in a

room with another person with whom you have often been
on the most bitterly hostile terms in the past, and
suppose that each of you has a pistol, you may find
yourself in a predicament in which both of you would like
to throw the pistols out of the window, yet it defeats
the intelligence to find a way of doing it." On the other side, however, as the slow but perceptible movement
toward disentanglement from this predicament shows, the
cost and the terror of nuclear armament have created common interest in peace and accommodation stretching across
sectors of both the Soviet and American governments as
well as their populations.

The realist emphasis on the rivalries in the interstate system, in short, confuses a part of the international scene, although admittedly a most important part,
with the whole. Attention is thereby diverted from those
aspects of international affairs moving toward new forms
of transnationalism and internationalism. Practitioners
of the philosophy of realism——Mr. Kissinger is an example——
can properly be criticized for not paying sufficient attention to the problems of international economic governance that have been created by the transnational movement
of corporations, investments, technicians, and currencies.
It is hard to think of any actions in the past decade,
other than the Vietnam war, which have more greatly dam-
aged our international position or the economies of the
world than the brusque unilateral decisions taken by
Secretary John Connally and the Nixon Administration regarding the dollar and the trade deficit. In the present
world setting talk about the inevitability of national
rivalries is like doctors sitting around and sagely pre-
dicting everyone's death. It does not deal with the
problem at hand.

Nor is it clear what the term "national interest" means when it is used as Mr. Morgenthau uses it, to name the defining object of foreign policy. It is an algebraic formula. The phrase was more useful as a technical term of diplomacy when diplomats were the servants of dynasties with identifiable family lines. The imperatives it defined were those involved with keeping a large, rich family going—a lustrous family name, more money, more land, sound marriages, dependable retainers, a household service on whose competence and loyalty the family could count. Even so, difficult judgments had to be made as to what the best interests of the client were. But in principle one could turn to the permanent head of the family to ask his decision. Things are different if one is superintending the external policy of a large heterogeneous nation and of a democratic one led by a figure whose expected term of office is four or eight years.

Even a nation's geographic position remains fixed only in an abstract sense. The realities of distance, resources, needs, military dangers, and opportunities are all affected by changes in technology, population movements, and other circumstances. In the definition of national interests even more elusive considerations are pertinent—the military intentions of others, the minimal economic standards that have to be preserved domestically, the traditional objectives of the nation, the extent and nature of what is perceived as a "congenial" political-cultural environment. Not one of these can be given concrete meaning without making value judgments. Among the variety of competing concerns felt and expressed in the nation, decision makers must select by deliberate choice or by default those which in their judgment are most

important to its well-being. A national interest is not
a chart pinned to the wall from which one takes one's
sense of direction. The heart of the decision-making
process, in which the professional foreign service officer inescapably plays a part, is not the finding of
the best means to serve a national interest already perfectly known and understood. It is the determining of
that interest itself: the reassessement of the nation's
resources, needs, commitments, traditions, and political
and cultural horizons—in short, in calendar values.

In its most systematic form, that given to it by
Professor Morgenthau, the doctrine of political realism,
it appears to this writer, is an ideology whose consequence, though not intended, is to justify a posture of
professional privilege, of immunity from decisions about
ends and principles. In making the central concept of
international politics "the concept of interest defined
in terms of power" Professor Morgenthau attempts to establish both a clearly defined *theory* of politics separate
from other spheres, "such as economics, ethics, aesthetics
or religion," and also a separate *"sphere of action."*
Political realism, he says, has "a normative element....
It considers a rational foreign policy (i.e., one that
maximizes the national interest defined in terms of power)
to be a good foreign policy. "The fallacy in this position is illustrated by the scene in Molière's *Les Femmes
Savantes* in which ladies impressed by their knowledge of
newly discovered laws of gravitation lecture a servant
for being so foolish as to have fallen down. When an
economist says that economic fluctuations are rendered
intelligible by making the concept of profit-maximization
central, that is a piece of economic theory; when he says
that businessmen are "irrational" or follow a bad policy

when they let ethics, aesthetics, religion, or politics
affect their behavior, that is a value judgment dressed
up as a scientific finding. Nobody is under an obligation, moral or otherwise, to behave in accordance with
the rules that students of society lay down in order to
make their fields of study systematically intelligible.
Nor is there a conceptual sleight of hand by which, when
a diplomat or soldier offers his judgment as to what is
in the best interest of the nation, he can be let off
the moral hook and treated as a mere technician. *Real-
politik* is a version of morals; it is not a leave of
absence from morals.

POLITICAL ACTION:
THE PROBLEM OF DIRTY HANDS[1]

MICHAEL WALZER

The preceding essays first appeared in *Philosophy
& Public Affairs* as a symposium on the rules of war which
was actually (or at least more importantly) a symposium
on another topic.[2] The actual topic was whether or not
a man can ever face, or even has to face, a moral dilemma, a situation where he must choose between two courses
of action both of which it would be wrong for him to undertake. Thomas Nagel worriedly suggested that this
could happen and that it did happen whenever someone was that
forced to choose between upholding an important moral
pinciple and avoiding some looming disaster.[3] R. B.
Brandt argued that it could not possibly happen, for there
were guidelines we might follow and calculations we might
go through which would necessarily yield the conclusion
that one or the other course of action was the right one
to undertake in the circumstances (or that it did not matter which we undertook). R. M. Hare explained how it was
someone might wrongly suppose that he was faced with a
moral dilemma: sometimes, he suggested, the precepts and
principles of an ordinary man, the products of his moral
education, come into conflict with injunctions developed
at a higher level of moral discourse. But this conflict
is, or ought to be, resolved at the higher level; there
is no real dilemma.

I am not sure that Hare's explanation is at all
comforting, but the question is important even if no such
explanation is possible, perhaps especially so if this is
the case. The argument relates not only to the coherence
and harmony of the moral universe, but also to the relative ease or difficulty—or impossibility—of living a
moral life. It is not, therefore, merely a philosopher's
question. If such a dilemma can arise, whether frequently
or very rarely, any of us might one day face it. Indeed,
many men have faced it, or think they have, especially men
involved in political activity or war. The dilemma, exactly as Nagel describes it, is frequently discussed in
the literature of political action—in novels and plays
dealing with politics and in the work of theorists too.

In modern times the dilemma appears most often as
the problem of "dirty hands," and it is typically stated
by the Communist leader Hoerderer in Sartre's play of that
name: "I have dirty hands right up to the elbows. I've
plunged them in filth and blood. Do you think you can
govern innocently?"[4] My own answer is no, I don't think
I could govern innocently; nor do most of us believe that
those who govern us are innocent—as I shall argue below—
even the best of them. But this does not mean that it
isn't possible to do the right thing while governing. It
means that a particular act of government (in a political
party or in the state) may be exactly the right thing to
do in utilitarian terms and yet leave the man who does it
guilty of a moral wrong. The innocent man, afterwards, is
no longer innocent. If on the other hand he remains innocent, chooses, that is, the "absolutist" side of Nagel's
dilemma, he not only fails to do the right thing (in utilitarian terms), he may also fail to measure up to the

duties of his office (which imposes on him a considerable responsibility for consequences and outcomes). Most
often, of course, political leaders accept the utilitarian calculation; they try to measure up. One might offer
a number of sardonic comments on this fact, the most obvious being that by the calculations they usually make
they demonstrate the great virtues of the "absolutist"
position. Nevertheless, we would not want to be governed
by men who consistently adopted that position.

The notion of dirty hands derives from an effort to
refuse "absolutism" without denying the reality of the
moral dilemma. Though this may appear to utilitarian
philosophers to pile confusion upon confusion, I propose
to take it very seriously. For the literature I shall
examine, is the work of serious and often wise men, and
it reflects, though it may also have helped to shape, popular thinking about politics. It is important to pay attention to that too. I shall do so without assuming, as
Hare suggests one might, that everyday moral and political discourse constitutes a distinct level of argument,
where content is largely a matter of pedagogic expediency.[5] If popular views are resistant (as they are) to
utilitarianism, there may be something to learn from that
and not merely something to explain about it.

                           i

Let me begin, then, with a piece of conventional
wisdom to the effect that politicians are a good deal
worse, morally worse, than the rest of us (it is the
wisdom of the rest of us). Without either endorsing it
or pretending to disbelieve it, I am going to expound
this convention. For it suggests that the dilemma of
dirty hands is a central feature of political life, that

it arises not merely as an occasional crisis in the career of this or that unlucky politician but systematically and frequently.

Why is the politician singled out? Isn't he like
the other entrepreneurs in an open society, who hustle,
lie, intrigue, wear masks, smile and are villains? He
is not, no doubt for many reasons, three of which I need
to consider. First of all, the politician claims to
play a different part than other entrepreneurs. He does
not merely cater to our interests; he acts on our behalf,
even in our name. He has purposes in mind, causes and
projects that require the support and redound to the benefit, not of each of us individually, but of all of us
together. He hustles, lies, and intrigues for *us*—or so
he claims. Perhaps he is right, or at least sincere, but
we suspect that he acts for himself also. Indeed, he
cannot serve us without serving himself, for success
brings him power and glory, the greatest rewards that men
can win from their fellows. The competition for these
two is fierce; the risks are often great, but the temptations are greater. We imagine ourselves succumbing. Why
should our representatives act differently? Even if they
would like to act differently, they probably cannot: for
other men are all too ready to hustle and lie for power
and glory, and it is the others who set the terms of the
competition. Hustling and lying are necessary because
power and glory are so desirable—that is, so widely de-
sired. And so the men who act for us and in our name are
necessarily hustlers and liars.

Politicians are also thought to be worse than the
rest of us because they rule over us, and the pleasures
of ruling are much greater than the pleasures of being
ruled. The successful politician becomes the visible

architect of our restraint. He taxes us, licenses us,
forbids and permits us, directs us to this or that distant goal——all for our greater good. Moreover, he takes
chances for our greater good that put us, or some of us,
in danger. Sometimes he puts himself in danger too, but
politics, after all, is his adventure. It is not always
ours. There are undoubtedly times when it is good or
necessary to direct the affairs of other people and to
put them in danger. But we are a little frightened of
the man who seeks, ordinarily and every day, the power to
do so. And the fear is reasonable enough. The politician has, or pretends to have, a kind of confidence in his
own judgment that the rest of us know to be presumptuous
in any man.

The presumption is especially great because the
victorious politician uses violence and the threat of
violence——not only against foreign nations in our defense
but also against us, and again ostensibly for our greater
good. This is a point emphasized and perhaps overemphasized by Max Weber in his essay "Politics as a Vocation"[6]
It has not, so far as I can tell, played an overt or obvious part in the development of the convention I am examining. The stock figure is the lying, not the murderous,
politician——though the murderer lurks in the background,
appearing most often in the form of the revolutionary or
terrorist, very rarely as an ordinary magistrate or official. Nevertheless, the sheer weight of official violence
in human history does suggest the kind of power to which
politicians aspire, the kind of power they want to wield,
and it may point to the roots of our half-conscious dis-
like and unease. The men who act for us and in our name
are often killers, or seem to become killers too quickly
and too easily.

Knowing all this or most of it, good and decent
people still enter political life, aiming at some specific reform or seeking a general reformation. They are
then required to learn the lesson Machiavelli first set
out to teach: "how not to be good."[7] Some of them are
incapable of learning; many more profess to be incapable.
But they will not succeed unless they learn, for they
have joined the terrible competition for power and glory;
they have chosen to work and struggle as Machiavelli
says, among "so many who are not good." They can do no
good themselves unless they win the struggle, which they
are unlikely to do unless they are willing and able to
use the necessary means. So we are suspicious even of
the best of winners. It is not a sign of our perversity
if we think them only more clever than the rest. They
have not won, after all, because they were good, or not
only because of that, but also because they were not good.
No one succeeds in politics without getting his hands
dirty. This is conventional wisdom again, and again I
don't mean to insist that it is true without qualification.
I repeat it only to disclose the moral dilemma inherent in
the convention. For sometimes it is right to try to succeed, and then it must also be right to get one's hands
dirty. But one's hands get dirty from doing what it is
wrong to do. And how can it be wrong to do what is right?
Or, how can we get our hands dirty by doing what we ought
to do?

ii

It will be best to turn quickly to some examples. I
have chosen two, one relating to the struggle for power
and one to its exercise. I should stress that in both
these cases the men who face the dilemma of dirty hands

have in an important sense chosen to do so; the cases
tell us nothing about what it would be like, so to speak,
to fall into the dilemma; nor shall I say anything about
that here. Politicians often argue that they have no
right to keep their hands clean, and that may well be
true of them, but it is not so clearly true of the rest
of us. Probably we do have a right to avoid, if we possibly can, those positions in which we might be forced to do
terrible things. This might be regarded as the moral equivalent of our legal right not to incriminate ourselves.
Good men will be in no hurry to surrender it, though there
are reasons for doing so sometimes, and among these are or
might be the reasons good men have for entering politics.
But let us imagine a politician who does not agree to that:
he wants to do good only by doing good, or at least he is
certain that he can stop short of the most corrupting and
brutal uses of political power. Very quickly that certainty is tested. What do we think of him then?

     He wants to win the election, someone says, but he
doesn't want to get his hands dirty. This is meant as a
disparagement, even though it also means that the man being criticized is the sort of man who will not lie, cheat,
bargain behind the backs of his supporters, shout absurdi-
ties at public meetings, or manipulate other men and women.
Assuming that this particular election ought to be won, it
is clear, I think, that the disparagement is justified.
If the candidate didn't want to get his hands dirty, he
should have stayed at home; if he can't stand the heat,
he should get out of the kitchen, and so on. His decision
to run was a commitment (to all of us who think the election important) to try to win, that is, to do within rational limits whatever is necessary to win. But the candidate is a moral man. He has principles and a history of

adherence to those principles. That is why we are supporting him. Perhaps when he refuses to dirty his hands,
he is simply insisting on being the sort of man he is.
And isn't that the sort of man we want?

Let us look more closely at this case. In order to
win the election the candidate must make a deal with a
dishonest ward boss, involving the granting of contracts
for school construction over the next four years. Should
he make the deal? Well, at least he shouldn't be surprised by the offer, most of us would probably say (a conventional piece of sarcasm). And he should accept it or
not, depending on exactly what is at stake in the election.
But that is not the candidate's view. He is extremely reluctant even to consider the deal, puts off his aides when
they remind him of it, refuses to calculate its possible
effects upon the campaign. Now, if he is acting this way
because the very thought of bargaining with that particular ward boss makes him feel unclean, his reluctance isn't
very interesting. His feelings by themselves are not important. But he may also have reasons for his reluctance.
He may know, for example, that some of his supporters
support him precisely because they believe he is a good
man, and this means to them a man who won't make such
deals. Or he may doubt his own motives for considering
the deal, wondering whether it is the political campaign
or his own candidacy that makes the bargain at all tempting. Or he may believe that if he makes deals of this
sort now he may not be able later on to achieve those
ends that make the campaign worthwhile, and he may not
feel entitled to take such risks with a future that is not
only his own future. Or he may simply think that the deal
is dishonest and therefore wrong, corrupting not only himself but all those human relations in which he is involved.

Because he has scruples of this sort, we know him
to be a good man. But we view the campaign in a certain
light, estimate its importance in a certain way, and hope
that he will overcome his scruples and make the deal. It
is important to stress that we don't want just *anyone* to
make the deal; we want *him* to make it, precisely because
he has scruples about it. We know he is doing right when
he makes the deal because he knows he is doing wrong. I
don't mean merely that he will feel badly or even very
badly after he makes the deal. If he is the good man I
am imagining him to be, he will feel guilty, that is, he
will believe himself to be guilty. That is what it means
to have dirty hands.

All this may become clearer if we look at a more
dramatic example, for we are, perhaps, a little blasé
about political deals and disinclined to worry much about
the man who makes one. So consider a politician who has
seized upon a national crisis—a prolonged colonial war—
to reach for power. He and his friends win office pledged
to decolonization and peace, they are honestly committed
to both, though not without some sense of the advantages
of the commitment. In any case, they have no responsibility for the war; they have steadfastly opposed it. Immediately, the politician goes off to the colonial capital
to open negotiations with the rebels. But the capital is
in the grip of a terrorist campaign, and the first decision
the new leader faces is this: he is asked to authorize
the torture of a captured rebel leader who knows or probably knows the location of a number of bombs hidden in
apartment buildings around the city, set to go off within
the next twenty-four hours. He orders the man tortured,
convinced that he must do so for the sake of the people
who might otherwise die in the explosions—even though he

believes that torture is wrong, indeed abominable, not
just sometimes, but always. [8] He had expressed this belief often and angrily during his own campaign; the rest
of us took it as a sign of his goodness. How should we
regard him now? (How should he regard himself?)

Once again, it does not seem enough to say that he
should feel very badly. But why not? Why shouldn't he
have feelings like those of St. Augustine's melancholy
soldier, who understood both that his war was just and
that killing, even in a just war, is a terrible thing to
do? [9] The difference is that Augustine did not believe
that it was wrong to kill in a just war; it was just sad,
or the sort of thing a good man would be saddened by.
But he might have thought it wrong to torture in a just
war, and later Catholic theorists have certainly thought
it wrong. Moreover, the politician I am imagining thinks
it wrong, as do many of us who supported him. Surely we
have a right to expect more than melancholy from him now.
When he ordered the prisoner tortured, he committed a moral crime and he accepted a moral burden. Now he is a
guilty man. His willingness to acknowledge and bear (and
perhaps to repent and do penance for) his guilt is evidence, and it is the only evidence he can offer us, both
that he is not too good for politics and that he is good
enough. Here is the moral politician: it is by his dirty
hands that we know him. If he were a moral man and nothing else, his hands would not be dirty; if he were a politician and nothing else, he would pretend that they were
clean.

iii

Machiavelli's argument about the need to learn how
not to be good clearly implies that there are acts known

to be bad quite apart from the immediate circumstances
in which they are performed or not performed. He points
to a distinct set of political methods and stratagems
which good men must study (by reading his books), not
only because their use does not come naturally, but also
because they are explicitly condemned by the moral teach-
ings good men accept——and whose acceptance serves in turn
to mark men as good. These methods may be condemned because they are thought contrary to divine law or to the
order of nature or to our moral sense, or because in pre-
scribing the law to ourselves we have individually or
collectively prohibited them. Machiavelli does not commit himself on such issues, and I shall not do so either
if I can avoid it. The effects of these different views
are, at least in one crucial sense, the same. They take
out of our hands the constant business of attaching moral
labels to such Machiavellian methods as deceit and betrayal. Such methods are simply bad. They are the sort of
thing that good men avoid, at least until they have
learned how not to be good.

        Now, if there is no such class of actions, there is
no dilemma of dirty hands, and the Machiavellian teaching
loses what Machiavelli surely intended it to have, its
disturbing and paradoxical character. He can then be
understood to be saying that political actors must sometimes overcome their moral inhibitions, but not that they
must sometimes commit crimes. I take it that utilitarian
philosophers also want to make the first of these statements and to deny the second. From their point of view,
the candidate who makes a corrupt deal and the official
who authorizes the torture of a prisoner must be described
as good men (given the cases as I have specified them),
who ought, perhaps, to be honored for making the right

decision when it was a hard decision to make. There are
three ways of developing this argument. First, it might
be said that every political choice ought to be made solely in terms of its particular and immediate circumstances
—in terms, that is, of the reasonable alternatives, available knowledge, likely consequences, and so on. Then the
good man will face difficult choices (when his knowledge
of options and outcomes is radically uncertain), but it
cannot happen that he will face a moral dilemma. Indeed,
if he always makes decisions in this way, and has been
taught from childhood to do so, he will never have to
overcome his inhibitions, whatever he does for how could
he have acquired inhibitions? Assuming further that he
weighs the alternatives and calculates the consequences
seriously and in good faith, he cannot commit a crime,
though he can certainly make a mistake, even a very serious mistake. Even when he lies and tortures, his hands
will be clean, for he has done what he should do as best
he can, standing alone in a moment of time, forced to
choose.

This is in some ways an attractive description of
moral decision-making, but it is also a very improbable
one. For while any one of us may stand alone, and so on,
when we make this or that decision, we are not isolated
or solitary in our moral lives. Moral life is a social
phenomenon, and it is constituted at least in part by
rules, the knowing of which (and perhaps the making of
which) we share with our fellows. The experience of
coming up against these rules, challenging their prohibitions, and explaining ourselves to other men and women is
so common and so obviously important that no account or
moral decision-making can possibly fail to come to grips
with it. Hence the second utilitarian argument: such

rules do indeed exist, but they are not really prohibitions of wrongful actions (though they do, perhaps for
pedagogic reasons, have that form).   They are moral guidelines, summaries of previous calculations.   They ease our
choices in ordinary cases, for we can simply follow their
injunctions and do what has been found useful in the past;
in exceptional cases they serve as signals warning us
against doing too quickly or without the most careful calculations what has not been found useful in the past.   But
they do no more than that; they have no other purpose, and
so it cannot be the case that it is or even might be a
crime to override them.[10]   Nor is it necessary to feel
guilty when one does so.   Once again, if it is right to
break the rule in some hard case, after conscientiously
worrying about it, the man who acts (especially if he
knows that many of his fellows would simply worry rather
than act) may properly feel pride in his achievement.

        But this view, it seems to me, captures the reality
of our moral life no better than the last.   It may well
be right to say that moral rules ought to have the character of guidelines, but it seems that in fact they do
not.   Or at least, we defend ourselves when we break the
rules as if they had some status entirely independent of
their previous utility (and we rarely feel proud of ourselves).   The defenses we normally offer are not simply
justifications; they are also excuses.   Now, as Austin
says, these two can seem to come very close together—indeed, I shall suggest that they can appear side by side
in the same sentence—but they are conceptually distinct,
differentiated in this crucial respect: an excuse is typically an admission of innocence.[11]   Consdider a well-
known defense from Shakespeare's *Hamlet* that has often
reappeared in political literature: "I must be cruel only

to be kind."[12] The words are spoken on an occasion when
Hamlet is actually being cruel to his mother. I will
leave aside teh possibility that she deserves to hear
(to be forced to listen to) every harsh word he utters,
for Hamlet himself makes no such claim——and if she did
indeed deserve that, his words might not be cruel or he
might not be cruel for speaking them. "I must be cruel"
contains the excuse, since it both admits a fault and
suggests that Hamlet has no choice but to commit it. He
is doing what he has to do; he can't help himself (given
the ghost's command, the rotten state of Denmark, and so
on). The rest of the sentence is a justification, for
it suggests that Hamlet intends and expects kindness to
be the outcome of his actions——we must assume that he
means greater kindness, kindness to the right person, or
some such. It is not, however, so complete a justification that Hamlet is able to say that he is not *really*
being cruel. "Cruel" and "kind" have exactly the same
status; they both follow the verb "to be," and so they
perfectly reveal the moral dilemma.[13]

When rules are overridden, we do not talk or act as
if they had been set aside, canceled, or annulled. They
still stand and have this much effect at least: that we
know we have done something wrong even if what we have
done was also the best thing to do on the whole in the
circumstances.[14] Or at least we feel that way, and this
feeling is itself a crucial feature of our moral life.
Hence the third utilitarian argument, which recognizes
the usefulness of guilt and seeks to explain it. There
are, it appears, good reasons for "overvaluing" as well
as for overriding the rules. For the consequences might
be very bad indeed if the rules were overridden every time
the moral calculation seemed to go against them. It is

probably best if most men do not calculate too nicely,
but simply follow the rules; they are less likely to make
mistakes that way, all in all. And so a good man or at
least an ordinary good man) will respect the rules rather
more than he would if he thought them merely guidelines,
and he will feel guilty when he overrides them.   Indeed,
if he did not feel guilty, "he would not be such a good
man."[15] It is by his feelings that we know him. Because
of those feelings he will never be in a hurry to override
the rules, but will wait until there is no choice, acting
only to avoid consequences that are both imminent and almost certainly disastrous.

     The obvious difficulty with this argument is that
the feeling whose usefulness is being explained is most
unlikely to be felt by someone who is convinced only of
its usefulness. He breaks a utilitarian rule (guideline),
let us say, for good utilitarian reasons: but can he then
feel guilty, also for good utilitarian reasons, when he
has no reason for believing that he is guilty? Imagine
a moral philosopher expounding the third argument to a
man who is likely to feel guilty. Either the man won't
accept the utilitarian explanation as an account of his
feeling about the rules (probably the best outcome from
a utilitarian point of view) or he will accept it and then
cease to feel that (useful) feeling. But I do not want to
exclude the possibility of a kind of superstitious anxiety,
the possibility, that is, that some men will continue to
feel guilty even after they have been taught, and have
agreed, that they cannot possibly be guilty. It is best
to say only that the more fully they accept the utilitarian account, the less likely they are to feel that (useful)
feeling. The utilitarian account is not at all useful,
then, if political actors accept it, and that may help us

to understand why it plays, as Hare has pointed out, so
small a part in our moral education.[16]

iv

One further comment on the third argument: it is
worth stressing that to feel guilty is to suffer, and
that the men whose guilt feelings are here called useful
are themselves innocent according to the utilitarian account. So we seem to have come upon another case where
the suffering of the innocent is permitted and even encouraged by utilitarian calculation.[17] But surely an innocent man who has done something painful or hard (but
justified) should be helped to avoid or escape the sense
of guilt; he might reasonably expect the assistance of his
fellow men, even of moral philosophers, at such a time.
On the other hand, if we intuitively think it true of some
other man that he *should* feel guilty, then we ought to be
able to specify the nature of his guilt (and if he is a
good man, win his agreement). I think I can construct a
case which, with only small variation, highlights what is
different in these two situations.

Consider the common practice of distributing rifles
loaded with blanks to some of the members of a firing
squad. The individual men are not told whether their own
weapons are lethal, and so though all of them look like
executioners to the victim in front of them, none of them
know whether they are really executioners or not. The
purpose of this stratagem is to relieve each man of the
sense that he is a killer. It can hardly relieve him of
whatever moral responsibility he incurs by serving on a
firing squad, and that is not its purpose, for the execution is not thought to be (and let us grant this to be
the case) an immoral or wrongful act. But the inhibition

against killing another human being is so strong that even
if the men believe that what they are doing is right, they
will still feel guilty. Uncertainty as to their actual
role apparently reduces the intensity of these feelings.
If this is so, the stratagem is perfectly justifiable,
and one can only rejoice in every case where it succeeds—
for every success subtracts from the number of innocent
men who suffer.

     But we would feel differently, I think, if we ima-
gine a man who believes (and let us assume here that we
believe also) either that capital punishment is wrong or
that this particular victim is innocent, but who nevertheless agrees to participate in the firing squad for some
overriding political or moral reason—I won't try to suggest what that reason might be. If he is comforted by the
trick with the rifles, then we can be reasonably certain
that his opposition to capital punishment or his belief in
the victim's innocence is not morally serious. And if it
is serious, he will not merely feel guilty, he will know
that he is guilty (and we will know it too), though he
may also believe (and we may agree) that he has good reasons for incurring the guilt. Our guilt feelings can be
tricked away when they are isolated from our moral beliefs,
as in the first case, but not when they are allied with
them, as in the second. The beliefs themselves and the
rules which are believed in can only be *overridden*, a
painful process which forces a man to weigh the wrong he
is willing to do in order to do right, and which leaves
pain behind, and should do so, even after the decision has
been made.

                               v

     That is the dilemma of dirty hands as it has been

experienced by political actors and written about in the
literature of political action. I don't want to argue
that it is only a political dilemma. No doubt we can
get our hands dirty in private life also, and sometimes,
no doubt we should. But the issue is posed most dramatically in politics for the three reasons that make political
life the kind of life it is, because we claim to act for
others but also serve ourselves, rule over others, and use
violence against them. It is easy to get one's hands
dirty in politics and it is often right to do so. But it
is not easy to teach a good man how not to be good, nor
is it easy to explain such a man to himself once he has
committed whatever crimes are required of him. At least,
it is not easy once we have agreed to use the word "crimes"
and to live with (because we have no choice) the dilemma
of dirty hands. Still the agreement is common enough, and
on its basis there have developed three broad traditions
of explanation, three ways of thinking about dirty hands,
which derive in some very general fashion from neoclassi-
cal, Protestant, and Catholic perspectives on politics and
morality. I want to try to say something very briefly
about each of them, or rather about a representative example of each of them, for each seems to me partly right.
But I don't think I can put together the compound view
that might be wholly right.

The first tradition is best represented by Machiavelli, the first man, so far as I know, to state the paradox that I am examining. The good man who aims to found
or reform a republic must, Machiavelli tells us, do terrible thin's to reach his goal. Like Romulus, he must murder his brother; like Numa, he must lie to the people.
Sometimes, however, "when the act accuses, the result excuses."[18] This sentence from *The Discourses* is often

taken to mean that the politician's deceit and cruelty
are justified by the good results he brings about.   But
if they were justified, it wouldn't be necessary to learn
what Machiavelli claims to teach: how not to be good.   It
would only be necessary to learn how to be good in a new
more difficult, perhaps roundabout way.   That is not Mach-
ivelli's argument.   His political judgments are indeed
consequentialist in character, but not his moral judgments. ·We know whether cruelty is used well or badly by
its effects over time.   But that it is bad to use cruelty
we know in some other way.   The deceitful and cruel politician is excused (if he succeeds) only in the sense that
the rest of us come to agree that the results were "worth
it" or, more likely, that we simply forget his crimes
when we praise his success.

It is important to stress Machiavelli's own commitments to the existence of moral standards.   His paradox
depends upon that commitment as it depends upon the general stability of the standards—which he upholds in his
consistent use of words like good and bad.[19]   If he wants
the standards to be disregarded by good men more often
than they are, he has nothing with which to replace them
and no other way of recognizing the good men except by
their allegiance to those same standards.   It is exceedingly rare, he writes, that a good man is willing to employ bad means to become prince.[20]   Machiavelli's purpose
is to persuade such a person to make the attempt, and he
holds out the supreme political rewards, power and glory,
to the man who does so and succeeds.   The good man is not
rewarded (or excused), however, merely for his willingness
to get his hands dirty.   He must do bad things well.   There
is no reward for doing bad things badly, though they are
done with the best of intentions.   And so political action

necessarily involves taking a risk. But it should be
clear that what is risked is not personal goodness—*that
is thrown away*—but power and glory. If the politician
succeeds, he is a hero; eternal praise is the supreme
reward for not being good.

What the penalties are for not being good, Machiavelli doesn't say, and it is probably for this reason
above all that his moral sensitivity has so often been
questioned. He is suspect not because he tells political
actors they must get their hands dirty, but because he
does not specify the state of mind appropriate to a man
with dirty hands. A Machiavellian hero has no inwardness.
What he thinks of himself we don't know. I would guess,
along with most other readers of Machiavelli, that he
basks in his glory. But then it is difficult to account
for the strength of his original reluctance to learn how
not to be good. In any case, he is the sort of man who
is unlikely to keep a dairy and so we cannot find out what
he thinks. Yet we do want to know; above all, we want a
record of his anguish. That is a sign of our own conscientiousness and of the impact on us of the second tradition of thought that I want to examine, in which personal anguish sometimes seems the only acceptable excuse for
political crimes.

The second tradition is best represented, I think,
by Max Weber, who outlines its essential features with
great power at the very end of his essay "Politics as a
Vocation." For Weber, the good man with dirty hands is a
hero still, but he is a tragic hero. In part, his trage-
dy is that though politics is his vocation, he has not
been called by God and so cannot be justified by Him.
Weber's hero is alone in a world that seems to belong to
Satan, and his vocation is entirely his own choice. He

still wants what Christian magistrates have always wanted,
both to do good in the world and to save his soul, but now
these two ends have come into sharp contradiction. They
are contradictory because of the necessity for violence in
a world where God has not instituted the sword. The politician takes the sword himself, and only by doing so does
he measure up to his vocation. With full consciousness of
what he is doing, he does bad in order to do good, and surrenders his soul. He "lets himself in," Weber says, "for
the diabolic forces lurking in all violence." Perhaps
Machiavelli also meant to suggest that his hero surrenders
salvation in exchange for glory, but he does not explicitly
say so. Weber is absolutely clear: "the genius or demon
of politics lives in an inner tension with the god of love
...[which] can at any time lead to an irreconcilable conflict."[21] His politician views this conflict when it comes
with a tough realism, never pretends that it might be
solved by compromise, chooses politics once again, and
turns decisively away from love. Weber writes about this
choice with a passionate high-mindedness that makes a concern for one's flesh. Yet the reader never doubts that his
mature, superably trained, relentless, objective, responsible, and disciplined political leader is also a suffering
servant. His choices are hard and painful, and he pays
the price not only while making them but forever after. A
man doesn't lose his soul one day and find it the next.

        The difficulties with this view will be clear to any-
one who has ever met a suffering servant. Here is a man
who lies, intrigues, sends other men to their death—and
suffers. He does what he must do with a heavy heart.
None of us can know, he tells us, how much it costs him
to do his duty. Indeed, we cannot, for he himself fixes
the price he pays. And that is the trouble with this view

of political crime. We suspect the suffering servant of
either masochism or hypocrisy or both, and while we are
often wrong, we are not always wrong. Weber attempts to
resolve the problem of dirty hands entirely within the
confines of the individual conscience, but I am inclined
to think that this is neither possible nor desirable.
The self-awareness of the tragic hero is obviously of
great value. We want the politician to have an inner
life at least something like that which Weber describes.
But sometimes the hero's suffering needs to be socially
expressed (for like punishment, it confirms and reinforces
our sense that certain acts are wrong). And equally important, it sometimes needs to be socially limited. We
don't want to be ruled by men who have lost their souls.
A politician with dirty hands needs a soul, and it is
best for us all if he has some hope of personal salvation,
however that is conceived. It is not the case that when
he does bad in order to do good he surrenders himself
forever to the demon of politics. He commits a determinate crime, and he must pay a determinate penalty. When
he has done so, his hands will be clean again, or as clean
as human hands can ever be. So the Catholic Church has
always taught, and this teaching is central to the third
tradition that I want to examine.

Once again I will take a latter-day and a lapsed
representative of the tradition and consider Albert Camus'
The Just Assassins. The heroes of this play are terror-
ists at work in nineteenth-century Russia. The dirt on
their hands is human blood. And yet Camus' admiration
for them, he tells us, is complete. We consent to being
criminals, one of them says, but there is nothing with
which anyone can reproach us. Here is the dilemma of
dirty hands in a new form. The heroes are innocent crim-

inals, just assassins, because, having killed, they are
prepared to die——*and will die*. Only their execution, by
the same despotic authorities they are attacking, will
complete the action in which they are engaged: dying,
they need make no excuses. That is the end of their guilt
and pain. The execution is not so much punishment as
self-punishment and expiation. On the scaffold they wash
their hands clean and, unlike the suffering servant, they
die happy.

Now the argument of the play when presented in so
radically simplified a form may seem a little bizarre,
and perhaps it is marred by the moral extremism of Camus'
politics. "Political action has limits," he says in a
preface to the volume containing *The Just Assassins*, "and
there is no good and just action but what recognizes those
limits and if it must go beyond them, at least accepts
death."[22] I am less interested here in the violence of
that "at least"——what else does he have in mind?——than in
the sensible doctrine that it exaggerates. That doctrine
might best be described by an analogy: just assassination,
I want to suggest, is like civil disobedience. In both
men violate a set of rules, go beyond a moral or legal
limit, in order to do what they believe they should do.
At the same time, they acknowledge their responsibility
for the violation by accepting punishment or doing penance.
But there is also a difference between the two, which has
to do with the difference between law and morality. In
most cases of civil didobedience the laws of the state
are broken for moral reasons, and the state provides the
punishment. In most cases of dirty hands moral rules are
broken for reasons of state, and no one provides the punishment. There is rarely a Czarist executioner waiting
in the wings for politicians with dirty hands, even the

most deserving among them. Moral rules are not usually
enforced against the sort of actor I am considering,
largely because he acts in an official capacity. If
they were enforced, dirty hands would be no problem. We
would simply honor the man who did bad in order to do
good, and at the same time we would punish him. We would
honor him for the good he has done, and we would punish
him for the bad he has done. We would punish him, that
is, for the same reasons we punish anyone else; it is not
my purpose here to defend any particular view of punishment. Short of the priest and the confessional, there are
no authorities to whom we might entrust the task.

I am nevertheless inclined to think Camus' view the
most attractive of the three, if only because it requires
us at least to imagine a punishment or a penance that fits
the crime and so to examine closely the nature of the crime.
The others do not require that. Once he has launched his
career, the crimes of Machiavelli's prince seem subject
only to prudential control. And the crimes of Weber's
tragic hero are limited only by *his* capacity for suffering.
In neither case is there any explicit reference back to
the moral code, once it has, at great personal cost to be
sure, been set aside. The question posed by Sartre's
Hoerderer (whom I suspect of being a suffering servant) is
rhetorical, and the answer is obvious (I have already given
it), but the characteristic sweep of both is disturbing.
Since it is concerned only with those crimes that ought to
be committed, the dilemma of dirty hands seems to exclude
questions of degree. Wanton or excessive cruelty is not
at issue, any more than is cruelty directed at bad ends.
But political action is so uncertain that politicians
necessarily take moral as well as political risks, commit-
ting crimes that they only think ought to be committed

They override the rules without ever being certain that
they have found the best way to the results they hope to
achieve, and we don't want them to do that too quickly or
too often. So it is important that the moral stakes be
very high—which is to say, that the rules be rightly
valued. That, I suppose, is the reason for Camus' extremism. Without the executioner, however, there is no one to
set the stakes or maintain the values except ourselves,
and probably no way to do either except through philosoph-
ic reiteration and political activity.

   "We shall not abolish lying by refusing to tell
lies," say Hoerderer, "but by using every means at hand
to abolish social classes."[23] I suspect we shall not
abolish lying at all, but we might see to it that fewer
lies were told if we contrived to deny power and glory to
the greatest liars—except, of course, in the case of those
lucky few whose extraordinary achievements make us forget
the lies they told. If Hoerderer succeeds in abolishing
social classes, perhaps he will join the lucky few. Meanwhile, he lies, manipulates, and kills, and we must make
sure he pays the price. We won't be able to do that however, without getting our own hands dirty, and then we
must find some way of paying the price ourselves.

FOOTNOTES

[1]An earlier version of this paper was read at the annual meeting of the Conference for the Study of Political Thought in New York, April 1972. I am indebted to Charles Taylor, who served as commentator at that time and encouraged me to think that its arguments might be right.

[2]*Philosophy & Public Affairs* I, no. 2 (Winter 1972).

[3]For Nagel's description of a possible "moral blind alley," see pp. 23-24. Bernard Williams has made a similar suggestion, though without quite acknowledging it as his own: "many people can recognize the thought that a certain course of action is, indeed, the best thing to do on the whole in the circumstances, but that doing it involves doing something wrong" (*Morality: An Introduction to Ethics* [New York, 1972], p. 93.

[4]Jean-Paul Sartre, *Dirty Hands* in *No Exit and Three Other Plays*, trans. Lionel Abel (New York, n.d.), p. 224.

[5]See pp. 53-58, esp. p. 54: "the simple principles of the deontologist...have their place at the level of character-formation (moral education and self-education.)"

[6]In *From Max Weber: Essays in Sociology*, trans. and ed. Hans H. Gerth and C. Wright Mills (New York, 1946), pp. 77-128.

[7]See *The Prince*, chap. XV; cf. *The Discourses*, bk. I, chaps. IX and XVIII. I quote from the Modern Library edition of the two works (New York, 1950), p. 57.

[8]I leave aside the question of whether the prisoner is himself responsible for the terrorist campaign. Perhaps he opposed it in meetings of the rebel organization. In any case, whether he deserves to be punished or not, he does not deserve to be tortured.

[9]Other writers argued that Christians must never kill, even in a just war; and there was also an intermediate position which suggests the origins of the idea

12

                                                                            Political Action: The
Problem of Dirty Hands

of dirty hands. Thus Basil The Great (Bishop of Caesarea
in the fourth century A.D.): "Killing in war was differentiated by our fathers from murder...nevertheless, perhaps
it would be well that those whose hands are unclean ab-
stain from communion for three years." Here dirty hands
are a kind of impurity or unworthiness, which is not the
same as guilt, though closely related to it. For a general survey of these and other Christian views, see Roland
H. Bainton, *Christian Attitudes Toward War and Peace* (New
York, 1960), esp. chaps. 5-7.

[10]Brandt's rules do not appear to be of the sort that
can be overridden—except perhaps by a soldier who decides
that he just won't kill any more civilians, no matter what
cause is served—since all they require is careful calculation. But I take it that rules of a different sort,
which have the form of ordinary injunctions and prohibitions, can and often do figure in what is called "rule-
utilitarianism."

[11]J. L. Austin, "A Plea for Excuses," in *Philosophical Papers,* ed. J. O. Urmson and G.J. Warnock (Oxford,
1961), pp. 123-152.

[12]*Hamlet* 3-4-178.

[13]Compare the following lines from Bertold Brecht's
poem "To Posterity": "Alas, we/ Who wished to lay the
foundations of kindness/ Could not ourselves be kind..."
(*Selected Poems,* trans. H. R. Hays [New York, 1969], p.
177). This is more of an excuse, less of a justification
(the poem is an *apologia*).

[14]Robert Nozick discusses some of the possible effects of overriding a rule in his "Moral Complications
and Moral Structures," *Natural Law Forum* 13 (1968): 34-
35 and notes. Nozick suggests that what may remain after
one has broken a rule (for good reasons) is a "duty to
make reparations." He does not call this "guilt", though
the two notions are closely connected.

[15]Hare, p. 59.

[16]There is another possible utilitarian position,
suggested in Maurice Merleau-Ponty's *Humanism and Terror,*
trans. John O'Neill (Boston, 1970). According to this
view, the agony and the guilt feelings experienced by the
man who makes a "dirty hands" decision derive from his
radical uncertainty about the actual outcome. Perhaps

the awful thing he is doing will be done in vain; the
results he hopes for won't occur; the only outcome will
be the pain he has caused or the deceit he has fostered.
Then (and only then) he will indeed have committed a crime.
On the other hand, if the expected good does come, then
(and only then) he can abandon his guilt feelings; he can
say, and the rest of us must agree, that he is justified.
This is a kind of delayed utilitarianism, where justification is a matter of actual and not at all of predicted
outcomes.   It is not implausible to imagine a political
actor anxiously awaiting the "verdict of history."   But
suppose the verdict is in his favor (assuming that there
is a *final* verdict or a statute of limitations on possible verdicts): he will surely feel relieved—more so, no
doubt, than the rest of us.   I can see no reason, however,
why he should think himself justified, if he is a good
man and knows that what he did was wrong.   Perhaps the
victims of his crime, seeing the happy result, will ab-
solve him, but history has no powers of absolution.   Indeed, history is more likely to play tricks on our moral
judgment.   Predicted outcomes are at least thought to
follow from our own acts (this is the prediction), but
actual outcomes almost certainly have a multitude of
causes, the combination of which may well be fortuitous.
Merleau-Ponty stresses the risks of political decision-
making so heavily that he turns politics into a gamble
with time and circumstance.   But the anxiety of the
gambler is of no great moral interest.   Nor is it much
of a barrier, as Merleau-Ponty's book makes all too
clear, to the commission of the most terrible crimes.

[17]Cf. the cases suggested by David Ross, *The Right
and the Good* (Oxford, 1930), pp. 56-57, and E. F. Carritt,
Ethical and Political Thinking (Oxford, 1947), p. 65.

[18]*The Discourses,* bk. I, chap. IX (p. 139).

[19]For a very different view of Machiavelli, see
Isaiah Berlin, "The Question of Machiavelli," *The New
York Review of Books,* 4 November 1971.

[20]*The Discourses,* bk. I, chap. XVIII (p. 171).

[21]"Politics as a Vocation," pp. 125-128.   But sometimes a political leader does choose the "absolutist"
side of the conflict, and Weber writes (p. 127) that it
is "immensely moving when a mature man...aware of a
responsibility for the consequences of his conduct...
reaches a point where he says: 'Here I stand; I can do
no other.'"   Unfortunately, he does not suggest just

where that point is or even where it might be.

[22]*Caligula and Three Other Plays* (New York, 1958),
p. x.   (The preface is translated by Justin O'Brian, the
plays by Stuart Gilbert.)

[23]*Dirty Hands,* p. 223.

PART II

PUBLIC ETHICS INFORMED BY PRIVATE ETHICS

REVISIONIST PERSPECTIVES

DUTIES OF STATION[1] VS.
DUTIES OF CONSCIENCE:
ARE THERE TWO MORALITIES?*

DAVID LITTLE

We have no difficulty forming a rough first impression of what the title is driving at. We have in our mind a picture of a conscience-stricken government official or business executive driven, by the pressures and requirements of his occupation, to carry out a directive that contradicts his deepest-held moral convictions. He is called upon, let us say, to deceive the public in order to protect what are considered vital activities of his agency or company, an act he regards as detestable, yet in some sense necessary. A straightforward enough dilemma.

Our problem is how properly to describe and understand this dilemma. One familiar and still influential suggestion is that we have before us an example of a conflict between two systems of practical guidance that are, in effect, self-contained and divergent from each other. Reinhold Niebuhr, for one, made his reputation, in part, by elaborating this assumption and by reflecting on social life in relation to it. He puts his point most starkly in *Moral Man and Immoral Society:*

> The thesis to be elaborated in these pages is that a sharp distinction must be drawn between the moral and social behavior of individuals and of social groups; and that this distinction justifies and necessitates political politics which a purely

> individualistic ethic must always find embarrassing
> ...[In other words,] individuals have a moral code
> which makes the actions of collective man an out-
> rage to their conscience (Niebuhr, 1932: pp. xi, 9).

So defined, Niebuhr appears to advocate the view
that there are, after all, "two moralities," or, in his
words, "two moral perspectives" (1932: p. 257).
The one—the 'duty of conscience'—is looked at from the
individual or "internal perspective;" it consists of disinterested motives or intentions, which is to say intentions governed by self-sacrificial regard for the well-
being of the other (neighbor love). "Unselfishness," says
Niebuhr, "must remain the criterion of the highest
morality" (1932: p. 258), and by unselfishness he
means "heedless" and spontaneous self-sacrifice for the
good of the other. This sort of love is relevent to the
moral and social behavior of individuals in that it is
feasible to expect that individuals, acting privately or
on their own behalf, can behave heroically toward others,
can heedlessly sacrifice all for the other. It is also
feasible in face-to-face relationships (family-life,
friendships), where sacrificial love is, in part, consti-
tutive of the relationship.

The second—the 'duty of social life'—is viewed
from the external perspective, or from the point of view
of the external conditions and necessities of life in this
world. These are the constraints imposed by one's position
in the social and natural environment. One of the primary
constraints or realities of social life is, for Niebuhr,
the satisfaction of self-interest, of egoistic impulses.
By self-interest or egoism Niebuhr appears to mean the unavoidable disposition to be partial to, to protect and favor, the special interest of oneself or one's group over
competing interests in a situation of scarcity. He under-

stands the word self in an individualistic or collective
way. There are collective egos just as there are individual ones. The only difference is that the collective ego,
whether one's country, corporation or occupational team,
is more constraining, more inescapable, in determining
one's action in the public world than the individual ego
is. As we mentioned, it is possible on rare, but conceiv-
able, occasions for individuals, acting on their own, or
in uniquely intimate social settings, to forsake self-
interest out of love for another. But it is emphatically
not possible for people acting in roles that are representative of group interests to avoid by very far protecting and favoring their group's special interest, or going
to extreme lengths, if necessary, to satisfy that interest.

This is, if I understand Niebuhr, a matter of definition. Action in a collective context must be conceived of
from the external perspective, that is, from the point of
view of the outward necessities of social action, including,
as primary, the motive of self-interest.

We need to be clear on what sort of necessity
or constraint group self-interest is for Niebuhr.
It is not in a class with what might commonly be called
physical constraints—like the inability of human beings
to jump to the moon. It is, rather, like Kant's notion of
a "pragmatic necessity": If one chooses to act in a collective context, then one must (of necessity) act in reference
to group self-interest. That means that all planning and
decision-making on behalf of groups must be prudential and
preferential (1932: pp. 170-1). A person does not have to
take on a social role; one may follow exclusively the dictates of conscience, in which case he will not, of course,
be acting collectively, but in another way. The option of
following one's conscience by turning away from the real-

ities of collective life, is always open, and, historically, saints and heroes have chosen it.

So mapped out, we can see the root of the distinction and conflict between the two moralities. We can understand why, for Niebuhr, it is never possible "completely [to] eliminate *certain irreconcilable elements* in the
two types of morality, internal and external, individual
and social" (1932: p. 258; italics mine). These are two
mutually exclusive ways of viewing morality. One way,
from the internal perspective, sees action as a matter of
pure conscience, involving heedless and unselfish intentions. Resulting action can only be performed in the private world of oneself and two or three neighbors or family
members. The other way, from the external perspective,
sees action as constrained by the play of partiality and
preferentialism, and as unavoidable for actors in a collective context. Around these two perspectives are organized
two self-contained and divergent moralities.

But Niebuhr holds an additional view which modifies the
stark distinction between these two moralities, and, to a
degree, harmonizes them. It is never quite clear how this
second position gets on with the one we have just summarized. According to the second view, "the highest moral
insights and achievements of the individual conscience are
both relevant and necessary to the life of society" (1932:
p. 257). It appears that the duties of conscience are not,
after all, exclusively applicable to the intentions and
private life of the individual. In an adjusted form, the
conscience can, Niebuhr now says, give direction to actors emersed in social life. On the way toward realizing
the criterion of the highest morality, unselfishness, the
conscience, apparently, supplies proximate and mediate
direction to the occupants of social roles, direction that

moderates and balances, though naturally never eliminates, the self-interest that is a necessary feature of collective life. Here we have Niebuhr's doctrine of justice. The "adjusted" conscience translates the idea of heedless unselfishness into the language of the public arena. Something is lost, but something is also gained. An alien and withdrawn conscience suddenly speaks an ameliorating word. The individual must never forget the difference between the pure and the adjusted conscience, but so long as that lesson is remembered, his conscience does not leave him adrift on the stormy sea of social conflict.

Niebuhr himself clearly favors this way of compromising between the duties of conscience and the duties of social life. To view collective life solely from the external point of view, and without regard, therefore, to the internal virtues of disinterestedness and impartiality, would jeopardize even the minimum achievements of mutuality and welfare in social life. On the other hand, to follow the duties of pure conscience, indifferent to the external conditions of collective life, would be escapist.

In the light of this compromise view, what becomes of the two moralities? If there are, any longer, two moralities, they do not now match the distinction between the duties of conscience and the duties of social life. On the contrary, for the compromise view, the two sets of duties are harmonized. Conscience, in its adjusted form, helps to organize the requirements and conditions of social life according to certain moral standards. Any residual division in the moral life would appear to be located in the conflict between the two principles of conscience. The pure conscience dictates an uncompromising duty of self-sacrificial neighbor love, exclusive of

the motive of self-love. The adjusted conscience dictates
proximate forms of neighbor love which take explicit account of self-love and endeavor to control and modify it.
Both of these sets of duties are in some sense binding on
the individual actor, though I confess I do not understand
how they both can be binding at the same time. If each
individual is ultimately bound by pure conscience to engage in acts of heedless unselfishness, and if participation in the social world systematically prevents such acts,
and, finally, if it is possible to escape the corruption
of the social world by cultivating only private, intimate
contacts, why isn't one bound to do that? As I say, how
the duties issuing from the two notions of conscience get
along with each other is not self-evident. Nevertheless,
Niebuhr holds both notions.

        It is clear, then, that though a person like Niebuhr
talks about splitting up the duties of conscience and the
duties of social life into two moralities, he does not
consistently sustain that view. He does believe that the
duties of pure conscience are practicable in highly re-
stricted social settings. But it is the duties of adjusted conscience, with their positive direction for collective life, that are for Niebuhr of predominant practical importance and interest.

        In a recent essay, Professor Charles Frankel has
tried his hand at this issue. He agrees that "the morality appropriate to the performance of a [complex] social
role, and the morality of small-scale, face-to-face relations are different" (Frankel, 1975: p. 19). Duties among
family members and friends are dissimilar from those of
"large-scale social relations," such as government agencies
and business corporations. In stressing this difference,
Niebuhr and others, Frankel believes, made an important

point. Presumably, the point is that simple social roles are simple precisely in the sense of being free of a variety of divergent, and possibly conflicting, duties. The role requirements of father or friend are, as a rule, relatively uncomplicated and unstressful, at least in comparison with roles in complex organizations. In simple roles, one can, it is suggested, more readily and more consistently be oneself. By contrast, a complex role is defined according to the existence of an intricate network, and sometimes a tangle, of duties. The greater the complexity, the greater the probability that a role-occupant will experience a conflict of duties, and consequently, greater stress and strain. Under those conditions, he will naturally find it harder to live a consistent, integrated life.

Frankel does not, however, wish to suggest that the difference between the duties of simple and complex roles amounts to two moralities, at least in the strict sense. Rather, it is simply the case that different moral rules and considerations—different uses, that is, of the *same* moral system—apply to these contrasting roles. There is, Frankel believes, that much truth in Niebuhr's original insight, and in the thoughts of others, like George Kennan and Hans Morgenthau, who say the same things.

This is an interesting and suggestive point. In one respect, however, I find it misleading. I am not convinced that certain face-to-face institutions, like the family, consist of unambiguously simple roles, composed of uncomplicated duties. On the contrary, family experience seems to display conflicts of duty analogous to those notoriously present in large-scale social relations. Parents and spouses are frequently torn up over contradictory responsibilities to their children and to each other in the distribution of affection, goods and interest.

In fact, the duty of distributive justice is often as
compelling in family affairs as the duty of beneficience,
the duty of promise-keeping as compelling as the duty to
repay a kindness. The parental responsibility to discipline and direct one's children does not always harmonize
with the duty to tolerate and respect autonomy, and so on.

On reflection, the complexity of family roles is
self-evident. The point, therefore, is that we may not
continue to use family-life, and possibly other face-to-
face relations, as examples of simple roles, at least not
without very careful examination and defense. We must
add to this the more important point that individuals who
occupy parental roles are never simply parents, but occupants of all sorts of cross-cutting roles, each with its
own intricate web of duties, and each duty competing in
certain ways, and at certain points, with the implicit
duties of the other roles. As citizen, a parent must honor
the duty to protect and preserve the welfare of his family,
but also to honor a similar concern on the part of other
parents, even though such concern may cost him and his
family something. In a situation of economic disparity,
in which one's own family is well off, it might be
argued that the appropriate objects of additional benefic-
ence and self-sacrifice on the part of the parents are the
children of deprived families.

All this brings us to a general remark about duties
and social life, and, more precisely, about our use of
the word, "station." Properly understood, the term expresses the point we have just been making. Persons
acting in the social world ought not to be understood as
one-role occupants (whether those roles be simple or complex), but as multi-role occupants, confronted with a
vast, often tangled, web of duties. The word station,

accordingly, designates the *general social location* of an individual, the position that he occupies at the center of an intricate network of duties. In a felicitous phrase from *Webster's New International Dictionary,* a station is an individual's "sphere of duty."

This understanding of the duties of station helps to correct the common, but misleading, impression that moral dilemmas faced by government or corporation officials, or others are normally role-specific, that is, that they are produced by a conflict of duties in respect, exclusively, to carrying out an occupational role. While some moral dilemmas are role-specific in that sense, many are not. Frequently, a high government official, for example, is bound not only by loyalty to the team of which he is a member, or by a commitment to the requirements of his job, but also by a commitment of fidelity to the officer who appointed him, a debt of gratitude to those who recommended him, an obligation to provide for his family, and, perhaps, to care, at great expense, for his infirm mother. To repeat, the term "duties of station" is usefully understood as the combination of all these social duties, as one's sphere of duty in the widest sense.

I stress the utility of this understanding of the notion of station because, with it, we can begin to clarify the relations between the duties of station and the duties of conscience. One of the troubles with Reinhold Niebuhr's account of conscience is that he did not reflect carefully enough on what we ordinarily take the concept and function of conscience to be. He recommends a particular view of conscience, or two views, to be exact. The pure conscience represents for everyone the criterion of highest morality, namely, heedless selflessness. The adjusted conscience provides moral guidance for individ-

uals in collective life who, for some reason, do not try
to conform to the highest criterion. But however adequate or inadequate all this may or may not finally be,
it does not represent an altogether coherent or well-
developed theory of conscience. I am going to assume,
and try by what comes after to demonstrate, that the best
way to work our way toward a satisfactory view of conscience is at least to *start* from our ordinary impressions,
and to try to clarify and systematize those impressions.
It may be that having done that, we will want then to make
alterations and renovations in our ordinary view. That is
another matter. But we ought not rush to those changes before we have spent time getting to know how the notion of
conscience *does* operate for us, and what we seem to have
at stake in having it perform the functions it does.

In line with this directive, we ought, I believe, to
commence our examination of conscience against the background of the idea of station I have put forward. According to that idea, a person's station, or general social
position, should be seen as a web, usually tangled, always
intricate, of various duties which stretch him this way
and that. Persons encountering this profusion of duties
experience the need *to integrate* these duties, to achieve
some measure of coherence and consistency among them all,
and to do that according to a set of basic practical standards or principles.

Now I contend that an individual confronts conscience,
at least in one of its central functions, at the same time
that he confronts a significant conflict of duties thrown
up to him out of this array of commitments and responsibilities. He is suddenly torn, let us say, by the clash of
commitment to tell the truth in public with the commitment to protect his teammates or the vital functions
of his agency, as well as his responsibility to care

for his family, his infirm mother, etc. How shall he
bring all these duties into harmony with one another, or,
barring that, how shall he reach a judgment, satisfying to
him, according to which he can determine the priority of
one over the others?

It is interesting that we do not invoke, or refer
to, conscience, unless we are faced with conflict situations of which the clash of duties is one sort. In fact,
conscience seems to have no explicit job to do until we
do face such conflicts. For eample, the "cases of conscience," which consumed the attention of Puritan thinkers
in the seventeenth century, were often precisely dilemmas
of this sort: "Whether a man may lawfully and with good
conscience, use Policie [that is, use pretense or deception
to further the interests of his worldly calling]," or,
"Whether a man may reskue himself or others by combate"
(Perkins, 1972: pp. 485, 501). And in more recent times,
appeals to conscience have characteristically gained prom-
inence in times of intense strain among duties. The campaigns of civil disobedience during the sixties against
racial discrimination or protest against United States'
action in Indochina illustrate the strain, deeply felt
on the part of many, between a duty to obey the law of
the land and a commitment to higher duties. In short, it
is only when we encounter some strife over our commitments
and responsibilities—and those characteristically in our
stations—that the subject of conscience arises.

This observation provides background for two useful
summary accounts of our experience of conscience, one by
Immanuel Kant, and one by the eighteenth-century philosopher, Bishop Joseph Butler, though both accounts need
here and there to be sharpened and amended. For Kant,
"consciousness of *an inner court (or tribunal) in man is*

conscience" (Kant, 1964: p. 103). Incidentally, Kant explicitly reinforces this adversarial and judicial image
by citing one of St. Paul's allusions to conscience in the
Epistle to the Romans (2:15): "/The gentiles/show that
what the law requires is written on their hearts, while
their conscience also bears witness, and their conflicting
thoughts accuse or perhaps excuse them..." (*The New English
Bible* brings out the adversarial flavor of the same words
even more strikingly: "Their conscience is called as witness, and their own thoughts argue the case on either side,
against them or even for them...")

Butler, in turn, describes the conscience as follows:
"There is a principle of reflection in men by which they
distinguish between, and approve and disapprove, their own
actions. We are plainly constituted such sort of creatures
as to reflect uoon our own nature.... This principle in man
by which he approves or disapproves his heart, temper, and
actions is conscience" (Butler, 1950: p. 26).

Given these two descriptions, we may construct the
following generalizations regarding the *functions and jurisdiction,* the *content,* and the *procedures* of conscience.

Functions and Jurisdiction. The court of conscience
is, so to speak, called into session by a conflict (either
prospective or retrospective) in the practical life of an
individual. The prupose or function of the court session
is to resolve the conflict by rendering a judgment of approval or disapproval concerning the pertinent courses of
action, and by determining the degree of responsibility
of the individual for taking (or for thinking of taking)
the right or wrong course.

We need to underscore the distinction, and yet the
relation, between judgments of approval/disapproval, according to which the conscience appraises courses of

action, and judgments of the individual's responsibility for doing approved or disapproved actions. Let us resort to the following diagram for clarification:

		Individual Actor	
		Responsible	Not Responsible
Action	Good	Approved (credit	Approved (no credit)
	Bad	Disapproved (guilt)	Disapproved EXCUSE

We must not forget that judgments of conscience involve both axes of our diagram, no doubt in highly subtle combinations. I call special attention to the place and character of excuse, as an assessment not of the goodness or badness of acts, but of the condition and capability of the actor. We shall want to come back to excuses and conscience in our concluding remarks.

There are two sorts of conflicts that are actionable in the court of conscience: (1) conflicts of duties which we have been referring to all along; (2) conflicts between one duty and some contrary inclination an individual may experience against doing that duty. Once the issues of approval and disapproval, and the responsibility of the actor have been resolved in these conflicts, the court exerts a sentencing or sanctioning function; it measures out the so-called feelings of conscience. A good conscience involves a rewarding emotional state (credit), while a bad one is notoriously associated with acute distress, or pangs of conscience (guilt).

Finally, the conscience functions in peculiar relation to the possessor of the conscience, to his identity as a person or self. In Professor Ryle's words, the conscience is a *private monitor*. I do not have pangs of conscience if you do something which happens to be

against your conscience, and perhaps even against mine.
I would only have such pangs, would only feel the
sentencing power of the court conscience, if I were tempted, of felt committed, to follow in your footsteps, or
in some other way felt obliged myself to repeat your
deed. In other words, *a person's conscience monitors
only that action over which he as an individual actor has
control or responsibility.*[2] So intimate is the connection between conscience and self. Please understand, the
phrase, "private monitor," does *not* mean that an individual's private (that is, nonsocial) actions are the only
things monitored by conscience. Rather, it means that
only those actions responsibly performed or performable
by the individual—whether done toward others or in private—are monitored by the conscience.

This intimate relation between self-identify and
conscience partly explains why, as we mentioned earlier,
a central function of the conscience is to integrate conflicting duties in one way or another, to achieve a measure of coherence and consistency among the disjunctive
requirements and responsibilities, thrown up to one by
his station. If, as Erik Erikson says, a sense of self
or ego identity "provides the ability to experience oneself as something that has continuity and sameness, and
to act accordingly" (Erikson, 1950: p. 38), then the
notion of conscience appears to be in the very business of
sustaining that identity and continuity, of protecting the
integrity of the person as actor, at the deepest levels
of the self. So much for the functions and jurisdiction
of the conscience.

In carrying out these functions, the conscience appears to be understood to have two sides or aspects, an

objective and a subjective side. The objective side refers to the content, or the basic standards and principles,
the cluster of moral convictions, that undergirds the
judgments of conscience. The subjective side refers,
roughly, to the procedures followed by an individual undertaking to be conscientious. I shall deal, briefly,
with these two sides as the content and the procedures of
conscience.

    Content. Bishop Butler's statement, quoted earlier,
that "there is a principle of reflection in men by which
they distinguish between, approve and disapprove their
own actions," presupposes that every person's conscience
rests on some set of basic moral convictions. These provide the basis for the *authority* of conscience; they are,
so to speak, the constitution for the court of conscience.

    The content contains not only criteria for assessing
the value of actions, but also priority rules by which to
attribute relative weights to competing courses of action.
In a case of conscience one consults the content to decide
whether a commitment to be at an important meeting on time
or to aid one's ailing child takes precedence, whether
the duty of loyalty to one's team is prior or not to a
duty to tell the truth in public. The content also contains material relevant to the assessment of responsibility for action, including some of the criteria for distinguishing between good and bad excuses.

    It is important to note that the content of con-
science frequently varies from person to person, and even
within the lifespan of an individual. Presumably because
of this variability, it is in respect to the content of
conscience that the principle of tolerance is most directly acknowledged. Nevertheless, so far as a given individual at a given time is concerned, the content of conscience

provides for that individual a sort of *unified master
model* of the self, and the conscience in its judicial
role prompts conformity, or, failing it, demands to know
the reason why. Though the content of conscience may
change, any basic change is difficult and is associated
with nothing short of a crisis of the self.

    Procedures. Bishop Butler's comment, that "we are
plainly constituted such sort of creatures as to reflect
upon our own nature," highlights the so-called subjective
side of conscience, or conscientiousness, which is separ-
able from, though related to, the content. Butler goes
on: "The mind can take a view of what passes within itself, its propensions, aversions, passions,...and of the
several actions consequent thereupon." In a word, *to be
conscientious* (in the relevant sense) *is to be reflective
in the fullest possible way in face of a case of conscience.*

    What does that mean? Professor C. D. Broad has pro-
vided us with an outline of the features of conscientiousness that, in my opinion, cannot be improved upon:

> An action is conscientious if the following condi-
> tions are fulfilled. (i) The agent has reflected
> on the situation, the action, and the alternatives
> to it, in order to discover what is the right
> course. In this reflection he has tried his ut-
> most to learn the relevant facts and to give each
> its due weight, he has exercised his judgment on
> them to the best of his ability, and he has striven
> to allow for all sources of bias. (ii) He has
> decided that, on the factual and ethical informa-
> tion available to him, the action in question is
> probably the most right or the least wrong of all
> those open to him. (iii) His belief that the action
> has this moral characteristic, together with his
> desire to do what is right as such, was either the
> only motive or a sufficient and necessary motive for
> doing it (1970: p. 75).

    This is a parsimonious model of what it means to be
self-critical in relation to an action done or contem-

plated—a feature of conscience that is completely conson-
ant with the adversarial and judicial function examined
earlier. We may adduce from Broad's observations, four
specific *rules of conscientious procedure,* which we pre-
suppose in our ordinary understanding.

> 1) To determine which of several conflicting
>   directives is the right or approved course,
>   as well as how much responsibility one has
>   for doing or not doing it, one must consult
>   and clarify the content of conscience, care-
>   fully ascertain its relevance to the case at
>   hand, and act on the resulting dictate.
>
> 2) One must scrupulously search out and weigh,
>   within the limits of one's power, all rele-
>   vant factual evidence bearing on the decision.
>
> 3) One must strive for impartiality and ob-
>   jectivity.
>
> 4) One must clarify as rigorously as possible
>   all pertinent and operative motives—flat-
>   fering and unflattering—for undertaking
>   the respective courses of action. In the
>   case of the approved action, one must attempt
>   to bring the real motives for action into
>   line with the "conscience-felt" concern to
>   act in accord with the content of conscience,
>   and to exclude or neutralize, as much as pos-
>   sible, ulterior and countervailing motives.
>   In the case of disapproved action, one must
>   attempt to identify prodigal motives, and
>   determine the degree of one's responsibility
>   for yielding to them. [3]

These rules of conscientiousness call to mind some
of the traditional moral and intellectual virtues, such
as wisdom, courage, justice, honesty and temperance.
They all have their place, it seems, in our idea of conscientiousness. The wise agent has a clear, organized
understanding of his basic convictions; he is perspicacious
regarding the circumstances as consequences of his actions;
and on the basis of such a grasp of his situation, he is able to

derive the most fitting action. Having adjudged what he
ought to do, the courageous agent possesses the tenacity
of will to persevere despite the cost, to act, as we say,
on principle. The notion of justice includes a number
of things, but among them is the requirement of impartiality and objectivity, of judging one's actions in accord
with impersonal or transsubjective standards. An agent is
said to be honest when he gives evidence of knowing himself, of clearly perceiving the full range of motives,
flattering and unflattering, that underlies his action,
and of having the strength of character to admit to himself and others the operation of prodigal motives, when
they are present. He is not self-deceived of self-deluded.
Finally, an agent is temperate in that he exemplifies self-
control in face of the distractions and disruptions of
prodigal motives.

Accordingly, conscientiousness is a composite virtue, combining aspects of the more familiar virtues. Because it is such, it has a special status among the terms
of our moral vocabulary. To call someone conscientious
is to use a term of high moral commendation.

That we use the notion of conscientiousness in a
commendatory way indicates something of great interest
about the notion. It means we assume there are *public evaluative criteria* for applying it. The jurisdiction of conscience
may be private in the sense that it reaches only to those
actions over which an individual has control, and the content of the conscience is, up to a point, the private
responsibility of each individual. Each person has a right to determine the character of his basic convictions, and must
take the consequences for so doing. But whether someone
is to be called conscientious in obeying his conscience
is a matter for public scrutiny and determination; it is

something observers properly judge, rather than being
simply a private affair. We ascribe the term to others
when they give evidence of having met, to the best of
their ability, the tests laid out above, the various
tests of virtue, as they turned out to be.

Thus, while the content of conscience is, we believe, properly subject to private discretion, and to be
respected accordingly, compliance with the procedures of
conscience is publicly assessed. Because there exists
this sort of distinction in our understanding of conscience, we have allowed for what is traditionally known
as the doctrine of erroneous conscience (see, e.g., Kolnai,
1958). According to this doctrine, an observer might, in
a given instance, disagree with an individual's moral decision because of a disagreement with the *content* of his
conscience, with his basic substantive moral convictions.
At the same time, the observer might concede that the individual has been conscientious in following the *rules* of
conscience: on inspection, he passes the tests of virtue
specified above. On such occasions, the observer would
conclude that the individual is, to be sure, suffering
from an erroneous conscience, but that, because he is
satisfactorily conscientious, his decision ought, nevertheless, to be respected, and he ought to act as he sees fit.[4]
This is, I take it, the attitude of many non-pacifists,
even those strongly committed to fighting a given war,
toward conscientious objectors.

It is this distinction between the content and procedures of conscience that enables us, in holding a doctrine of the freedom of conscience, to adopt a spirit of
tolerance within certain agreed upon limits. Each person,
we assume, has a duty to follow consistently the verdict
of conscience, but he also has a duty to conform to the

commonly accepted tests of conscientiousness in arriving
at the verdict.

But while we do detach the content and procedures
of conscience in the way I suggest, and seem to have something at stake in doing so, the detachment is qualified
in some important ways. The content and procedures also
appear to overlap. Presumably, we would not adjudge a
person conscientious who did not include somewhere among
his basic convictions (within the content of conscience)
a commitment to principles, articulated in some recogniza-
ble way, of honesty, wisdom, truth, courage and the other
procedural virtues that comprise the concept of conscientiousness. How could a person be genuinely conscientious unless he valued and demonstrated loyalty to the
principles of conscientiousness?

It seems clear, then, that to have a conscience
means that its content must include these principles.
Therefore, it is not entirely at the private discretion
of each individual to compose the content of conscience
as he sees fit. If he ignores, systematically excludes,
or contradicts what we commonly understand by these principles, he does not have a different conscience from
others; he has no conscience at all. The concept as we
employ it does not apply to such a person. In other words,
the procedures of conscience impose significant restrictions on what may go into the content. For this reason,
it would not be intelligible to refer to an individual
like Hitler, knowing what we do about him, as a man of
conscience. Not only by his own testimony did he disbelieve in conscience ("a Jewish invention, a blemish like
circumcision"), but his life gives no evidence of even minimal conformity or allegiance to the procedures of conscience
or the principles which lie behind them. He was a man who
"had neither scruples nor inhibitions" (Bullock, 1964: p. 380

He characteristically distrusted rational criticism, particularly of his own views and positions (Bullock, 1964, p. 372), and he had an enormous capacity for self delusion (Bullock, 1964: pp. 376, 385).[5]

On the other hand, while there are surely some commonly understood limits to what those principles lying behind the procedures of conscience may mean, we also assume that they are subject to different interpretations and various possible combinations and applications. In other words, it is the particular way an individual organizes and construes these principles, in combination, of course, with other substantive principles, that varies from person to person, and, indeed within the life of one individual. In fact, it is often in the process of practicing conscientiousness that an individual comes to clarify, modify, reinterpret, and even reorganize some of his basic convictions, and the way they are combined. Professor Leavell's description of the changes in President Theodore Roosevelt's moral convictions while in office offers a pertinent example.[6] In his younger days, Roosevelt laid stress on the duties of honesty, courage, and self-reliance, all in a personalistic sense. The content of his conscience was, at that point, defined in the light of Yankee individualism and the deep-seated belief that personal uprightness exhausted one's moral responsibility. But, as Roosevelt attempted conscientiously to harmonize the duties of his office with the duties dictated by his Yankee conscience, he came to revise and reinterpret his basic convictions to include a broadening sense of social responsibility, as Professor Leavell shows so ably.

According to the analysis so far, then, our understanding of conscience appears to have both a private and a public side to it. The conscience is a private monitor in that it reaches only those actions over which an indi-

vidual has control. At the same time, it monitors *all*
of an individual's actions, whether they are public or
private in character. The conscience is pertinent to an
individual's whole sphere of duty. Beyond that, we respect the right of an individual (within limits) to private discretion in formulating the particular content of
his conscience. At the same time, however, we hold ourselves and others to public account with regard to obeying
the procedures of conscience.

     The fact that we assume public tests for conscienti-
ousness indicates one reason why our prevailing notion of
conscience can never, properly understood, be construed
as necessarily favoring an atomistic, isolated view of
the self. Conscientiousness is plainly an art that is
learned in communication with others. It is learned by
testing one's own self-appraisal against the criticism of
others, by learning—slowly and painfully—to see ourselves as others see us. Through enlightened social interaction, one begins to recognize, and to correct for,
the persistent enemies of conscientiousness: bias, short-
sightedness, inconsistency, inconstancy, dishonesty and
self-deception, among others. I say enlightened social
interaction, because it is only those social encounters
that themselves impose and support the procedures of conscience that help to cultivate the capacity for self-re-
flection and self-criticism. It is easy to think of social situations which accomplish the opposite, which re-
enforce bias and self-deception, which encourage the
individual to evade conscience, and to be satisfied with
poor excuses for doing so. But just as social experience
can impede the functioning of the procedures of conscience,
so, under the right conditions, social surveillance, criticism and support is indispensable for the internalization

of those procedures.

Having sketched out the functions and jurisdiction, the content, and procedures of conscience, we may now draw some conclusions about the duties of conscience and their relation to the duties of station. Above all, our analysis indicates that we normally understand *the preeminent duty of conscience to be the achievement and maintenance through time of the personal integrity or self-identity of an individual actor.* Conscience is in the business of unity and continuity. It drives toward overcoming contradictions, conflicts, inconsistencies of action; it struggles to illuminate the causes of deviation, and to justify, redress or dispel them. It has these functions or it isn't a conscience.

So understood, the conscience could hardly in principle tolerate two moralities. The very notion of two moralities implies a systematically divided self, with systematically divergent spheres of duty. We have argued that far from being set apart, or over against, the duties of station, the conscience moves into action precisely in response to the array of duties that comprises an individual's "station." Duties of station and duties of conscience are interdependent. It is not surprising, therefore, that thinkers like Reinhold Niebuhr cannot sustain a two-moralities position, even though they flirt with it.

On the other hand, Niebuhr does seem to be getting at something. It is our task, now, to try to understand the kernal of truth in the two-moralities talk, and to locate it in relation to the thoughts we have worked out so far. Niebuhr makes the point, not always in the most clear-headed way, that in worldly occupations what a person's conscience approves of as ideal is frequently incapable of realization or, at best, realizable at

enormous cost. Actors, particularly in the political
world, must frequently tolerate the sacrifice of many of
conscience's preferred actions, for they act in an area
where "dirty hands" are unavoidable (see Walzer, 1973).

On the other hand, Niebuhr winds up providing us
with an adjusted conscience that adapts, up to a point,
to the necessities and realities of the social world, and
thereupon gives some direction in that context. I suggest
that the adjustment of conscience taking place here is
best understood in reference to the category of excuse,
as we identified it earlier. In fact, the basic strategy
of Niebuhr's social commentary, not to mention that of his
sympathizers, Kennan and Morgenthau, is to offer a series
of excuses intended to diminish, though not entirely eliminate, the responsibility of individuals, who, occupying
political and other collective roles, cannot seem to clean
their dirty hands.

There are, in particular, two sorts of excuses that
Niebuhr employs: the excuse of *understandable weakness* and
the excuse of the *understandable commitment to a prior duty*.
The excuse of understandable weakness means that an individual falls short of living up to his ideally approved duty
because he is only human. For Niebuhr, as we saw, human
beings, especially in their social roles, are motivated
by self-interest; they are partial, preferential, short-
sighted, etc. These conditions apply no matter what individuals may do, and it is realistic to understand this
fact, and to allow for it. Thus, we must not expect too
much of ourselves if we are politicians or businessmen.
Participating in deception and manipulation, in compro-
mises, in lesser evils of all sorts is simply one's lot.
Of course, as we mentioned, these conditions are pragmatic
necessities: If one decides to take on a social role, he

cannot avoid this sort of weakness.

However, while the excuse of understandable weakness is meant to diminish an individual's responsibility for misdeeds, it does not, for Niebuhr, completely eliminate responsibility. As miserable offenders, our weakness may be understandable, but it is something for which we may still, up to a point, be blamed. Such awareness drives us to seek divine help and forgiveness, beyond our own understandable weakness.

The second sort of excuse, of understandable commitment to a prior duty, is really more important to Niebuhr in his day-to-day moral reflection. It is directly linked to his idea of an adjusted conscience. It means that, faced with two conflicting, and contradictory duties, such as we often encounter in our station, we are bound by conscience to perform the *prior* duty, which then becomes an excuse for defaulting the other one. An example is the instance mentioned above in which a parent must choose between a duty to attend an important meeting and a duty to aid his ailing child. In this example, it will be noted that if he chooses to aid his child, he still is forced to do a disapproved thing—he does not attend the meeting which he is committed to do. He has, we would probably say, a good excuse for missing the meeting, an excuse which removes his responsibility for defaulting on his commitment. Still, it is an excuse, which he owes to the participants at the meeting; and, in addition, he may owe some special effort to make up the inconvenience at a later time.

Over and over, according to Niebuhr, this is the sort of predicament the politician encounters. As between conflicting duties, he must select whichever he believes to be the prior one, thereby defaulting on another duty.

He must lie or misrepresent something to do a greater
good (or a lesser evil), etc. Whichever duty he chooses,
the politician finds himself in a tragic situation: to do
an approved thing he must do a disapproved thing! This
sort of excuse (not unlike excuses often given for defaulting on more ordinary duties) diminishes the politician's
responsibility for doing didapproved acts; it is, after
all, supposed to be understandable that he would make the
choice he did, according to which he defaulted on one of
his responsibilities. Again, Niebuhr does not wish to
eliminate guilt for the default altogether, but simply to
diminish it. A guilty conscience of some sort is still
in order.

By showing that Niebuhr's social thought is actually
an exercise in moral excuse-making, I wish to contend that
he is operating squarely within the province of our ordinary notion of the conscience. One of the tasks of the
conscience is, as we saw, to entertain excuses for doing
disapproved things. But excuses are offered precisely in
order to try to achieve and maintain, through time, the
personal integrity or self-identity of the actor. Excuses
simply provide reasons why a putatively discrepant or inconsistent action is, after all, consistent, and is coherent with the master model according to which an individual claims to be operating, and with which he identifies himself. There is no flavor of two moralities here;
on the contrary, there is nothing but the struggle to
achieve a truly consistent, coherent and understandable
image of the self, that encompasses one's station, one's
whole sphere of duty.[7]

Having provided, we hope, the beginnings of a fuller
and more adequate analysis of the conscience than proponents of the two moralities view, like Reinhold Niebuhr,

have done, I wish to close by drawing attention to a timely discussion of one of the central duties of conscience
that emerges from our study, the duty to exercise and cultivate conscientiousness. We have suggested that to have a
conscience is to be required to live in keeping with the
procedures of conscience. Moreover, as conscientiousness
involves public assessment of one anothers' appeals to
conscience, the cultivation of conscientiousness is a matter of general social concern. But that concern is intensified when it comes to assessing the conscientiousness of
individuals whose station includes positions of institutional and social responsibility. In these contexts, its
presence or absence has a direct and telling effect on
constituents or clients.

When we learn, for example, as we do from the important study by Edward Weisband and Thomas M. Franck, *Resignation in Protest*, that the formal and informal arrangements and expectations at the top levels of the United
States government discourage, impede and disguise conscientiousness, we need to be especially troubled. Weisband
and Franck contend in their book, significantly subtitled,
*Political and Ethical Choices between Loyalty to Team and
Loyalty to Conscience,* that in contrast to British political experience, the American system predisposes officials
against resigning from public office on grounds of conscience, and, still more, against making public the reasons
for any such resignation, should it occur. The pressures
of office, outlook, and background are in the direction of
going along with the team. That frequently means the
evasion or betrayal of conscience. If resignation for
conscience' sake takes place, and, as often happens, that
fact is suppressed, then the resigner's deliberative process, his factual and normative reasons for resignation,

is hidden from public view.

It is not so much the content of conscience—the
particular substantive reasons for objecting and resigning—that concerns the authors, as the reasons why so few
high public officials in the history of this country have
been true to themselves, have stuck to their guns, in face
of deeply felt and conscientiously determined disagreements
with established policy. Smothered in an ethos of team
loyalty, the official is not encouraged to distinguish
and clarify his own basic convictions, let alone to act
upon them courageously. Nor is he encouraged to search
out and weigh serupulously all relevant factual information.
nor to strive for impartiality and objectivity in respect
to justifying or excusing the team's policies, nor to clarify
and face up to all pertinent and operative motives behind
the requirement of team loyalty.

Resignation in Protest, then, vivifies the two central points we have tried to make about the relation of
the duties of conscience and the duties of station. First,
the conscience is properly understood, not as set apart
from political and other social responsibilities, but as
something that arbitrates and adjusts the tangles of social duties and loyalties that comprise one's station.
Official duties which cover the public actions of individuals are every bit as fit for adjudication by the conscience as private actions are.

Second, along with the duties that flow from the
particular basic convictions or content of a person's
conscience, there are procedural duties of conscience.
These duties specify the requirements of exercising conscientiousness. Furthermore, since the cultivation of
conscientiousness is favored or impeded according to one's
reference groups, excessive emphasis by a group on certain

kinds of loyalties and duties systematically retards the
development of conscientiousness and leads to evasion of
conscience. The implication of this observation is that
all groups—religious, political, educational, etc.—
should be scrutinized for their contribution to the cultivation of conscientiousness, much as Weisband and Franck
have done in respect to certain groups of political officials.

We have attempted little more than to provide a
"phenomenological" account of conscience. We have not
offered compelling reasons why this account should be af-
firmed. But before that necessary job is undertaken, it
is perhaps useful to clarify our ordinary, working understanding of conscience in relation to the requirements
of social life, and to investigate a little the commitments and ideals that seem to underlie it.   In any case,
that has been our objective.

FOOTNOTES

*This is a revised version of the paper delivered
at the conference. Changes and additions have been made
in the light of the other papers and some of the comments
uttered during the sessions. My remarks on virtue were
stimulated by Professor Long's fine paper, and my observations on the social context of conscientiousness were
prompted by some insightful comments by Professor Max
Stackhouse. I mention my debt to Professor Leavell in
footnote 6. I also benefitted greatly from private con-
versations with several participants.

May I add, too, that in the light of the papers by
Ms. Janeway and Professor Brown, I am particularly sensitive to the problem of using the masculine pronoun
throughout this chapter. I do not regard this a trivial
matter, but I have so far not found a felicitous or
economical way to improve upon that usage.

* * *

[1] I have a special reason for choosing the rather
archaic phrase, "duties of station," over "duties of role,"
or "duties of office or occupation." I shall clarify why
as we go along. Briefly, I think we need a more inclusive
term respecting the requirements and responsibilities
(duties) of social life, and the word station may provide
that.

[2] In discussion, I was asked about the problem of
"collective guilt." The issue, as I understand it, is,
can one be considered morally guilty for culpable deeds
performed, beyond one's own direct control, by members of
one's group (family, nation, etc.)? The notion of collective guilt remains murky and confused, unless, in applying
it, a case is made that the culpable deeds were not in
fact beyond the control of other group members. Perhaps
the others were negligent for not undertaking to resist
the performance of the culpable deeds. Of course, if
that case is made, then the argument is that the individual, after all, *did* have the capacity to affect the actions
taken, and he may therefore be held guilty because he did
not exercise that capacity as he ought to have done. In
this sense, one member is understood to bear responsibility
for controlling the actions of other members of his group.

However, even this interpretation would exclude some group
members (e.g., infants, incapacitated individuals, etc.).
Therefore, membership in the group cannot alone constitute
grounds for responsibility. Anything beyond this sort of
construction seems to me to be full of mystification.

[3] In ch. 17, "Conscientiousness," Nowell-Smith (1961)
considers conscientiousness to amount to little more than
devotion to duty. That seems to me a seriously deficient
account of what we understand by the notion.

[4] The notion of erroneous conscience has produced
what has been thought to be a contradiction. An observer
may believe that the action contemplated by an actor is
wrong and ought not to be done, but, according to the
doctrine, the observer must, nevertheless, counsel the
actor that he ought to go ahead and do the act, providing
he is conscientious about it. In other words, in the
observer's eyes, the actor ought to do what he ought not
to do! However, I do not believe this is a proper statement of the position. Rightly stated, the observer would
hold the following: In a situation in which the observer's
assessment of the right thing to do conflicts with the
actor's assessment, the actor ought to go ahead and do
what he thinks is right, providing he has been conscientious in determining it. So far as deciding what the
actor himself ought to do, the actor's conscientious decision ought to take precedence over the observer's
assessment of the right thing to do. That formulation is
not contradictory. On the contrary, it provides a "priority rule" for favoring one judgment over another in a
conflict situation.

A somewhat different problem with the doctrine arises when
the observer must decide what he himself ought to do in
response to the actor's decision. Suppose the observer
is convinced the actor is deeply conscientious, but has
decided to perform an act that the observer believes is
gravely immoral, and ought to be coercively resisted.
Then, it appears, the observer ought not allow the actor
to do what, from the observer's point of view, the actor
ought to do! But, again, there is no real contradiction
here, if the matter is properly stated. It is not contradictory for the observer to say to the actor, "Given that
both you and I are conscientious in evaluating the situation, you must try to do your duty as you see it, and I
must try to resist you, according to my lights." Dramas
and novels are filled with such perfectly intelligible
predicaments. Interestingly, the mutual ascription of
blame and guilt will, according to our understanding, be
mitigated to the extent each party believes the other to be

conscientious in acting as he sees fit. That is, in part,
what it means to continue to *respect* a person with whom, on
substantive moral issues, one disagrees. It appears, then,
that a judgment that someone is conscientious about performing
erroneous acts constitutes an excuse; it diminishes guilt in
the eyes of the observer. Incidentally, the doctrine of erroneous conscience would not apply to a person like Hitler,
for, as I suggest below, Hitler could not pass the tests of
conscientiousness.

[5]At the same time, the case of Adolf Eichmann, as portrayed by Hannah Arendt (1964), is somewhat more difficult to
classify. Was Eichmann a conscientious person in implement-
ing a policy of mass murder against the Jews? Measured against
our list of rules of conscientious procedures, the correct answer seems to be that he was partly so.

On the one hand, Eichmann appears to have had a clear
principle ("duty to the Führer") which he applied consistently,
even to the point of reproaching himself and confessing his
"sins" to his superiors, when he several times yielded, out of
sympathy, to the "temptation" to exempt certain victims in violation of Hitler's orders. "For the sad and very uncomfortable
truth of the matter probably was," Arendt writes, "that it was
not his fanaticism but his very conscience that prompted Eichmann to adopt his uncompromising attitude [toward the extermination of the Jews] during the last year of the war..." (p.
146). Or, "...as for his conscience, he remembered perfectly
well that he would have had a bad conscience only if he had
not done what he had been ordered to do—to ship millions of
men, women and children to their death with great zeal and the
most meticulous care" (p. 25). In short, the first rule of
conscientious procedure seems satisfied.

On the other hand, Arendt records some rather striking
examples of hypocrisy on Eichmann's part (pp. 54-5) which appear to have been related to "the aura of systematic mendacity
that had constituted the general, and generally accepted, at-
mosphere of the Third Reich." Accordingly, "...German society
of eighty million people had been shielded against reality and
factuality by exactly the same means, the same self-deception,
lies, and stupidity that had now become ingrained in Eichmann's
mentality" (p. 52). It would, consequently, be difficult to
characterize Eichmann's devotion to the policies of the Third
Reich as *fully* conscientious: the second, third and fourth
rules of conscientious procedure appear, if these observations
of Arendt's are accurate, to have been rather seriously violated

This selective compliance with the rules of conscientiousness seems to account well for what I would take as a
common disposition to assess Eichmann as conscientious *in some
sense* (but certainly not fully so).

[6]See J. Perry Leavell, Jr., "Theodore Roosevelt's
Practical Idealism: A Case Study of Morality and Politics,"
included in this volume.

[7]In his stimulating essay, Walzer makes a significant point wbout Machiavelli in this regard (1973: p. 175).
He cites Machiavelli's reliance on the notion of excuse in
relating political action to morality. Sometimes, according to Machiavelli, the magistrate must be excused from
prohibitions against cruelty and deceit (*Discourses*, bk. I,
ch. IX), in order to prevent greater cruelty and deceit
(*Prince*, ch. XVII). "It is important," says Walzer, "to
stress Machiavelli's own commitment to the existence of
moral standards" (p. 175). To the extent that this represents his consistent position, there is no basis at all for
a "two-moralities" view. However, this position needs
rigorously to be compared to other relevant statements
throughout the *Discourses* and the *Prince* before we can be
certain that Machiavelli is either consistent or clear-
headed on this issue.

REFERENCES

Arendt, Hannah. *Eichmann in Jerusalem* (New York: The Viking Press, 1964).

Broad, C. D. "Conscience and Conscientious Action." Pp. 74-79 in Joal Feinberg (ed.), *Moral Concepts* (New York: Oxford University Press, 1970).

Bullock, Alan. *Hitler: A Study in Tyranny* (New York: Harper & Row, 1964).

Butler, Joseph. *Five Sermons* (New York: Bobbs-Merill Co., 1950).

Erikson, Erik. *Childhood and Society* (New York: W. W. Norton & Co., 1950).

Frankel, Charles. "Morality and U.S. Foreign Policy." Pp. 13-23 in *Worldview* 18, 2 (April 1975).

Kant, Immanuel. *The Doctrine of Virtue*. Trans. by Mary J. Gregor (New York: Harper & Row, 1964)

Kol Aurel. "Erroneous Conscience." Pp. 171-198 in *Proceedings of the Aristotelian Society*. New Series, LVIII (1958).

Niebuhr, Reinhold. *Moral Man and Immoral Society* (New York: Charles Scrib   1932).

Nowell-Smith, P. H. *Ethics* (London: Penguin Books, 19

Perkins, William. *The Whole Treatise of the Cases of Conscience*. Reprinted (Amsterdam: Theatrum Orbis Terrarum, Ltd., 1972).

Walzer, Michael. "Political Action: The Problem of Dirty Hands." Pp. 160-180 in *Philosophy and Public Affairs* 2, 2 (Winter 1973).

Weisband, Edward and Franck, Thomas M. *Resignation in Protest: Political and Ethical Choices between Loyalty to Team and Loyalty to Conscience* (New York: Penguin Books, 1975).

THE SOCIAL ROLES OF THE MORAL SELF

EDWARD LeROY LONG, JR.

Much of our thinking about the relationship between personal morality and social ethics has been influenced by a catchy title and a more serious thesis advanced in 1932 by Reinhold Niebuhr. The opening paragraph of the Introduction of *Moral Man and Immoral Society* encapsulates the argument:

> ...a sharp distinction must be drawn between the moral and social behavior of individuals and of social groups, national, racial, and economic; ...this distinction justifies and necessitates political policies which a purely individualistic ethic must always find embarrassing.[1]

To be sure, Reinhold Niebuhr did not create the issue nor originate an entirely new way of looking at these matters. Many before him—often a long time before him—were keenly aware of the differences between the relationships that can be created and sustained in face-to-face encounters and those which inhere in intergroup situations. For example, even though Luther contended that the state is divinely ordained rather than a pagan or ungodly construct, he still drew sharp distinctions between the harsh and negative behavior of the state in repressing evil and the outpouring of love possible between individuals.

Nor was Reinhold Niebuhr alone among his contemporaries in suggesting dichotomies between the norms which govern individual morality and those which govern social interactions. Emil Brunner, in a consistent extension of

premises found in Luther, contrasted the moral imperative
in personal relationships with those which are determinative for the exercise of official roles. For Brunner,
"The State is primarily not a moral institution but an
irrational product of history; the Christian State never
has existed and never will. Where the State is concerned
ethics always lag behind."[2] Hence, argued Brunner, the
duties of station or office differ from the duties of
person. "If the Christian's 'official duty' causes pain
and perplexity to his conscience," he wrote, "it simply
must be endured."[3]

From different perspectives, George Kennan and Hans
Morgenthau in not dissimilar lines of argument, pointed
to several ways in which moral scruples cherished by individuals in their idealism can be ineffective in forming
and conducting a realistic foreign policy. They argued
that nations must be governed more by interests than by
ideals. When nations determine their policy by moral
criteria they are tempted, among other things, to force
other nations to patterns of behavior dictated by moral
scruples. Policy should be pursued only for the purpose
of insuring that some nations do not behave adversely to
the rights and interests of other nations, not to make
nations conform to moral agenda. George Kennan put the
point this way:

> It is a curious thing, but it is true, that the
> legalistic approach to world affairs, rooted as it
> unquestionably is in a desire to do away with war
> and violence, makes violence more enduring, more
> terrible, and more destructive to political stabil-
> ity than did the older virtues of national interest.
> A war fought in the name of high moral principle
> finds no early end short of some form of total
> domination.[4]

Not only considerations of foreign affairs, but
analyses of domestic political life depended upon a dis-

tinction between personal and social morality. William
Muehl stood in the stream when he criticized the moralistic approach to politics with the following anecdote and
commentary.

> Some years ago the editors of a magazine published
> by one of the largest Protestant denominations de-
> cided to honor an American politician as 'Christian
> Statesman of the Year.' After much thought they
> chose for this designation Governor J. Throm Thurmond
> of South Carolina, the Dixiecrat candidate for Presi-
> dent in 1948.

> Truly remarkable was the principle reason given to
> support this choice. He neither drinks himself,
> nor allows alcohol to be served in his home.

Comments Muehl:

> At first hearing one could be disposed to dismiss
> this incident as nothing more than the quaint ex-
> pression of a provincial morality. But it would be
> unwise to do so. The selection of Governor Thurmond
> on the basis of his stand against liquor is fully in
> keeping with the traditions of Protestant individualism.[5]

In *Moral Man and Immoral Society*, Niebuhr charged
that those who look at the human situation with only personal ideals in mind are incapable of understanding "the
brutal character of the behavior of all human collectives."[6] Therefore they underestimate the stubborn resistance of group egotism and arrive at sentimental judgments about political reality that often betray the very
purposes they would affirm. In *The Children of Light and
the Children of Darkness* he made use of another metaphor
and observed: The [children of darkness] are evil because
they know no law beyond the self. They are wise, though
evil, because they understand the power of self interest.
The children of light are virtuous because they have some
conception of a higher law than their own will. They are
usually foolish because they do not know the power of
self-will."[7] In this formulation wisdom and virtue are

counterposed.

Some of those who accepted and adopted the dichotomy between personal and social morality concluded that the
corporate areas of human life are governed by a different
morality than individual affairs. Others concluded that
corporate life—and particularly that between autonomous
collectives—was governed by no scruples at all. In
either event the standards of individual morality came to
be viewed as either inappropriate or irrelevant to social
affairs. At times scruples based upon personal morality
were judged to be dysfunctional and often counterproduc-
tive for ordering social existence; at still other times
personal scruples were suspect because they caused hesitation in the performance of official duty.

* * *

The frame of mind that we have sketched all too
briefly has been highly influential and has given moral
reflection over the past several decades certain qualities
that need to be re-examination. For one thing, face-to-
face relationships have not been given sufficient attention as ethical problems. Some writers, like Carl F. H.
Henry, have spoken to Christian personal morality from a
conservation evangelical persuasion.[8] When others have
written about such matters, as for example William F. May
has done in his *A Catalogue of Sins*,[9] the result has often
been considered more of a contribution to pastoral theology than to Christian ethics. One can almost go so far as
to say that the treatment of the field of Religion and
Personality—a field not without its importance for theological education—as something apart from and unrelated
to Christian ethics may well be a consequence of the split
between the personal and the social aspects of morality.

For a second thing, too much thinking about face-
to-face relationships has oversimplified the nature of
these relationships. The "moral man" side of the Niebuhrian catch phrase has been misleading. It has caused
us to overlook or to prematurely discount the profound
difficulties that often inhere in being fully moral in
personal relationships as well as in social responsibilities. I think that the experience with bio-medical ethics is proving a corrective here. Bio-ethics has been
concerned to a large (and in my judgment too large) extent with dilemmas on a relatively low level of political
complexity. The dilemmas are often horrendous—but not
because large collectivities are involved. Some of the
situations with which biomedical ethics deals are face-
to-face ones in which all the participants can reason together, yet they permit of no easy solutions. Face-to-
face morality does not proceed without problems of compromise, ambiguity, and doubt.

For another thing the polarization of thinking about
these matters into individual and social moralities has
placed too great attention upon institutions of sovereign
power, like the state, and has occasioned inattention to
a range of societal and institutional realities that occupy a complex middle spectrum between solitary existence
and overarching sovereignties. While thinkers well-versed
in social analysis, like Troeltsch, Weber, and James Luther Adams, have dealt with the role and functions of voluntary associations, many Christian ethicists have either
neglected such associations altogether or have too easily
plugged them into the same pidgeon hole with power collectives and labelled the undifferentiated grouping "immoral
society." Just as political science should not study merely governmental units, so Christian social ethics should

not concern itself with only political sovereignties.
Granted that voluntary associations often present problems analogous to those created by governmental units
with power, they also have features, problems, and resources that can only be treated with different categories of analysis and insight. Consider, to cite an example from the educational world, how relatively little attention has been paid by academics to the problems of
governing the very institutions in which they do their
work. Much more has been written about how dictatorships,
congresses, presidencies, and the courts function than
about faculties or administrations. Similarly, many seminary students—taking the usual regimen of courses—are
more fully exposed to the working of macro-public groups
than to considerations of how ecclesiastical bodies function. The course in polity—if offered or required—tends
to be more of a practical advance course on the periphery
of theological inquiry than the place where social ethics
is learned.

* * *

Many problems and difficulties flow from an over-
simplistic contrast of private and public morality. The
considerations which follow in this paper are but one way,
and by no means the only way, along which we should work
to correct and supplement the ethical reflections of the
past fifty years.

The task before us can be defined in terms of several questions. The largest of these is: "What are the
social functions of the moral self?" Stated differently:
"It is possible to conceptualize any virtues that are
commonly associated with private morality in ways that

will have significance for social process?" Is it possible to discern any correlation between moral maturities
in individuals and social health in groups? What can social ethics learn and utilize from personality theory and
the concern for mental and spiritual health of individuals that can be transferred to help in understanding and
creating healthy social behavior? Does the individual
character of a person bear any relationship to possible
usefulness as a policy maker or public administrator?

     To put the description of this chapter's agenda into
the terminology introduced by Professor Little would be to
suggest that it attempts the difficult task of thinking
about private and public morality in terms of the *content*
of conscience rather than the *functions* of conscience
alone. This is an immensely difficult task in a pluralistic society and even within a Christian ethic dominated
by a presumed dichotomy between private and public deline-
ations of behavior. It is attempted in but an admittedly
tentative and exploratory fashion.

                         * * *

     The rubric "virtue" denotes certain attributes of
character. I wish there was an equivalent term which was
not clouded by gender implications but believe that we
can surely employ the term to apply equally to qualities
in both male and female persons. In traditional philosophy the most mentioned virtues are wisdom, temperance,
courage, and justice. In the Christian tradition faith,
hope and love (or charity) were added. The contemporary
world may not think of virtue in terms of either list.
For instance, wisdom has come to mean a more intellectual
thing—a kind of skill or breadth of information—rather
than a capacity for moral judgment. Did not Reinhold

Niebuhr reveal as much when he spoke of the Children of
Darkness as "wise, though evil?" Faith is not commonly
considered a virtue today, but an intellectual stance—a
way of looking at meaning. It is scrutinized in episte-
mology rather than in ethics. To be sure justice con-
tinues to be regarded as an important term in ethics, but
it is conceived less as a virtue possessed by individuals
than as a requirement in a healthy social system. We
think of a prudent person more as a skillful operator who
can get things done without false counterproductivities
than as a virtuous person whose decisions embody moral
good. Except as interpreted by a few recent theologians,
hope is for dreamers. It relates to *esprit de corps* and
morale rather than to morals.

The virtues that are respected on Main Street, or in
the board room of the corporation, around the union hall,
or in the governmental bureaucracy would more likely be
honesty, dependability, loyalty and consideration for others. These virtues are important clues to the kind of
individual believed most functional in the working world.
A Wall Street brokerage house looking for an account executive would probably seek honesty, dependability, loyalty and politeness rather than faith, justice, or charity.
(Prudence would be given a rather special meaning.) A
labor union selecting a negotiator would probably not
look for temperance and charity. (Wisdom would be given
a very operational connotation.) Professors Weisband and
Franck have documented for us how important loyalty is
among those selected for posts in governmental bodies, as
it is also within the worlds of finance and industry.
Professor Rubenstein has pointed out how the quality of
loyalty can be perverted by bureaucratic necessity and
actually occasion gross immorality. Other qualities, like

shrewdness or coolness, could be added to this list, but
these would stand in the same tension with the traditional virtues, if not indeed, more so.

In exploring the relationship of the virtues to social functions we might argue that it is important to recapture the significance of the classical virtues as contrasted with the newer ones. Another approach would be
to transvaluate those qualities identified with the contemporary worlds of practical affairs. What follows is a
combination of these approaches but mainly an effort to
redefine the prevailing virtues of Main Street to make
them more socially significant.

a] We begin with honesty: From the perspective of
an individualistic approach, honesty implies the obligation to yield technically correct answers to specifically
posed questions, particularly when under oath or in formalized settings. The opposite of honesty in this sense is
lying, deliberate deceit. The folklore for teaching it:
George Washington and the cherry tree. When asked, the
child answered honestly—but he never volunteered the information.

But honesty can have far broader meanings. Consider
by way of illustration a meaning of honesty that comes
from the practice of architecture. A brick or stone wall
laid upon a steel supporting lintel may be said to be dishonest. A church constructed in gothic style on steel
supports may be similarly judged dishonest. I confess
that for years I resisted this use of the term, but have
slowly come to see what it connotes. Since masonry is
strong only in compression, its use can be authentic only
when it is used in buildings under compression—not when
it is hung upon steel merely as a curtain. A Gothic
building built without steel is honest; a suspension

bridge built of steel is honest, wood paneling printed on
cardboard is not, whereas ordinary wall paper is.

We are broadening the term honesty to mean authenticity. Honesty is a wholistic integrity at odds with pretense, sham, and hypocrisy. The oblique representations
upon which so much commercial advertising depends become
dishonest under such rubrics even when they raise no problems of false statements. Technical correctness is not
sufficient. Or, to illustrate from another kind of practice: the use of superlatives when simple comparatives
will do is not merely exaggerated rhetoric but a form of
dishonesty and, if our logic holds, even a kind of moral
malfeasance. Honesty demands chaste and judicious language
faithful to the reality portrayed. Representations passing
the test of authenticity are quite different from those
which only qualify as technically correct answers to specific questions.

Another transvaluation of honesty turns it into a
demand for exposure. Secret and clandestine ways of doing
things are too prevalent in contemporary life—as we discovered so dramatically in Watergate. Honesty requires a
more open style in which decisions are publicly made and
public accountability is required in the performance of
duty. Who is not more comfortable making comments about
others in a close and confidential circle of friends? Who
would rather not deal with controversial matters behind
closed doors rather than in a town meeting? Who would
rather not use a secret ballot when deciding a personnel
matter or policy controversy than go on record with a vote?
The advent of sunshine laws represents a stirring toward
making honesty a function of exposure and accountability
and not merely personal intentionality. There are limits
to sunshine laws and dangers in blowing some decisions into

a public circus, but the future will probably bring increased demands for exposure and accountability in public
and quasi-public functions. Many matters not treated as
confidential will become matters on which the public expects to know the record. Such is the case already with
hiring practices under affirmative action procedures.
Such is the case with codes of ethics for public officials
requiring them to disclose financial holdings. Such is
the case within the governance of institutions where constituency involvement enables groups to know what other
groups do. To live exposed and accountable is a demanding
experience. It will require the cultivation of quite new
traits of character and will also raise the risks and
agonies involved in becoming active in social processes.

        Consider in this connection the difference between
being honest and achieving credibility. It is far more
difficult to become trusted than merely to meet the test of
telling the truth. But success with becoming trusted is
precisely the stuff of which personal success in social
interaction is made. Credibility is seldom obtained by
pleading for it; it must be earned. A society that gives
credibility too easily is often unstable and prone to being
led astray by stuntmanship. Credibility can occasionally
be staged——the more so in immature and unhealthy social
circumstances——but situations in which it can be staged
are situations in which it may also quickly wither. Sometimes credibility is falsely denied where it is due. There
is not much that can be done in such circumstances except
to steer a steady course in the hope that suspicions will
dissipate. We know more about the importance of credibility than about how it is sustained. On balance, however,
I do believe credibility must correlate more with personal
integrity, openness, and accountability than any sharp

dichotomy between private and public morality can account
for.

b] Some considerations concerning loyalty: The
concept of loyalty is often taken to mean team play and
the subordination of individual autonomy to the common
purposes of a larger group, such as the nation. In the
baser versions of this understanding subservience and
obedience become the accepted pattern. This idea of loyalty is made a virtue in boot camps, plebe years, and novi-
tiate periods in nunneries. It is also engendered by pro-
bationary periods in many professions and enforced by arrangements in commercial worlds whereby people serve almost entirely at the whim of superiors.

While we give lip service to individual initiative
and independence, few institutional arrangements truly
honor autonomy. We raise children on television shows in
which the Lone Ranger enforces justice and dispenses mercy
better than the sheriff's department but we have ways of
dealing with people in sheriff's department (and in most
other structures) who act too much like lone rangers.

This sets up a strange dichotomy in which loyalty
and criticism are seen to work in opposition to each other.
Much social behavior is therefore caught on the dilemma of
having either to exhibit a loyalty that does not criticize
or to engage in criticism that does not know how to be
loyal. The criticism rendered under such conditions becomes a frantic kind of shrill protest rather than a set
of suggested alternatives. As long as this is the case
the problem remains whether to be a sycophant or a rebel
and the dichotomy between individual morality and social
behavior is perpetuated.

Ethically speaking the criticism made from within
an institution or an organization is a far deeper expres-

sion of loyalty than disassociation.   If one cares deeply
one criticizes for the potential benefit which that criticism can have for the institution of which one is a part.
If one ceases to care one either quietly withdraws, or,
as contemporary parlance puts it, "cops out." Criticism
is a deeper expression of loyalty than obedience or ac-
quiescence—though rulers may not think so. Both those
who acquiesce and those who merely slip away break covenant.

The union of loyalty with criticism is seen most
pointedly in the prophetic stance. A prophet brings loyalty and criticism into a symbiotic relationship by boring
from within rather than yacking from without. Prophets
criticize a given situation because it does not measure up
to that which they believe it should by the ideals to which
both the prophet and his society are professedly loyal.
Prophecy is possible only under covenant, that is, in a
situation in which a society is defined by common expectations more lofty than its own accomplishments or the policies of its immediate leaders. One of the important premises of democracy is that it should make possible internal
self-correction. The British think of this as coming from
Her Majesty's loyal opposition. In America, we have a
less adequately conceived place for in-house criticism, as
Professors Weisband and Franck have documented for us.

Consider, in the way of an illustration, how we have
structured the civil service system. In America we make a
very clear decision to protect competent workers who deal
with routine matters but explicitly exclude policy makers
from the protection of the system. This makes political
sense on the ground that democracy must be able to throw
out those who make policy whenever the ground swell of
discontent from below is great enough. But it also tends

to raise the risk and increase the hazards of speaking out
against policies from bureaucratic positions.

We need to fashion a middle kind of social role con-
sisting of policy-advising. This should have the protection surrounding it that would engender candor yet not
bear the functional responsibility for deciding policy.
We are actually coming to something like this by the creation of policy study centers ("think-tanks") which have
a detached position of protection yet an obligation to
criticize and suggest alternatives and to render necessary
judgments upon shortcomings in an existing order. Persons
employed in such agencies can, when conditions are favor-
able, be considered loyal without being rendered neutral.
In contrast with bureaucrats, they can suggest strategies
without becoming dangerous.

I want to say something here about the current discussion of the tenure system in the academic world. Tenure
has several functions, the most commonly cited being the
protection of academic freedom. Academic freedom may
presently be somewhat secure and is secure for many even
without tenure, though it cannot be taken for granted and
would be less secure for all if not protected strongly by
tenure for some. But freedom to discuss the implications
of issues within the subject matter competency of the classroom is not the only freedom protected by tenure. Tenure
also engenders a security from which, ideally, faculty
members will be able to be loyal critics of policies within their own institutions, particularly matters of governance and procedures upon which the health of the intellectual community depends. Tenure is one of the most institu-
tionalized ways of acknowledging the importance of loyalty
that couples responsibility to a group with the protection
of criticism that is designed to improve the life and the

integrity of the group from within. Whatever the case
against it on operational or managerial grounds, its value as a paradigm for a richer conception of loyalty than
that cherished by many institutions in our culture makes
it crucially important both to uphold and to reinterpret
as a symbol. In this instance, tenure protects not only
against arbitrary administrative action, but against removal by peer pressure or action.

    Pluralistic societies are more likely to enable
criticism to be coupled with loyalty because they diversi-
fy loyalty and thus provide interactions that support
prophetic judgments against the dominant group. The confessing church has more than once played such a role of
support for those called to say "no" to a social policy
or to a tyranny. I was pleased to have Professor Rubenstein, who is not noted for soft illusions, recognize the
importance of this role in what seemed to be his main
meagre hope of stemming bureaucracy.

    We have not heard as much in this conference as we might
have of the special kind of religiously inspired vocational witness to a moral vision symbolized and practiced
in sectarian traditions such as the Mennonite. These traditions engage, not in protest resignation, but in protest
detachment. They refuse to accept duties of station within the political order to the end that they may bear a
special witness to the morality of their ideals. I find
it significant that Professor Stanley Hauerwas, who is now
writing a Christian ethic of virtue,[10] expresses much appreciation for Professor John Howard Yoder's restatement
of the importance of the Christian witness to the state.
The witness of which Yoder speaks is possible because
radical disjuncture is voluntarily assumed while rebellion
against the state is simultaneously eschewed. What is

even more interesting is that Reinhold Niebuhr frequently
expressed appreciation for the particular brand of moral
earnestness that stems from vocational witness. Although
we know from studies of intentional communities that they
sometimes are as rigid against criticism made from within
their fellowship as the larger society is impatient with
criticism, it remains that purists can contribute to social health even when they disclaim any social effectiveness.

     c] Some social dimensions to kindness: I pick
"kindness" as a term with a long history of negative con-
notations associated with individualistic morality. Brunner uses the term when discussing how the actions of a
Christian judge will differ when done as an individual than
when performed as an official. The term has been given
perjorative meaning in the commentary made upon political
processes by Christian realism. How a person treats children or pets—not infrequently cited in political cam-
paigning—is hardly a measure of how policy decisions will
be made when that person has power. Often those who seem
most kindly or polite in personal relationships are least
willing to back policies designed to alleviate injustice
or human distress on a systemic level. Several personal
attributes associated with kindness—decorum, poise, an
ability to get along well with others, responsibility with
assets, etc.—often illustrate the sharp distinction between personal qualities that are frequently admirable
and official actions that work against the needs of others.

     But kindness need not be a simple antithesis to so-
cial responsibility. For instance, empathy (which has
some affinities to kindness) may be the seed bed of mercy
and should not be easily ridiculed as socially dysfunctional. The line from kindness to compassion is not a

valuational U-turn, but a progressive deepening and en-
richment of the same qualities of character. Love expresses itself socially through mercy and compassion more
directly than through some vividly contrasting traits
felt to be justified as duties of office or station. In
moving from individual to social morality as much is to
be gained by amplifying and extending the same genre of
virtues as by looking for radical discontinuities. The
setting of love and justice into antithetical, or at least
polarized, terms (which was sometimes done by the theological realists) was at best of limited usefulness. Sometimes
justice permits actions less sweepingly heroic than love;
But those who must express a social concern born of love
resort to justice—not to contradict but to implement their
intentions. The mileage had by setting individual behavior
as kindness or compassion into a dichotomy with toughness
or justice as unpleasant duty, while at times useful and
important, is meager as compared with the mileage to be
had from raising politeness of kindness from limited virtues to the morally inclusive and socially important qualities of caring, compassion and justice-loving concern.

        A side effect of the kind of thinking that sets in-
dividual and social morality into antithetical terms is
the almost complete lack in contemporary theological ethics of any serious attention to the significance of philanthropy for the social order. Philanthropy, which often
stems from caring and kindness (sometimes from guilt or
self-serving), has been an important social fact in a
pluralistic society. Voluntary associations exist wholly
on the foundation of freely offered gifts. If philanthropy
is the life blood of voluntary associations, and if voluntary associations are communities from which significant
independent social analysis and social criticism stem,

then philanthropy is fundamental to the maintenance of an
open and healthy society. We have all, I suspect, ridiculed the simplistic formula "earn all you can and give
all you can." It isn't clear whether Wesley or Franklin
deserves to be credited or blamed for it. But "give all
you can" is not bad social advice in a society where the
strength of voluntary associations devoted to all levels
of public impact—from caring for animals to making policy
studies—is an essential ingredient of social health and
perhaps the most promising of all the slim hopes for a
viable future.

The reasoning in this chapter is presented as a pre-
liminary paradigm for putting personal and social morality
into interactional rather than antithetical terms. It
suggests that a symbiosis rather than a dichotomy is the
more fruitful model with which to work. Nothing which
has been suggested should comfort the idea—still prevalent in certain places—that the conversion of individuals
to a religious perspective is a sole and sufficient solution to social ills. That view was decisively discredited
by those whose work has furnished the springboard for the
appreciative demurrers of this colloquim. Moreover, nothing suggested here should abet a new kind of moralism by
which the public careers of individuals can be axed by
finding purely personal indiscretions that have no functional relationship to the public performance of duty and
no bearing on policy. Blackmail by morals does not truly
join personal and public morality but uses one to thwart
the workings of the other.

Institutional patterns must be systematically judged,
and where necessary, changed. But in changing institutional patterns we can bear in mind—not only the ways in
which justice is aligned behind policy—but also the ways

by which individuals are reinforced in the kinds of personal qualities that contribute to social health. Results
from thinking and working with these matters will not come
quickly, nor will they be free of ambiguity or miscarri-
ages of intention. The stakes are high and the risks
enormous, but so are the dangers of escalating the deper-
sonalization and irresponsibilities of bureaucracies that
operate with immunity from moral scrutiny.

      While it is true that individual moral scruples can
sometimes be dysfunctional to the performance of duty there
is another side to the problem of the interface between
private and public behavior. Our attention is yanked to
it every time we hear of a widespread scandal or a "rip
off" in a public project. Lack of scruples and violation
of just procedures can seriously undercut institutional-
ized justice. Corruption and personal irresponsibility
illustrate how immoral persons can thwart the achievement
of a more moral society. When any group, in white collar
or blue collar or no collar, comes to feel that ripping
off the system is perfectly legitimate because others do
it and moral sanctions deal only with personal matters anyway, it has to be called up short. Societies which lack
internal moral disciplines invite rule by terror.

      Few societies in the course of human history have
attained the personal and social disciplines that make a
high degree of freedom possible. It may be that religious
or quasi-religious convictions are crucial for inculcating
this quality in the general public. And, it may also be
that the Judeo-Christian ethos has lost its capacity to
engender such rudimentary moral behavior in western society as makes possible the continuation of political and
social systems of the type we cherish. If so, nothing will
stave off the technological terror that will arise to

maintain the kind of social control necessary for societal functioning. It may also be that the new regime in
Communist China reveals the power of a new ideology to
engender individual responsibility supportive of social
betterment, although I do not have the necessary information to judge all the present dynamics or the prospects
of that phenomenon. I do know that there is a cause for
great worry about much that is going on within our society,
even on the local scene. Walzer's book, *Obligations,* has
been lifted unsigned from the reserves in the library for
several days, possibly by a student wanting to be sure
he has it for a long enough period to write a peper in
ethics! Mention of this is not merely moralistic prattle
or socially irrelevant carping. Such behavior invites a
checkout system, which is a first step toward transforming
the society of which we are locally a part, to one in
which externally imposed restraints are more evident than
internalized decency.

   Kohlberg and others who study moral development suggest that social responsibility is acquired with the approach of adulthood. In contrast, Toynbee suggested that
the breakdown of moral standards is one mark of a society
that has passed its prime and is on the way toward disso-
lution. Are we to conclude that individuals seem to become more socially responsible as they age while societies
move toward the disintegration of morals after they have
passed their primes? Perhaps this a new way of seeing
the distinction between private and public morality, but
rather than assume it condemns societies to the "downhill"
path once the zeal and fervor of their founding impulses
have worn off, these observations should alert us to how
crucially important for societies it is to nourish their
moral commitments for as long as possible.

The kind of intensified ethical expectations which
are being discussed today for public figures will do little unless they are complemented by a general toning of
behavior in all the citizenry. Expectations that public
policies will be correctly or fairly made only by those
who have technically freed themselves from possible conflict of interest will not suffice to save the social
welfare if private citizens continue to milk the system.
To believe, as ethical realism tended to, that the main
task of social thought is to remove the debilitating
shackles of moralism so that public figures can perform
the harsh duties required of office, will not meet the
needs of these times. The biblical prophets were less
concerned to suggest how public officials could be
shrewder than they were concerned to insist that the
people as a whole should be more faithful and just. Our
task is to stand in their stead.

FOOTNOTES

[1]Niebuhr, Reinhold, *Moral Man and Immoral Society* (New York: Charles Scribner's Sons, 1932), p. xi.

[2]Brunner, Emil, *The Divine Imperative* (Philadelphia: Westminster Press, 1947), p. 463.

[3]*Ibid.*, p. 222.

[4]Kennan, George F., *American Diplomacy 1900-1950* (Chicago: University of Chicago Press, 1951, 1953), p. 101f.

[5]Muehl, William, *Politics for Christians* (New York: Association Press, 1956), p. 37f.

[6]Niebuhr, *op. cit.*, p. xx.

[7]Niebuhr, Reinhold, *The Children of Light and the Children of Darkness* (New York: Charles Scribner's Sons, 1944), p. 10f.

[8]Henry, Carl F. H., *Christian Personal Ethics* (Grand Rapids, Mich.: Wm. B. Eerdmans, 1957).

[9]May, William F., *A Catalogue of Sins* (New York: Holt, Rinehart and Winston, 1967).

[10]Hauerwas, Stanley, *Vision and Virtue: Essays in Christian Ethical Reflection* (Notre Dame, Ind.: Fides Publishers, 1974).

CONGRESS AND THE CONCEPT
OF ETHICAL AUTONOMY

THOMAS M. FRANCK
EDWARD WEISBAND

In *Resignation in Protest,* we noted that a person who sacrifices team loyalty to pursue a competing value of personal conscience is likely to have brought to bear against him or her the coercive weight of society's historically conditioned sense of self-preservation. Loyalty, and conformity, play an important part in group perception of what is necessary to survival. Societies, groups, organizations tend to systematize the process of making value-judgments; indeed, they systematize the very process by which they perceive reality. Few individuals deliberately choose to set themselves against this process. The result, in decision-making circumstances, has been described by the psychologist Irving Janus as "group think."

Fortunately, there are exceptions. Thoreau grumbled that "The mass of men serve the state...not as men, mainly, but as machines...there is no free exercise whatever of the judgment or the moral senses.... Others—as most legislators, politicians, lawyers, ministers, and office-holders—...rarely make any moral distinctions...." Still, he was prepared to concede, "a very few, as heroes, patriots, martyrs, reformers in the great sense, and *men,* serve the state with their consciences also, and so necessarily resist it for the most part." However, "they are commonly treated as enemies by it."

In *Resignation in Protest,* we went on to observe
that instrumental values, the need for efficiency and the
dynamics of "belonging" are all-powerful weapons time and
again used against the conscience of an obstreperous individual when he or she strives to maintain ethical autonomy
by creating distance from the team and criticizing it openly.

By *ethical autonomy* we mean the willingness to assert one's own principled judgment against the group even
if in doing so the rules, values, or perceptions of the
organization, peer group, or team, are offended. Individuals are ethically autonomous to the degree that they
"stick to their guns" about what they think, believe, see,
sense, or know, even when it puts them in conflict with
such team values as conformity, loyalty, and institutional
efficiency.

When we use the term ethical autonomy, we do not
mean to imply approval of the individual's actual judgment.
Nor does it suggest that we believe that the ethically autonomous individual's ethical standards, in any particular
instance, are better or higher than those of the peer
group. The social importance of ethical autonomy, we believe lies not in what is asserted, but in the act of asserting.

This is because the ethical autonomy of an individual is an institution's and society's safety valve, a corrective that protects against malfunction and social disintegration. When a group's way of seeing, evaluating,
and deciding cease to be based on a free and open flow of
information and instead, for example, reflect simplistically what some dominant persons within the group may prefer to think is so then conformity leads to miscalculations

that can be disastrous to the society that follows its
blind leader into the swamp. The ethically autonomous
individual, in such circumstances, risks unpopularity
and may even be forced to leave the group. He may even
have to be willing to incur onerous penalties. But he
is an essential social safeguard. Even if he is wrong,
the dissident compels rational evaluation of policies
that thereby become better understood and more intelli-
gently buttressed by a better informed public.

In *Resignation in Protest,* we dealt with the phenomenon of the cabinet and sub-cabinet official who, in the
exercise of ethical autonomy, resigns from the government
in order to be able to speak out against one or more of
its policies. We found that the penalties for such autonomous conduct could be very severe. Consequently,
few were willing to incur these costs to their professional, political and even social lives.

In this paper, we will examine ethical autonomy in
all the context of another "group": The Members of Congress.

The Watergate investigations conducted by Congress
have inevitably led to public scrutiny of the ethical
standards of the investigators. Unhappily, most of this
concern about the ethical standards of Congress has been
directed at the easy, and, for the most part, irrelevant
or trivial ethical questions arising from the work—or,
more often and most irrelevantly, the play—of the Members.
It requires no profound insight to discover ethical and
even legal problems in a Member's placing on the public
payroll someone whose services are strictly private.
However, as the British playwright, Tom Stoppard, has observed in his recent play "Dirty Linen": What is needed
is investigation not of what members of Parliament do in

public. The emphasis on private scandal is a red her-
ring—however pungent—and a poor substitute for a search-
ing investigation of more profound ethical dilemmas.

We propose that you join us in focusing on a few of
these. Since our research concern has been with the new
activism of Congress in the field of foreign relations,
it is from this area that our nuts-and-bolts examples are
drawn; but the sorts of major ethical quandries they illustrate are probably endemic.

One further caveat. We have deliberately chosen
ethical dilemmas. It is, of course, a matter of public
concern if Members of Congress are being bribed or otherwise suborned to perform their constitutional functions
in an illegal manner. Here, however, the ethical questions are identical with questions of legal responsibility
and the lawyers have already occupied the field in passing
judgment on such activities. The really difficult questions are those in which the public has not crystallized
its thinking sufficiently to write law and as to which
the lawyers thus far remain silent. It is here, in the
interstices between what is *legal* and what is *ethical,*
that moral philosophy has its major social task.

In our study of ethical autonomy among senior officials in the Executive Branch, we identified several factors which, quite aside from the cost of non-conformity,
helped contain the urge to ethically autonomous behavior.
Among these are professional conditioning (especially
among lawyers and businessmen with their strong sense
of client-ship), awe of the majestic presidency, an awareness of having been selected, not elected, to power.

Among members of Congress, we have detected four
different factors militating against ethical autonomy.
They are: (1) pressure-group politics, (2) the trap of

"effectiveness", (3) congressional discipline, and (4) the
tyranny of image.

   1. *PRESSURE-GROUP POLITICS.* Pressure-group politics are a relatively well-studied phenomenon in American
life, although most of the attention has been directed to
an examination of the political impact of big-business and,
perhaps to a lesser extent, big-labor influence groups. In
the past these have, indeed, been of overriding importance
because, in the cases of big business and the more influential trade unions, they have wielded considerable "power
of the purse" through massive campaign contributions.   In
recent years, however, that power has been circumscribed
by laws limiting aid for individual candidates to $5,000
per election and $5,000 per primary, as well as by exten-
sive reporting requirements. This has reduced, but
scarcely eliminated, their power over members.   Trade
union lobbies, in particular, have the additional advantage of being able at least to purport to deliver large
blocs of campaign workers and votes in some regions of the
country. Furthermore, in the 1940s and '50s, the big business and big labor lobbies were primarily locked in struggles against one another, as during the Taft-Hartly debate.
More recently, however, labor and industry, more often than
not, have been on the same side in advocating policies re-
strictive of international trade, as well as in support
for certain important defense industries. The power of
this "commerce" lobby is still very significant in certain
key areas of Congressional responsibility.

   Moreover, with the decline of some of the more traditional lobbies, new ones have appeared on the scene,
marshalling a different, but considerable, clout. These
include groups in Washington concerned with the so-called

"public interest" and ethnic lobbies.   The latter are particularly interesting.   The American-Hellenic Lobby,
AHEPA, working in Washington on behalf of the Greek-Amer-
ican-Israeli Public Affairs Committee, AIPAC, working on
behalf of American Jews and Israel, have both demonstrated
their sway over individual members of Congress, influencing
them to vote in ways which, some concede privately, they
might not otherwise have done.

Finally, there has appeared in Washington a cluster
of lobbies representing foreign governments with special
ties to Congress: ties usually resulting from a history
of U.S. foreign assistance, both economic and military.
The South Korean lobby is a currently visible instance.

These various kinds of lobbies, new and old, governmental and private, raise different ethical problems and
each instance in which they operate produces its own personal ethical equation for each member of Congress.   The
basic ethical issue, however, is always the same and very
simple: should a member vote his own mind's preference or
should he defer to the views being urged by the lobby?   In
answering this question, the member must decide: does it
matter, ethically, *which* kind of lobby?   Does it matter,
in this equation, *which* member of Congress?   Does it matter
which kind of issue?

A good example is afforded by the recent Cyprus crisis.   This confrontation was precipitated on July 15, 1974,
when Archbishop Makarios was overthrown as president of
Cyprus and replaced with Nikos Sampson.   Within two weeks
the Turkish army opened an offensive on Cyprus which, after
two days, succeeded in establishing Turkish control over
the entire northern third of the island.   It also trans-
formed more than 180,000 Greek Cypriots into homeless ref-
ugees.

     Pressure soon mounted in Congress to cut off U.S.
arms supplies that were being provided to Turkey under
bilateral and NATO arrangements. A campaign was led in
the Senate by Senator Eagleton and in the House of Representatives by Congressmen Brademas, Sarbanes, Yatron, and
Bafalis. Their efforts were facilitated by provisions of
the Foreign Assistance Act of 1961 and the Foreign Military Sales Act of 1968, which prohibit the delivery of
weapons to any country that uses them for purposes other
than internal security or "legitimate self-defense."

     Also supporting the forces pressing for a cutoff of
supplies to Turkey was the Greek-American lobby, AHEPA.
In opposition was virtually the entire foreign relations
establishment of Congress and the Administration, which
argued that Turkey would not compromise in response to
public armtwisting. Others opposed the cutoff as neo-
colonialist. In the words of Senator Mansfield, the Administration's refusal to take sides between Greece and
Turkey represented a low-profile policy that was essentially correct: "For once, we did not try to intervene."
He added, referring to the pressure groups, that "...there
seems to be a madness throughout the land. We are looking
for short answers, quick answers...." Defiantly, Mansfield
added, "I do not care how many telegrams we get from organizations in this country...."

     Not all members of Congress who continued to support
the arms cutoff were necessarily acting under such pressures. Nevertheless, many voted against their perception
of what was best for the United States or for Cyprus and
went along with the concentration of ethnic power.

     Ultimately, only fire was able to fight fire. By
mid-August, new lobbies were beginning to appear on the
scene. The American Legion, Veterans of Foreign Wars,

the Air Force Association began to urge Congress to "reverse this Congressional blunder and impress upon Congressional leadership the overriding stragetic importance of
Turkey, and the U.S. bases therein."

At the beginning of October, under intense counter-
lobbying, Congress partially rescinded the Turkish embargo. As of today, however, the issue is far from resolved
because the reopening of U.S. bases in Turkey has been
conditioned upon ratification of a new four-year U.S.-
Turkish aid agreement which lies blocked in the U.S. Senate, again vigorously opposed by the Greek-American lobby.

Is this vulnerability of members of Congress to
lobbies unethical? The answer is neither simple nor self-
evident. The power of AHEPA to influence a crucial core
of members of Congress can be interpreted as a manifestation of the very essence of the democracy ethic: the exercise of the power of Americans to compel their representatives to respond to their desires. Or it can be seen as
an effort to force members to submerge their ethical autonomy. Or both.

It is not our purpose to attempt to judge whether
the Greek lobby was ethically right or wrong about the
need for, or effect of, the Turkish embargo. That question, too, raises real ethical issues but the answers belong in the realm of political and ethical subjectivity.
Our reluctance to get into those "merits," however, does
not mean that we are totally cast adrift in a sea of relativism or of intense value conflicts. We believe there
are ethical imperatives to be found in the *procedural*
rather than in the substantive aspects of Congressional
behavior. Evaluative tests can be applied in assessing
the procedural issue of whether members of Congress should
be responsive to AHEPA or ignore it to vote their own

consciences.   The answers to such questions, we believe,
are to be found in *the economics of ethical autonomy.*

By this we mean the balance between external pressures against and internal force for, ethical autonomy.
When these forces are in balance, there will be some, but
not too much nor too little, ethically autonomous behavior.   In our study of resignation behavior of senior officials from the Executive Branch, for example, we found
that, of those cabinet level officials who resigned in
public protest against the policies of a president, virtually *none* was ever allowed to return to government office.   This was true throughout this century until the
recent case of Elliot Richardson.   It was our conclusion
that the costs of ethical autonomy were too high.   Senior
officials were aware that the costs of resigning and
speaking up publicly were so exorbitant as to make it impossible for the ordinary, reasonably ambitious person
to afford the path of ethical autonomy.   The economics of
ethical autonomy were thus skewed by pricing it out of
the reach of the reasonable person.

The objective rule of the economics of ethical autonomy comes to this: a system does not work properly if
it extracts so high a price for ethical autonomy as to
make it unaffordable to all but lunatic-fringe fanatics
or if ethical autonomy comes so cheaply as to promote the
disintegration of social cohesion.

Applying the economics of ethical autonomy to Congress, we hypothesize that a member's ethical autonomy
should not have to be purchased at a cost so high as to
discourage the ordinary, reasonably conscientious and ambitious member; nor so low as to make members idiosyncratic-
ally indifferent to the intense feelings of organized elements in the demos.   The pressures within which a member of

Congress exercises ethical judgment should be so balanced
as to permit but not unduly encourage ethical autonomy.
In short, there should be a balanced market, with the
costs of ethical autonomy floating in response to con-
sumer demand. Costs should go up or down depending on
the amount of ethical autonomy actually being exercised.
If no members are willing to defy the lobbies, then costs
must be lowered. On the other hand, if no members restrain their private ethical predilections in deference
to the passionate convictions of lobbies or other groups,
then the market is providing opportunities for ethical
autonomy too cheaply.

Let us attempt to employ this analytical framework
to the case of a member of Congress whose ethical imperatives are challenged by an organized lobby. In the first
place, distinctions are to be made between kinds of lobbies: the Lockheed Aircraft Corporation, AHEPA, the Greek-
American lobby, etc. The campaign contribution restrictions have probably lowered the cost of ethical autonomy
vis-à-vis the corporate lobbies. Commensurately, lobbying
organizations which exercise their clout through promising
to deliver or threatening to withhold voter support have
probably gained in their ability to extract costs from
members who insist on their ethical autonomy and who defy
those lobbies. It is these lobbies that are now in a
position to drive the costs too high. If so, corrective
action may be needed.

However, even the power of AHEPA or AIPAC or common
cause or a powerful trade union is likely to vary from
member to member. AHEPA is a national organization and
lobbies the Congress as a whole. Yet its effectiveness
is very uneven. If a member of Congress represents a predominantly Greek-American district, obviously AHEPA could

drive very high the costs of pursuing private ethical
autonomy to the point of voting against the Turkish
arms cutoff. Had Senator Pell or Senator Kennedy chosen
to vote on the Turkish side they would have had to reckon
with a significant loss of Greek vote and support. In
many Congressional districts, however, AHEPA can extract
only a very minor cost. Thus the economics of ethical
autonomy have a built-in stabilizing element. A member
of Congress elected to represent a minority interest—
be it Black, Greek or Jewish—ought to vote the feelings
of the national Black, Greek or Jewish communities since
there are relatively few districts in which those interests are sufficiently concentrated to return responsive
members to Congress. For him or her, the cost of autonomy
is high and this is as it should be. On the other hand,
the same lobbies are not able to extract such a high price
in most other areas. It is ethically appropriate for a
member elected to represent minority interests to have to
pay a very high price to express his ethical autonomy on
issues of great importance to that minority.

          Even so, those costs are not necessarily fixed at a
prohibitive level. Even in such circumstances, the member's ethical autonomy need not invariably be priced out
of the market. There is much the member can do to lower
the costs. First, the member should emphasize the positive. The cost of ethical autonomy in any particular confrontation with the powerful voting interests in his or
her constituency will vary to the extent that the member
has been able to convince his constituents that he is "on
their side" in a broad range of the other issues that matter most to them. To some extent, the costs of ethical
autonomy in a particular vote will then be averaged along
with the votes the member has taken in all other instances.

Secondly, the member should have staked out in advance
his right to ethical autonomy. If he or she is known to
be a person of strong convictions who on occasion reserves
the right to vote as conscience dictates, the chances of
forgiveness and survival are far greater than in the case
of one known as an ethical dwarf who suddenly stands on a
moral right to defy those he is supposed to represent.
Third, the chances of constituency forgiveness are greatly
enhanced if the congressperson has the integrity and conviction to take his case to the "home folk," explaining
with well-designed verbal stragety what he proposes to do
and his reasons for defying the lobbies.

Members of Congress in discussing their experiences
in confronting inner demands for ethical autonomy in the
face of strong voter pressure from organized groups in
their congressional districts, have confirmed that it is
possible to lower the costs of resisting those pressures
if one is widely known to be the sort who takes a stand
on principle and, even more specifically, if "one is known
to have strong, carefully enunciated and principled reasons
for the position being taken on the specific issue." One
congressman, representing a district where organized labor
exerts intense pressure against foreign aid and free trade,
nevertheless sticks by his guns and is regularly returned
because, as he puts it, "everyone knows I'm the sort of guy
who feels strongly about trade and aid for the Third World
and because I've always made my position clear on those issues, so that I wasn't sailing under false colors or pull-
ing a fast one. And, of course, I do labor a hell-of-alot
of other favors."

The point this member makes is essentially that of
the conscientious objector syndrome. Most persons are inclined to respect the religious conscientious objector who

has lived a life congruent with the professed principles
of his religion and there is wide tolerance for his refusal to serve in wartime combat. But the public is very
intolerant of those they perceive to be more converts of
opportunity: the : atheist who has never expressed Quaker
beliefs or pacifist conviction until the day he is summoned before his draft board.

2. *THE "EFFECTIVENESS TRAP"*. In our study of why
American cabinet officials are reluctant to resign in
protest, we found another prevalent reason for the submergence of ethical autonomy. Persons often went along
with group-think in order not to surrender their perceived
effectiveness.

Officials frequently told us that, although they on
occasion strongly opposed policies being pursued by the
President, they remained at their posts in the hope that
they would be able to influence matters for the better.
Mostly, these hopes proved ephemeral. George Ball, an
early opponent of the Vietnam war within the upper reaches
of presidential counsel, provided an instance of such reasoning, and remained the loyal house-critic of the Johnson
administration until its very end. Officials are loathe
to reject openly the bases of their power, and are reluctant to renounce their positions of authority.

In Congress, too, senators and representatives must
face the ethical dilemma of what to do when they strongly
disagree with policies being pursued by the executive
agencies they are trying to oversee: to go along in the
hope of modifying these policies, or to break ranks and
go into public opposition. Similarly, members who disagree with decisions reached by the majority of their congressional colleagues must also decide whether to "go

along" in the hope of preserving effectiveness or to "blow
the whistle." These ethical and political dilemmas of the
individual member of Congress who wants to blow the whistle on an executive agency or on his fellow members is well
illustrated by reference to congressional oversight in relation to the activities of the CIA. The recent history
of that oversight provides excellent illustrations of the
choices facing a member.

Let us begin with the events during the recent Angolan civil war. The struggle for Angola started with
the revolutionary Lisbon government's decision to give
independence to its colony on November 11, 1975. The
Soviet Union, which had for years been supporting the
Angolan Popular Movement for the Liberation of Angola
(MPLA) began in March 1975 to send plane loads of arms
and equipment to its client. The flow of Soviet supplies
increased substantially through April, May, and June,
with its efforts being augmented by Yugoslavia, East Germany, and Algeria. In early 1975, the CIA was authorized
to provide $300,000 in clandestine support to the rival
National Front for the Liberation of Angola (NFLA), headed
by Holden Roberto. After this initial commitment, U.S.
aid to NFLA escalated rapidly over the summer. Assistance
was also furnished to UNITA, headed by Jonathan Savimbi,
the group reported to have the largest Angolan tribal af-
filiation.

News of the U.S. covert activities in Angola was
first revealed by *The New York Times* in a story datelined
September 25. Once the story broke, public and congressional reaction was swift. This was the year following
the Vietnamese debacle—a fiasco to which parallels were
immediately, and perhaps superficially, drawn. Here, it
seemed, was the CIA again drawing us into a covert war on

the side forces we little knew or cared about: forces,
moreover, that appeared likely to lose the war.

On December 19, the Senate adopted an amendment to
the 1976 Defense Appropriations Bill sponsored by John
V. Tunney that had the effect of banning the use of all
defense funds "for any activities involving Angola directly or indirectly." On January 27, 1976, a similar
ban was imposed by the House of Representatives and the
bill was reluctantly signed by President Ford early in
February. Ford charged that "Congress had lost their
guts" and added ominously that "it was a serious mistake
and I think they will live to regret it...if and when the
Soviet Union and their Cuban mercenaries undertake another military operation...."

The Administration took the view that Congress had
violated its implied obligation to support the CIA operation. This implication, it was argued, arose from the
fact that key members had been briefed throughout, and
had not objected until after the operation had been publicized and attacked in the press. Secretary Kissinger
stated, "...we were determined to adhere to the highest
standards of executive-legislative consultation. Eight
congressional committees were briefed on twenty-four
separate occasions. We sought in these briefings to
determine the wishes of Congress. While we do not claim
that every Member approved our actions, we had no indication of basic opposition."

"Between July and December 1975," Kissinger continued,

> we discussed the Angolan situation on numerous
> occasions with members of the Foreign Relations
> Committees and the Appropriations Committees of
> both Houses that have CIA oversight responsibil-
> ities. The two committees investigating CIA ac-
> tivities—the Church Committee and the Pike Com-

> mittee—were also briefed. Altogether, more
> than two dozen Senators, and about a hundred
> staff members of both Houses were informed.

The members who were briefed must have sensed their particular "effectiveness." They were the ones who enjoyed the special confidence of the CIA. It is to them, a minority among their peers, that the CIA looked for approval. But implicit in this effectiveness is the concomitant that disapproval of the CIA action, especially any kind of public disapproval, would mark the member as untrustworthy, perhaps undermining his or her vaunted effectiveness. In this way the privileged position of the congressional overseer tends to make the overseer a captive of that which is to be overseen.

The problem is illustrated by a classical exchange regarding Angola between the Secretary of State and a whistle-blowing Senator Clark. Testifying before the Senate Foreign Relations Committee's Subcommittee on African Affairs, on January 29, 1976, Secretary Kissinger declared:

> The problem of how to conduct covert operations in
> relationship to congressional oversight is an ex-
> tremely complicated one...the President decided to
> proceed to brief the Congress meticulously. If,
> out of these briefings there emerged what appeared
> to us a determined opposition, we would reconsider
> our views, reconsider our policy."

Kissinger added,

> I always ask those who are briefing congressional
> committees what reaction they found and that the
> President and I thought that the degree of contin-
> uation of the action, at least in its early phases,
> was to some extent dependent on the mood we found
> in the Congress. But there could have been a mis-
> understanding.

Senator Clark then asked:

> So it would be well for these people who are
> being briefed to assume that if they do not
> take opposition on the occasion of the brief-
> ing, that it could be interpreted to mean that
> they may be favorable to it?

To this Secretary Kissinger replied, "...or at least
that they will not carry their opposition beyond a certain
point." It is perhaps not surprising that Senator Clark
speaks of his "frustration" at being caught in the position of being made privy to secret government information
regarding operations to which, by being informed, he becomes a sort of unwilling accessory, limited in his options to oppose in public.

"Classified briefings," he later wrote, "actually
become an impediment to effective oversight. Once the
information is made available, there is no way the Congress can properly use it to oppose or influence policy
without taking public action." To the extent this is true,
the costs of ethical autonomy have become too high in the
discharge of congressional oversight functions. These
functions should be inherently adversary, not co-optive,
if they are to be carried out at all.

3. *CONGRESSIONAL DISCIPLINE AND THE ETHICALLY AU-
TONOMOUS DISSIDENT.* More recently, this problem has
emerged in a new form. A new Intelligence Oversight Committee headed by Senator Inouye of Hawaii has been established and is not only briefed, but, in practice, briefed
before an intelligence operation begins. This committee
is charged with the responsibility of objecting to an
operation if it considers it ill-conceived, making its
objections known to the President and, if he persists,
to a secret session of Congress which, in turn, can act
either to cut off funding or to "go public."

This new responsibility sharply focuses the issue
of members' ethical responsibility. Suppose a senator
on the Oversight Committee is briefed regarding an operation which he or she comes to consider immoral. A majority of the committee, however, do not object, and the
operation proceeds on schedule. What are the ethical options? Having been briefed in secret, the senator's position is worse than that of someone who discovers the
same information through a newspaper or a leak. To what
extent may senators who disagree with the proposed covert
operation take their opposition to the rest of Congress
and to the public? May they use information to cross-ex-
amine government witnesses at public congressional hearings? Are they estopped by their roles as overseer and
by the procedures laid down by the overseers as a "team"?
To what extent does a failure to make opposition effective
or public constitute endorsement which can be used subse-
quently as a call on the senator's loyalty in support—or
at least in mitigation—of opposition to a covert operation?

A further question has to do with the role of senators, who, in accordance with procedures laid down by the
Senate itself, are not briefed. To what extent should
they consider themselves to be under moral obligation to
follow the lead taken by those chosen by the Senate as a
whole, to receive the briefings and to be the "judges"?
And, then, there are the ethics of timing. To what extent
are those briefed or not briefed free to reopen the question of an operation's wisdom once the operation is in
mid-stream? Is it fair to say to dissenters: "You should
have objected earlier. You didn't. Now you have an ethical duty to go along"?

Most covert operations obviously depend for their

utility on secrecy and surprise. Consequently, a single
senator, having been briefed before an operation is begun,
if he or she is truly opposed but cannot persuade the majority to join in quashing it through legislative process,
may still have the capacity to "blow the whistle" by the
simple expedient of leaking the planned operation to the
press. Nowadays, almost any newsman would feel himself
ethically obliged to publish the story: another ethical
dilemma beyond the scope of this paper. But the dissident
member of Congress' dilemma is central to our inquiry.
Under what circumstances, if any, is the member entitled
to take into his or her own hands the stopping of an operation which has been duly approved by the oversight procedures laid down by and for the whole Congress?

       Angola starkly illustrates the complex dilemma of
the individual legislator's conscience pitted against the
precept of "democratic majoritarian order," itself an
ethical principle most legislators have almost certainly
internalized.

       The preceding section dealt with instances that pit-
ted the individual member's conscience against the subtle
pressure exerted by the *executive* branch that is being
overseen by the member and which, inevitably, attempts to
turn oversight into co-option and co-responsibility. Closely related to this is the phenomenon of ethical autonomy
in opposition to *congressional* discipline and organization:
the individual versus his own peer group. The most celebrated recent instance of this in the foreign relations
field was the Daniel Schorr case.

       The House of Representatives as a whole, meeting in
closed session in accordance with its procedures established by the congressional majority, decided that the
report of the Pike Select Committee on the Intelligence

establishment should not be made public. Nevertheless,
a copy of the committee's controversial report was made
available to newsman Daniel Schorr. The House of Representatives made a determined, if ineffectual, attempt to
find out which of its members or staff (if any—the CIA
itself was also suspected) had been responsible for the
leak. Had the culprit been found, he could—and probably
would—have been punished at the bar of Congress.

The well-publicized leaks from the Pike Committee, as
well as the leak of its final report, in defiance of the
rules of the House, poses the ethical dilemma of a congressional member of such a committee who disagrees not only
with the policies of the Executive Branch agency being examined but also with the attitudes and policies being
struck by the majority of the committee and by Congress itself. This dilemma is not new. George Washington was an
optimist about the ability of congressional committees to
share and keep executive secrets, writing that his national security plans would be revealed to committee members,
"with more freedom and confidence than to a numerous body,
where secrety is impossible, where the indiscretion of a
single member by disclosing may defeat the project." However, for the most part, congressional committees have
taken a rather lenient view of the leaking of secrets.
Even Washington himself had to contend with opposition
members like Senators Pierce Butler of South Carolina and
Stevens T. Mason of Virginia, who smuggled copies of the
still-secret Jay Treaty out of the Senate Chamber before
it had been fully negotiated. The text was published in
the *Republican Aurora* before the states concerned had had
an opportunity to make the provisions public.

In the intervening years, the problem of maintaining

confidentiality was increasingly resolved by presidents
through the twin devices of secrecy and the co-option
of key congressional committees. More recently still,
both of these protective devices have been undermined by
congressional reassertiveness, investigative journalism,
and public opinion following the Vietnam debacle and the
Watergate scandals, culminating in the Pike Committee Report in violation of the express prohibition voted by the
House as a whole in executive (closed) session. The subsequent attempt to deal with this contempt by pilloring
newsman Daniel Schorr is no substitute for a more effective system of committee self-discipline. If costs of
disclosure are to be raised, then it is the discloser,
not the messenger, who should pay the price.

On another occasion, Congressman Michael Harrington
was dropped from the reconstituted House Committee inves-
tigating the CIA precisely as a mild disciplinary measure
for a suspected but unproven breach of confidentiality.

Breaches of confidentiality—"whistle blowing"—by
a member of the Standing Senate Intelligence Oversight
Committee could invoke far more serious penalties. Such
a member, at very least, would be ostracized from the "gentlemen's club." He could probably expect to be shunned in
making significant committee appointments and to be crippled in securing consideration of his constituents' interests. He could be expelled from Congress. Conceivably,
he might even be arrested and imprisoned unless—as would
ordinarily be the case—he made his disclosures under
constitutional protection in Congress.

So far, this problem of ethical autonomy versus congressional discipline has scarcely been examined. Senator
Gravel read the classified *Pentagon Papers* aloud in a committee room of Congress and was held immune to prosecution.

But he has been penalized on other, more subtle ways by
his peers. Yet there were few secrets in those documents,
and public as well as considerable congressional opinion
seems to have been on his side. On the other hand,
Gravel's ethically autonomous conduct is unusual in the
national security context. Through interviews we have
learned that there have already been occasions when a senator on the CIA Oversight Committee has vigorously opposed
a planned covert operation on ethical grounds, has been
outvoted, and has then kept utterly silent. That silence
makes him a partner in the operation he opposes. Is this
a tribute to "the system"? To the individual's respect
for his role as a responsible overseer? Is it a sign of
ethical maturity by dissidents, an indication that they
understand the proper limits of opposition? Is it an indication or respect for majority rule? Or does it merely
suggest that team pressures are so strong and costs of
deviation so high that the senator could not afford effective ethical autonomy?

The Inouye Committee has tried to raise the price of
ethical autonomy by providing that unauthorized leaks by
its members would be dealt with by the Select Committee
on Standards and Conduct. According to the charter of
the Intelligence Committee, unauthorized disclosure is
punishable by "censure, removal from committee membership,
or expulsion from the Senate, in the case of member, or
removal from office or employment or punishment for contempt, in the case of an officer or employee."

It is probably right that these costs of asserting
ethical autonomy in such peer-group situations involving
national security oversight should be high. Expulsion
from Congress is the most the Constitution permits. It
remains to be seen whether it will be necessary, and

whether Congress will be willing, that it be invoked. The
ethical dilemma of the committee member who is opposed to
an operation but overruled by the majority of the committee and, ultimately, by Congress, is clear and stark. His
conscience is pitted against the precept of democratic majoritarian order—another ethical imperative—which the
peer group and demos value highly. Hence, that imperative
should not be easily overridden. Indeed, as the power of
congressional committees to oversee executive action has
increased and as the costs of exercising ethical autonomy
in respect of the actions of executive agencies has de-
creased in general, so it is appropriate that the costs of
ethical autonomy should rise when an individual member of
a committee decides to exercise that ethical autonomy in
violation of the majoritarian procedures laid down by the
Congress itself. Were this not to be so, the increasing
power of Congress would become meaningless, for it would
translate into a power of individual, idiosyncratic members to paralyze the majority.

     This is not to say that the hypothetical member of
the Inouye Committee who is profoundly opposed to a covert
operation, but is unable to persuade the majority, should
under no circumstances "blow the whistle." But the costs
of doing so should be high enough to dissuade in all but
the rarest and most extraordinary of circumstances.

     4. THE TYRANNY OF IMAGE. Thus it seems proper to
us that the costs of ethical autonomy should ordinarily be
highest in national security situations where the ethical
autonomy is being exercised not to blow the whistle on the
organization being overseen but on the congressional overseers themselves. But in another peer group context, the
costs of ethical autonomy may currently be too high: in

instances where a member's conscience leads him to break
with an ideological group in Congress with which he is
normally identified.

The voting records of members of Congress identify
them on a scale of ideological and interest-group values.
"Teams" form around ideological biases: the Monday Club of
progressive Republicans and the Republican Study Group of
more conservative elements are balanced by comparable
groupings of Democrats who identify with others of similar political proclivity. The members of Congress for
Peace Through Law contrast with the less internationalist
views of the Study Group. Not all members of Congress
are "team players," of course, but there is a tendency to
achieve meaning, definition, and power through association
with a congressional grouping.

Also, in soliciting votes, members give out valuable
IOUs. When a member of the class of '74—youngish Democrats who won in the anti-Watergate backwash—calls on his
classmates for support on an issue of importance to that
member, he or she promises—implicitly or explicitly—to
return the favor at an appropriate time in the context of
some other issue. Underlying this well-established IOU
practice is a reification: "If you are the sort I think
you are, you can go along with me on this, and I'll be
able to go along with you on something else."

Even without such formal or informal coalition-build-
ing and alliance politics, members would be identified by
categorizations imposed on them by the media as a form of
shorthand labeling. Thus, Congressman Les Aspin is "anti-
military establishment" and Senator Jesse Helms is an
"arch-conservative." Such labels have their own prescrip-
tive power to affect a member's behavior. Even if Congressman Aspin, in a particular instance, wished to vote

in favor of a higher military appropriation, he would
find it difficult to break out of his assigned image-cate-
gory. His allies within and outside Congress and the media would find his pragmatism unsettling. He would risk
being perceived as unreliable or even unstable. Pragma-
tists do not make either good allies or good copy. The
pressure, hard to define but nonetheless real, therefore
militates in favor of a simplistic conceptual consistency
that may run counter to the member's ethical imperatives
in a particular situation.

Take the role of Congressman Don Fraser of Minnesota
in the fight to cut off funds for covert aid to Angola.
Fraser is correctly identified as a key House liberal. To
a man, these voted for the cutoff, against the CIA, against
"another Vietnam." Fraser is also known for his support
of independence for black Africa, his sympathy for African
freedom fighters, and his opposition to the South African
policy of apartheid. He is a principal advocate of human
rights as a factor in American foreign policy. In the
specific case of aid to Angola Fraser confronted his liberal team in the House. "I take a somewhat different view
of our potential involvement in Angola. I have difficulty
subscribing to Secretary Kissinger's cold war rationale.
But I am disturbed that in the civil war in Angola what is
essentially a minority group is going to overwhelm the majority group because of the enormous infusion of outside
funds and manpower," he declared. "I don't find any analogy with Vietnam here...I don't regard Angola as important
in a cold war context." He concluded that

> ...it is a matter of decency not to leave defenseless
> the majority group in Angola, not to subject them to
> a military outcome dependent upon an external power
> that has put in an enormous amount of money and man-
> power from Cuba...if we say that this is not our
> business, if we say that we don't care that a minor-

> ity group can jump on a majority group through
> external aggression, it seems to me we have
> abandoned very fundamental principles relating
> to the welfare of peoples around the world.

Walking this narrow line in pursuit of his ethical
imperatives must have been difficult and costly for Congressman Fraser. It put him at odds with virtually all
of his long-time allies in Congress, blurred the simplistic image of him that had been built up in the media, and
generally led to a sense of cognitive dissonance regarding his public stance on world issues. He could not have
been unmindful of the cost of taking a position so superficially but significantly at odds with what had generally been perceived to be his voting pattern.

Similar in this respect was the position taken by
Paul McCloskey of California, long regarded as one of the
most consistent and prominent of the congressional Vietnam
"doves." McCloskey, after a visit to Cambidia and Vietnam
with a congressional team in 1974, returned to vote *against*
a suspension of military and economic assistance to those
two countries. While he certainly did not favor prolonging
the war, neither was he in favor of imposing a cutoff that
would compel the premature surrender of the anti-Communist
regime while there was still an opportunity for humanitarian operations to alleviate the consequences of surrender.
Because of what he had seen, he found himself voting with
the dwindling core of die-hard "hawks" against what was,
by now, the large majority of his late-converted colleagues. There was a widespread impression that McCloskey,
a Republican and thus always a bit suspect among liberals,
had "sold out." When Fraser joined him, a fellow liberal
turned to him in astonishment and said, "Don, I thought
you were one of *us*."

Such situations can be painful and costly to a member

who chooses ethical autonomy. Fellow members, the press
and the public tend to treat as intellectual, moral and
political lightweights those in Congress who will not
stand still in the ideological groupings to which they
are assigned (or to which they assign themselves). They
tend to be perceived as ineffective, and the risk of that
is enough to cause too many members to vote with their
group and against their conscience for the sake of a consistency in which they do not really believe.

The costs of ethical autonomy from the ideological
stereotypes imposed on members is probably too high to
create a balanced market of ethical autonomy. But what
are the remedies? They are in the hands of the public and
of the media. Only a more politically sophisticated public can liberate the members from these stereotypes and
give them the freedom to be themselves: complex, inconsistent and propelled by a healthy regard for their inner
voice.

THEODORE ROOSEVELT'S "PRACTICAL IDEALISM": A CASE STUDY OF MORALITY AND POLITICS

J. PERRY LEAVELL, JR.

Amos Pinchot once advised Theodore Roosevelt that he would have to make a choice between two roles he wanted to perform. He could either be a great moral leader or he could be a great politician, but he could not be both. Roosevelt, however, disagreed and rejected Pinchot's advice for two reasons. He rejected Pinchot's advice, first, because he was constitutionally incapable of denying himself a role he wanted to play, and he clearly enjoyed the role of moral authority. He continually and even, one might say, promiscuously advised the American people on such disparate matters as the immorality of modern art, the evils of bachelorhood, and the moral virtues of war and motherhood. But he also rejected Pinchot's advice because he believed that politics was a moral profession and that the presidency especially was a moral as well as a political office—as he liked to put it, the presidency was a "bully pulpit."[1]

Because of his insistence on merging the roles of moral and political leader, Roosevelt stands exposed to us today as a prime candidate for the award of Great First-Class Hypocrite. He insisted on justifying and rationalizing even his most unscrupulous acts (like his role in the Panamanian revolt) in splendid moral terms, and, as a result, it is incredibly easy to interpret his life (as John Chamberlain has done)[2] as an exercise in

207

hypocrisy. But it is also because of his rejection of
Pinchot's advice that this paper is possible and that
Roosevelt makes an interesting case study of the relationship between morality and politics in the United States
of some seventy years ago.

Theodore Roosevelt's personality and early life influenced his quest for a moral life through politics and
played a role in shaping the context of his original decision to enter politics. He was born into an old, established, socially-prominent family. As a child he suffered from myopia and asthma and from a generally weak physical condition; he soon developed, under the tutelage of
his father, a program of physical exercise which led him
to become throughout his life an ardent exponent ot
strenuous physical activity. He also became a voracious
reader and a firm believer, again because of his father's
influence, in a kind of *noblesse oblige*. By the time he
left his tutors to attend Harvard he had already developed many of the character traits which would mark his
life—his belief in a strenuous physical life, his intellectual curiosity, a strong sense of morality and duty,
and a belief in activism.

When the young Roosevelt announced to a classmate
that he planned to enter politics after graduation from
Harvard, his friend wondered if Roosevelt had lost his
mind. After all, "everybody knew" that New York politics
were controlled by the liquor interests, the machine bosses, and gangsters supported by unscrupulous lawyers and
nouveau riche businessmen. How, asked Roosevelt's friend,
could "Teddie" (as Roosevelt was called by intimates)
consider a career in such a crude, profane, alcoholic,
sordid environment? Ever since the 1830s and the changes
in American politics associated with Andrew Jackson's

presidency, most of the "best people" like the Roosevelts
had gradually withdrawn from politics. The rise of the
common man had made politics "common," but the young
Roosevelt was clearly an aristocrat who even looked and
sounded out of place in politics—he was young, slender,
near-sighted in the extreme, wore a posh monocle, had
large prominent teeth and a high piping voice. As a
friend noted, to the typical politician of the day Roosevelt seemed "a joke, a dude, the way he combed his hair,
the way he talked—the whole thing."[3]

    The context of Roosevelt's decision to enter poli-
tics was important. Many Americans believed in the 1870s
and the 1880s that morality and politics had been divorced
as a consequence of a series of changes that began in the
1830s. The introduction of universal manhood suffrage,
the emergency of political parties, and especially the
rise of professional politicians—all of these appeared
to intellectuals like Mark Twain and Henry Adams and to
the publishers and editors of elite national journals like
the *Nation, Atlantic Monthly,* and *Harper's Weekly* to have
undermined the moral base of American republicanism. Politics had now become, they believed, a game, or a business, performed by the lowest elements of society rather
than a disinterested consideration of constitutional and
moral principles debated by gentlemen of intellect and virtue like George Washington, an arena of partisanship rather
than patriotism. There were many signs of this change—
the widespread corruption of the Grant years, the rise of
bosses and machines in the large cities, and the defeat of
virtually all reform measures. But the surest sign of the
decline of politics was that the "best people", the respectable "good citizens," had largely resigned from politics in the years since Andrew Jackson's presidency. Sure-

ly there was something wrong if the best citizens were
not only not running for political office; so-called
"good citizens" were not even voting.

Roosevelt was one of these "best people" by birth
and training. The elite national press believed that his
decision to enter politics might be the beginning of a
return by a whole class, and such a return to power by
men of high personal moral character might result in a
more moral politics in the nation. Roosevelt also hoped
that he would be a force for a more decent politics, but
he was aware that he would be on the defensive at first.
He later described the psychological context of his decision: "I intended to be one of the governing class.
If they proved too hard-bit for me I supposed that I would
have to quit, but I certainly would not quit until I had
made the effort and found out whether I was too weak to
hold my own in the rough and tumble."[4] He understood
that he was entering an alien world, that he would be out
of his element, that he would have to prove that a gentle-
man was not too effete for politics, that a man of education and high personal moral standards could survive in
politics, that he was not simply another ineffectual ama-
teur "goo goo", as do-gooders were called in the nineteenth century. Whereas the elite journals of the day
welcomed the arrival in politics of people like Roosevelt
as a change toward a more moral politics, Roosevelt intended to prove that he was not simply good but also sufficiently tough and effective to succeed in this strange
and hard world. He assumed morality; but he felt he had
to prove his effectiveness.

In some respects Roosevelt's psychological situation
was similar to that of many middle class women of the late
nineteenth century, like Jane Addams, who felt that they

were alienated from the real world of struggle, power,
and money because of their sex (in Roosevelt's case, it
was social class) and sought to break out of the cocoon-
like existence of idealized purity in which they found
themselves.[5] Like these women Roosevelt felt that the
members of the group to which he belonged were doomed to
lives of useless inactivity and parasitism unless they
were reinvigorated by association and communication with
issues of the real world. Unlike these women, of course,
Roosevelt had the opportunity to aim for the very top of
the power structure and therefore could aim toward a useful life as a governor, not simply as a participating
member of the governed.

Inevitably, conflicts soon emerged between Roosevelt
and his early supporters, the elite magazines, and this
conflict reflected an internal conflict between the conscience of Roosevelt (by which I mean his internalized
values) and the realities of party politics in the 1880s.
One such confrontation came in 1884 when the Republican
Party nominated James Blaine for the Presidency. Blaine
was, except for Ulysses Grant, the most popular Republican
in the country, but he had failed to win the Republican
Party nomination for the Presidency in 1876 and 1880 because he had been implicated in the *Credit Mobilier* scandals, the "Watergate" of its day. Now in 1884 Blaine and
the Republican Party clearly hoped that the nation had
forgotten *Credit Mobilier* and would remember only Blaine's
more recent record. But the "best people" had not forgotten, and many of them appealed to conscientious Republicans
to break with their party and elect Grover Cleveland President. These "mugwumps" or "Independents" or "Liberals"
included the publishers and editors of most of the elite
journals and newspapers of the day; they were precisely

the people who had welcomed Roosevelt's entrance into politics and who spoke for the high moral standards in which Roosevelt believed. What could (should) the young 26-year-old politician do?

Roosevelt had stated as a general principle, "I will not stay in public life unless I can do so on my own terms, and my ideal...is rather a high one." He concluded that Blaine, "Of all the men presented to the convention... by far the most objectionable," did not meet his ideal, and he worked before and during the convention to defeat Blaine. But when the convention voted, Roosevelt, after a brief hesitation, announced that he would support and campaign for the party's choice, James Blaine. To join the Mug-wumps, a decision which would have satisfied his conscience would in this very partisan age have destroyed his personal career in politics, would also have denied the legitimacy of the convention's vote for Blaine, and finally would have proven early critics right in their assertion that he was too much of a "goo goo" to survive in the rough and tumble of politics. So Roosevelt supported a party decision which he felt was unwise and a candidate he felt was immoral, a decision that he would repeat again in 1896 when the party nominated William McKinley. And, typically, Roosevelt, having made his decision, overstated his case and in 1884 denounced the Independents as traitors to the nation.

A key point to remember about these early years in politics and these conflicts is that on most issues Roose-velt agreed with the Mugwumps and Liberals. For example, he worked hard in the New York Assembly to outlaw certain corrupt practices; later, as Police Commissioner of New York City, he agreed with the Independents that police re-form was crucial and worked to achieve a more honest police force, non-partisan appointments and promotions, and more

modern police techniques. He especially agreed that civil service reform was a prerequisite for cleaner and more
honest politics, and during his years on the U.S. Civil
Service Commission he worked to expand the number of non-
partisan appointments to federal office and to create a
sound structure for the national civil service. On the
whole, Roosevelt had reason to feel proud of his accomplishments, but he was also aware of criticisms from the
Independent Mugwumps who argued that reforms came too
slowly and that Roosevelt was more interested in his own
career than in the principles of reform.

    Roosevelt, in other words, found himself in the
classic position of the reformer, and he remained in that
position as he moved on to become Assistant Secretary of
the Navy, Governor of New York, Vice-President, and in
1901 President of the United States. On the one hand, he
criticized and was criticized by those politicians who opposed change and reforms—the "standpatters" as they were
called at the time. Roosevelt felt that the standpatters
were too practical, too concerned with political technique,
too unwilling to apply moral principles, too devoted to
private interests and personal advantage. And, in return,
Roosevelt was frequently criticized by these groups as too
idealistic and reformist. On the other hand, Roosevelt
felt that the Independent idealists, who were outside of
government, were too unrealistic and impractical. They
insisted on total victory when only partial or proximate
solutions were possible, and they would never believe that
he was working for principles until he committed political
suicide and resigned. And, finally, he came to realize
that many of the idealists were not as pure as they liked
to appear. He agreed with Thomas Reed who once remarked
that Samuel Johnson, when he said that patriotism was the

last resort of scoundrels, must have been unaware of the
infinite possibilities and popularity of reform as a
refuge for scoundrels.

As a result of these disputes, Roosevelt developed
and articulated an interpretation of his role in politics,
arguing that he would try to walk a middle line between
what he called "efficiency" or "practicality" and "ideal-
ise" or "reform." Thus, the goal was to be a practical
idealist or an efficient reformer." He summed up this position in his *Autobiography:* "It seems to me that, for
the nation as for the individual, what is most important
is to insist on the vital need of combining sets of qualities, which separately are common enough, and, also useless enough. Practical efficiency is common, and lofty
idealism not uncommon; it is the combination which is
necessary and the combination is rare...." He deliberately set himself the task by 1900 of walking what he
called the "ridge crest, with the gulf of failure on each
side—the gulf of inefficiency on the one side, the gulf
of unrighteousness on the other.[7]

How successful was Roosevelt at walking the "ridge
crest"? And what was the impact on his life and career
of this attempt to balance morality and power? As you
might expect, there are many answers to these questions,
different evaluations made by both contemporaries and historians. Many political and business leaders concluded
that he was too idealistic, too prone to attempt what William Graham Sumner called "the absurd effort to make the
world over." They argued, for example, that it was his
irresponsible talk of reforms which undermined confidence
in the economy and caused the economic collapse in the
Panic of 1907.

Other contemporaries, both the late nineteenth cen-

tury Mugwumps and some of the twentieth century progres-
sives, concluded that Roosevelt was practical enough, but
not truly idealistic. They felt that he was too concerned
with personal success and always, when forced to choose,
followed the road of political compromise and expediency
rather than conscience. Note, for example, one verdict
offered in 1912 which compared Roosevelt with William Jennings Bryan, by this time a three-time loser of presidential elections:

> Mr. Roosevelt has taught the young men of this
> country that ideals can be successful, and for
> this we owe him much, but too often he has made
> success ideal, and in this he robs us of our
> birthright. There is success and there are
> ideals, but between the two there is nothing in
> common.... With Mr. Bryan [however], defeat is
> but an incident. To press on with undampened
> ardor, that is success indeed. We can hardly
> imagine Mr. Roosevelt fighting without the magic
> of popular applause. We can scarcely think of
> Mr. Bryan unpurified by popular defeat.... Per-
> sonal unselfishness has bestowed on Mr. Bryan a
> moral power which would have given his rival the
> strength of ten.[8]

What made Mr. Bryan's moral power greater than Mr. Roosevelt's political power, we might note, was the belief of
the author that real changes do not come about through
legislation or coercion but through slow changes in the
hearts and minds of people.

Still other contemporaries and historians agree with
Roosevelt that his mix of morality and politics, of practical idealism, was wise and appropriate and ultimately
beneficial to the nation as a whole. They argue that
business leaders confused their interests with the nation's
interest and that the idealists judged Roosevelt as a
moral leader rather than as a political leader. With regard to the latter point, note, for example, the dispute

that developed when Roosevelt, as Governor of New York,
met with Thomas Collier Platt, Republican boss of New York.
The *Nation* and *Atlantic Monthly* proclaimed that the meetings were a defeat for good government, for Roosevelt's
example suggested that an "evil man" could play a role in
the government of a great state and was acceptable in proper
society. Defenders of Roosevelt, however, argued that
Roosevelt had to meet with Platt or accept a position of
complete ineffectiveness, that specific legislative reforms
required negotiations with those who had political power.
Defenders of Roosevelt insisted that he be judged by political as well as moral criteria, and he would have been a
political failure if he had not met with Platt. The ultimate result of his entire career, they judged to be positive—as one contemporary concluded, before 1900 Americans
idealized captains of industry but after 1900 a new social
ideal emerged; in the person of Roosevelt this "ideal became the real, and to millions of his fellow countrymen, Mr.
Roosevelt, if not the Sir Galahad of politics, had at least
sought the Grail."[9]

It would be fruitless to pursue further these assessments of Roosevelt's career, for the effort would simply
lead deeper and deeper into the thicket of a vast histori-
ography on Roosevelt's life and presidency. Instead, attention should be focused on the emergence in Roosevelt of
what I will call a broadening ethical perspective which was
complete, perhaps, only in 1908 or 1912, and which had to
be incorporated by Roosevelt into the moral system in which
he already believed.

Theodore Roosevelt's career in politics spanned the
years when Americans first began to realize that industrial-
ization and urbanization were changing their environment.
Eric Goldman has noted that intellectuals responded to these

changes by developing a moral relativism which partially
rejected the older ideals of Americans, but most Americans,
Roosevelt among them, continued to believe absolutely in
the old moral values even as they developed new institutions
and adopted new techniques to deal with the new environment.
According to Henry May, this moral absolutism, the belief
that there was one moral code which applied to individuals,
groups, and nations, was a "pillar" of American culture up
to about 1912 when it began to crumble because of internal
flaws and external pressures.[10] By focusing on Roosevelt,
one of the leaders of the attempt to create new techniques
and institutions and one of the most articulate spokesmen
for moral absolutism, perhaps we can better understand how
most Americans maintained their consensus on moral absolutes and what some of the flaws were in that consensus.

One result of an examination of Roosevelt's
new ethical perspective is the realization that
those critics who said that Roosevelt should look more
to his conscience (by which they meant the ideals he had
internalized as a child) were offering the wrong advice;
Roosevelt's growth and broadening ethical perspective
emerged precisely because he chose career over conscience
and efficiency over idealism. In other words, his experience in the profession of politics plunged him into a
fuller association with the new industrial world and resulted in the discovery that his early ideals, while they
provided him with a useful base of personal honesty and a
generalized desire to do good, offered him no useful guides
to positive action which would effectively deal with the
problems and conditions which confronted Americans by the
turn of the century.

Essentially, Roosevelt's early ideals were rooted in
the rural past and what Richard Hofstadter calls the "Yankee-

Protestant Tradition."[11] This tradition emphasized the
virtues of duty, hard work, frugality, independence, honor,
and disinterestedness and assumed a direct connection between private and public morality; it also assumed a
laissez faire economy of the type described by Adam Smith
in the eighteenth century and a political community of
the size of the face-to-face communities that existed in
the United States prior to 1830 or so. The Yankee-Protestant tradition, then, was created in the early nineteenth
century and inevitably was challenged by the emergence of
an urban and industrial society in the late nineteenth
century.

In the early nineteenth century Americans believed
and could often document that there was a direct connection between individual morality, public decision-making,
and the moral good of the whole society. Call it the
Protestant Ethic or the Puritan Temper or whatever, but
Americans believed that a moral life was a precondition
for economic success and the absence of morality led to
economic failure. In an era when small businesses were
owned by individuals or families or partnerships and operated within small geographic areas, then the success of a
business was likely to be directly related to the character
of the owner. Credit, for example, was not likely to be
extended to a business if the owner was frequently drunk
or lazy or notoriously disreputable. The best public relations was a good character, and it was important that a
man's word be his bond, etc. The private morality of the
individual had public consequences; so public decision-
making and private morality were not distinct. Moreover,
the legitimacy of the whole economic system could be measured in terms of private morality. The capitalist market
economy was "good" because it encouraged individuals to be

good if they wanted to succeed. Thus, individuals seeking economic self-interest in the market were forced to
adopt the values of the Protestant Ethic. The consequence
of self-interest presumably was a society of moral people.

By 1900, however, much of this had changed. In a
world of national and international corporations, of
joint-stock ownership, of the growing separation between
ownership and management, gaps appeared between private
morality and economic consequences. John D. Rockefeller
might live a private life as a perfect Baptist even as
Standard Oil Corporation bribed legislatures and created
a giant monopoly over oil refining. Cornelius Vanderbilt
could proclaim and practice a policy of "the public be
damned" with no economic consequences, and Jim Fisk and
others could gain riches and credit even as they flaunted
all private moral standards of the day. The rising gaps
between the rich and the poor were certainly disproportion-
ate to any differences in individual morality; Andrew Car-
negie might be more moral than some West Virginia coal
miner but not $400,000,000 worth more. Indeed, some Amer-
icans were discovering that in the new industrial and urban economy poverty was a product of vast impersonal forces
(the size of the wheat crop in Russia or the collapse of a
railroad in Illinois) over which the individual had no control and of cultural traditions and training which again
were beyond individual accountability. There seemed to be
no direct connection between individual morality and public
consequences (Collis Huntington once claimed that the only
difference between honest and dishonest legislators was
that he had to *pay* the dishonest ones to do what he wanted.)
And if there were no connection between character and success, then the economy could be justified on the grounds of
efficiency, but not on the grounds that it promoted morality.

One response to this situation, the response of the
independent mugwumps, was simply to re-assert the old
values and protest against recent changes. They believed
in the old values and they were upset about many of the
problems confronting the United States and wanted to halt
what they believed to be the disintegration of American
values. But they were largely unable to develop a mean-
ingful program, unable to translate their anxieties about
the way things were going into a program of action. Particularly important, e.g., was the hostility of the Mugwumps
to mass democracy; they realized that universal manhood
suffrage created electorates too large to be dealt with
on an individualist base, that political organizations
would have to be created and strengthened if mass democracy continued; but they refused to accept political parties
as legitimate and, therefore, were left simply to protest
a change which had already occurred rather than developing
institutions to deal with the changes. They also resisted
the organization of the economy; they were especially and
consistently hostile to labor unions as intrusions on personal freedom; they were also anxious about the new power
of corporations, but significantly they were less consistent in their criticisms of corporations because frequently
their own self-interest was affected. Ultimately, the Independents had only one positive program—replace "bad"
men with "good" and "kick the rascals out." To do more
would be to recognize that the world had changed and that
political and economic organizations were facts of life
and the real question was what to do about them.[12]

Roosevelt's early training inclined him toward the
Independent liberals, but, as we have already seen, his
career led him to disagree with these Independents on
several specific issues and the disagreements increased

over time. Not that he ever rejected their belief in the
Protestant ethic and their individualist morality, for he
did not do that. He continued to believe, throughout his
life, in the private ethics he had been taught as a child,
but he did discover that they were not sufficient unto
themselves. In his *Autobiography,* he described what occurred. As a young man he was taught the

> individual virtues, and the necessity of character
> as the chief factor in any man's success—a teach-
> ing in which I now believe as seriously as ever,
> for all the laws that the wit of man can devise
> will never make a man a worthy citizen unless he
> has within himself the right stuff, unless he has
> self-reliance, energy, courage.... All this moral-
> ity I was taught at Harvard. But there was no
> teaching of the need for collective action, and of
> the fact that in addition to, not as a substitute
> for, individual responsibility, there is a col-
> lective responsibility.

Then he noted that fifty years earlier books like Herbert
Croly's *The Promise of American Life* and Walter Weyl's
New Democracy "would generally at that time have been
treated as unintelligible or as pure heresy.... The teach-
ing which I received was genuinely democratic in one way.
It was not so democratic in another."[13] Briefly, what
Roosevelt realized was the need for the development of
new ethical ideals.

The need for "collective action" and the recognition
of "collective responsibility"—these phrases were symptoms
of a broadening ethical perspective which for Roosevelt
emerged slowly in the nineties and early 1900s and reached
fruition around 1908 or 1912. Roosevelt, of course, was
not the only American to experience this different perspective—one thinks immediately of a whole generation of
Americans like Jane Addams or Frederic Howe or Lincoln
Steffens or Margaret Sanger. What happened to all of them
was that they discovered in the day-to-day life of the

new cities and factories a world which was almost totally inconsistent with the theories they had been taught
as children and young adults; as they decided to learn
from the new environment and try to create programs consistent with that environment. In the language of Robert
Wiebe, these Americans tried to go beyond "protest" to
"reform".

Roosevelt learned about the new environment because
as a politician he could not avoid it. Early in his career, e.g., as a member of the New York Assembly, he was
one of a committee of three appointed to investigate
a bill to prohibit the manufacture of cigars in tenement
houses in New York City. He began the investigation opposed to the bill, "for the respectable people I knew were
against it; it was contrary to the principles of political
economy of the *laissez faire* kind.... However, my first
visits to the tenement-house districts in question made me
feel that, whatever the theories might be, as a matter of
practical common sense I could not conscientiously vote
for the continuance of the conditions which I saw."[14] As
police commissioner of New York City, he toured the city's
underworld and slums with Jacob Riis. As President, he
sat in the middle of a labor dispute between the coal mine
owners and the UMW, and as a political candidate for various offices he visited immigrant associations, dealt with
urban bosses, and so forth.

As a consequence of his exposure to the environment
of time, Roosevelt's ideas changed on several issues. For
example, his views on labor unions shifted dramatically
over time—he began with a clear-cut hostility to unions,
though he felt a certain sense of *noblesse oblige* toward
workers; by the time he became President and went through
the anthracite coal strike of 1902, he concluded that

while unions might be dangerous because of their tendency
to dictate to individuals, they were no more tyrannical
than corporations; by 1912 he believed that collective
bargaining was the only road to industrial peace; and
in his *Autobiography* he indicated that if he were a labor-
er, he would unhesitatingly join the union of his trade.

Roosevelt learned other lessons as well. Like Lincoln Steffens, he learned that good men of high private
character and public respectability frequently provided
the bribes on which political machines flourished and
owned the breweries that owned the saloons that created
pigpens on city streets and managed corporations that paid
workers wages which in no way reflected the profits of the
company or the productivity of the workers. Judged by the
individualist ethics of the past, these men might be
"good," but the consequences of their actions were certainly not beneficial to the nation. Moreover, in politics,
it was not enough to "kick the rascals out" and replace
them with honest, decent men. Too often all that happened
as a result was that the new government would begin en-
forcing Blue Laws, like no drinking on Sundays, and would
then think that enough changes had been made. Inevitably,
the honest representatives would lose the next election to
the machine which understood, at least, that government involved decision-making and policy-making, not simply (or
even not at all) good private character. In particular,
Roosevelt learned that political machines, whatever their
faults, survived because they listened to the public on
issues like the price of public transportation and the
need for milk regulation. "Bread and butter" issues, if
you will, rather than moral principles like honesty.

Roosevelt concluded that the most important need was
that government be made efficient, capable of taking ac-

tion in what he called the "public interest." Perhaps
his most important actions as President were those which
created a stronger presidency. He realized that the
American government had been created on the assumption
that government would perform few functions, a view
which he regarded as outmoded by 1900. Thus, he said
later,

> In most positions the 'division of powers' theory
> works unmitigated mischief. The only way to get
> good service is to give somebody the power to
> render it.... What is normally needed is the con-
> centration in the hands of one man, or of a small
> body of men, of ample power to enable him or them
> to do the work that is necessary; and then dis-
> covering the means to hold these men accountable....
> I do not contend that my theory will automatically
> bring good government. I do contend that it will
> enable men...to get good government.[15]

By 1912, Roosevelt was prepared to support the view that
the national government would oversee the whole of the
American political economy, regulating relations between
labor and capital and passing special legislation to
benefit women (suffrage, work-day legislation), children
(child labor laws), and labor (minimum wages). In other
words, he had totally rejected the *laissez faire* ideas of
the past and anticipated parts of the New Deal.

Roosevelt also learned from his political career something at least of what the very disadvantaged in American
society were thinking. Richard Hofstadter has argued that
there were "two ethical systems" in the United States at
the turn of the century. One was the "Yankee-Protestant"
system; the other, an immigrant system. New immigrants,
partly because they came from Europe and partly because
their needs in America were so urgent, and partly because
their religious traditions were different, rejected the
Yankee-Protestant values. They tended to put more empha-

sis on the family, less on the individual, place loyalty
to people above loyalty to abstract moral codes or ideals,
tended to be relatively unconcerned about alcohol or the
honesty of governors and more concerned with satisfying
particular needs of their own. It was around this second
system that the boss and machine organizations were formulated.

Roosevelt, of course, had to work in a world where
the machines operated, work with the representatives
elected by the immigrants, and seek the votes of immigrants.
While he was never able to accept their views as a genuinely second or alternative ethical system to his own, he did
learn that their institutions were based on necessity, not
immorality or pure wrong-headedness, and perhaps the recognition of necessity is not far from the recognition of morality. It is important not to claim too much here, for
Roosevelt never became, as Jane Addams and some others did,
a convert to what might be called cultural pluralism. He
continued to believe in an organic society and cultural
unity rather than diversity, in cultural nationalism not
pluralism. But Roosevelt did go further than most of his
contemporaries in protesting racial prejudice (despite the
fact that he shared some of that prejudice) and in excluding new immigrants and some other disadvantaged groups
from judgments based on his own moral code on grounds
that they were environmentally and by necessity forced
to operate in ways deviant perhaps from the ideal.

And so Roosevelt learned, as others did and some of
them better than he, from immersion into the new urban and
industrial environment—an immersion, in his case, which
came about because he was a politician. His basic conclusion was that new institutional and structural changes
were necessary in the nation and that new collective

responsibilities had to be added to purely private ones
in order to make possible the creation of a government
which could act effectively in the political economy.
But Roosevelt received even more from his profession of
politics than that. John Blum has argued persuasively
that Roosevelt also received from politics a certain
structure, a role-model of sorts, which harnessed and disciplined his otherwise exuberant, boisterous, and vola-
tile self.[16]

Blum begins by delineating an important paradox between Roosevelt's words and his actions and between his
public acts and his private acts. Throughout his life,
Roosevelt's language and sometimes his actions when he
was outside of politics could be impulsive, extreme, and
even bizarre. Thus, Mark Hanna could plausibly call
Roosevelt a "madman" and warn against naming that "damn
cowboy" vice-president. One remembers, for example, the
near-duel over his fianceé, or his suggestion during the
Pullman Strike that the way to deal with strikers was to
line up their leaders and shoot them, or his ruthless pursuit of the Spaniards in Cuba and his determination to
kill a "rabbit", as he called the Spaniards, or, later in
his life, the irrational and vengeful criticism of Woodrow
Wilson. About many of Roosevelt's private acts and rhetoric hung an aura of obsession and fanaticism—his insistence on "manly virility", on the "strenuous life,"
and on the "citizen as soldier." Yet in contrast to his
strident rhetoric and his bizarre personal behavior,
Roosevelt's public record was cautious, expedient, moder-
ate, and, in some respects at least, even conservative.
Had Mark Hanna looked at the political record, had he
followed the old aphorism about politicians, to watch
their feet, not their mouths—then Hanna would not have

worried so much and it would have been clear that, whatever else he was, Roosevelt was far from a "madman."

Blum, then, argues that Roosevelt needed the structure and the limits of politics to restrain and guide and
shape his personality. Even the differences between
Roosevelt's exuberant and assertive actions as President
in foreign policy and his cautious and restrained domestic
policies provided evidence of the influence on Roosevelt of
institutional restraints. "Ultimately," concludes Blum,
"morality and information failed to restrain him." It was
as if his personality lacked all internal restraints save
one—a desire for power—and that one forced him to practice the profession of politics, which taught him a form
of effectiveness and ultimately made him a spokesman for
important new currents in American society.

By adding collective responsibilities to individual
ones, Roosevelt did not mean to say that public morality
is different from individual morality. Rather, he saw
the result as a seamless web. Indeed, he said repeatedly
that there is one moral code for individuals, groups, and
nations. In addition to the injunction to be honest,
frugal, hard-working, self-reliant, etc. in private life,
he called for Americans to adopt the duties of what might
be called a "new citizenship"—i.e., to recognize that we
are all of us interconnected in a great interdependent
network of large collectives (farm, labor, business) and
to act in such a way as to so structure government that we
can use the power of the state to rectify wrongs and to
create the best world we are capable of creating. The Ser-
mon on the Mount, however, is relevant to both aspects of
citizenship, and the two complement one another. For legislation and government, Roosevelt believed, can never do
everything; therefore, the governed must be sufficiently

reliant and courageous to be effective in other areas.

There were virtues to Roosevelt's structure, but there were defects as well. One virtue for Roosevelt and others of his generation was that by not denying the older Yankee-Protestant tradition, by insisting that the new fight was essentially a moral fight, and by asserting that all good men could by adopting this new vision work with a reasonable chance of success to create a more just society and achieve the "public interest"——by doing this Roosevelt was able to deny the growing view that class conflict might yet destroy America. If the new "collective" morality was but an addendum to the old individualist morality, then Roosevelt could appeal to men of good will from all classes, he could maintain the unity of democratic politics. Another virtue was that by casting the conflict in moral terms, by speaking of the need to distinguish good unions from bad and good trusts from bad, it was possible for political leaders to discuss relatively complex technical problems in a manner comprehensible to the broad, general public and sustain at least the image, and hopefully the reality, of public involvement in the central decision-making process.

There were some internal flaws, however. By making complex ideas comprehensible to the public, Roosevelt often over-simplified them and fostered only the illusion of understanding. More seriously, Roosevelt was not always logically consistent and his ideas lacked a certain precision and consideration of consequences. By simply adding "collective" virtues to "individualist" virtues and tying them all together in one absolutist view, Roosevelt failed to construct a vision that would endure the new relativistic notions of more rigorous intellectuals like Thorstein Veblen and John Dewey. Certainly the mix-

ture of old and new ideals galvanized by the force of his
own personality proved effective in the Progressive era,
but by the twenties, the ideas of Roosevelt proved vulnerable to logical inconsistencies and new pressures.

Soon, of course, assaults did come. Intellectuals by
the 1920s thought that the prescriptions of the Protestant
Ethic were too rigid, repressive (in the Freudian sense),
and parochial. Moreover, throughout the twenties and
thirties the pressure from the new immigrants and their
descendants increased, and a vision of cultural pluralism
gained ground on the cultural nationalsim of Roosevelt.
Finally, the acid of relativism continued its work—while
I could not possibly document it here, I think that many
Americans concluded something like this: the content of
our consciences is determined by culture and reflects
culture; if we are a culturally plural nation, and if all
cultures are equally good, then the contents of our consciences are plural and equal; and, finally, if all of
the above is the case, then we should focus on procedural
matters and processes like "due process" or "conscientous-
ness" rather than the content of any particular conscience,
with all of the strengths and weaknesses that go with
these efforts.[17]

FOOTNOTES

[1]Because of space limitations, this chapter treats only some aspects of Roosevelt's life and career. His ideas about foreign policy, e.g., are relevant to the theme of the chapter but could not be treated in depth and therefore were excluded as beyond the scope herein. The author's interpretation of Roosevelt was especially influenced by George Mowry, *The Era of Theodore Roosevelt and the Birth of Modern America 1900-1912* (New York: Harper and Row, 1958) and William Harbaugh, *The Life and Times of Theodore Roosevelt* (New York: Collier Books, 1963).

[2]See John Chamberlain, *Farewell to Reform* (New York: The John Day Company, 1932).

[3]Quoted in William Leuchtenburg, ed., *The Unfinished Century* (Boston: Little, Brown and Company, 1973), p. 4.

[4]Theodore Roosevelt, *An Autobiography* (New York: Charles Scribner's Sons, 1913), p. 56.

[5]See, e.g., Christopher Lasch, *The New Radicalism in America 1889-1963* (New York: Alfred A. Knopf, 1965), Chapter 1.

[6]John Blum, *The Republican Roosevelt* (New York: Atheneum, 1964), pp. 10-11.

[7]Roosevelt, *An Autobiography,* p. 7 and Theodore Roosevelt, "Latitude and Longitude Among Reformers," *Century Magazine* (June, 1900), 211-216.

[8]"Mr. Bryan," *Atlantic Monthly* (September, 1912), 289-294.

[9]E. S., "Mr. Roosevelt," *Atlantic Monthly* (March, 1912), 577-581.

[10]Henry F. May, *The End of American Innocence* (New York: Alfred A. Knopf, 1959) and Eric Goldman, *Rendezvous with Destiny.*

[11]See Richard Hofstadter, *The Age of Reform* (New York: Alfred A. Knopf, 1956), pp. 8-9.

[12] See John G. Sproat, *"The Best Men": Liberal Reformers in the Gilded Age* (London, Oxford, New York: Oxford University Press, 1968).

[13] Roosevelt, *An Autobiography,* pp. 25-26.

[14] *Ibid.*, pp. 79-80.

[15] *Ibid.*, pp. 170-171.

[16] See John Morton Blum, *The Republican Roosevelt* (New York: Atheneum, 1964).

[17] See, e.g., Richard Pells, *Radical Visions and American Dreams* (New York: Harper & Row, 1973).

PART III

PRIVATE AND PUBLIC ETHICS IN BUREAUCRACY

CASE STUDIES

REFLECTIONS ON THE HOLOCAUST
                                    Richard L. Rubenstein

FEDERAL REGULATION, THE ADVERSARY SYSTEM,
AND MISREPRESENTATION: THE WPIX CASE
                            Frank Wolf

REFLECTIONS ON THE HOLOCAUST

RICHARD L. RUBENSTEIN

Why should anyone bother to reflect once again on the extermination of Europe's Jews by the Germans 35 years ago? This world has witnessed new horrors aplenty since that time. And, given both the threat of global overpopulation and the scarcity of material resources, it will probably witness the death of far greater numbers in the foreseeable future.

Part of the answer lies in the fact that a hitherto unbreachable moral and political barrier in the history of Western civilization was successfully overcome by the Germans in World War II and that henceforth the extermination of millions of citizens and subject peoples will forever be one of the capacities and temptations of government, especially in times of extreme stress. Auschwitz has enlarged our understanding of the state's capacity to do violence.

On a more theoretical but no less important plane, the Holocaust serves as a datum whereby we can test the credibility of our conceptions of God, man and the political order. Since the Holocaust is as much a product of European civilization as the railroad, Goethe's *Faust,* Nietzsche's *Zarathrusta,* the nuclear bomb and Beethoven's Ninth Symphony, we ignore it at our intellectual and spiritual peril when we attempt to understand ourselves and our world.

Usually progress in death-dealing capacity in the

twentieth century has been reckoned in terms of technological advances in weaponry. Too little attention has been
paid to the "advances" in social organization that made it
possible to cross residual moral barriers and eliminate
millions. To understand these advances it is necessary to
consider the role of bureaucracy in modern political and
social organization. Writing in 1916, the great German
sociologist Max Weber observed:

> When fully developed bureaucracy stands...under the
> principle of *sine ira ac studio* (without scorn or
> bias). Its specific nature which is welcomed by
> capitalism develops the more perfectly the more
> bureaucracy is *'dehumanized,'* the more completely
> it succeeds in eliminating from official business
> love, hatred and purely personal, irrational and
> emotional elements which escape calculation. *This
> is the specific nature of bureaucracy, and it is
> appraised as its specific virtue.*[1] (Italics added.)

To the best of my knowledge, Weber never entertained
the possibility that the police and civil service bureaucracies of a modern state could be used as death machines
to eliminate millions who had been rendered superfluous
by political definition. Even Weber does not seem to have
foreseen state-sponsored, systematic, rationalized massa-
cres as one of the *dehumanized* capacities of bureaucracy,
although events have proved that there is no intrinsic
reason why such a capacity, once developed, could not be
used.

Too frequently the popular image of the Nazi extermination of the Jews is that of extreme sadists and bullies
visiting their sadism on their scapegoat victims. There
were, of course, bullies and sadists aplenty at every level
of the Nazi movement, and Nazi propaganda was calculated to
foster emotions of hatred and aggression against the Jews.
Nevertheless, the extermination project began in earnest
only after the bullies and hoodlums, many of whom were in

the brown-shirted SA, were put out of business and the
task of dealing with the Jews was turned over to the disciplined, bureaucratically-organized SS.

As is well known, the worst assault visited upon
Germany's Jews before World War II was *Kristallnacht,* the
program organized by Propaganda Minister Josef Goebbels
and the SA on November 10, 1938. In the wake of that
event leaders of the German state bureaucracy, as well
as Goering, expressed their vehement opposition to further
undisciplined, emotion-laden actions. Both the Nazi and
the non-Nazi bureaucrats were agreed that in the future
anti-Jewish measures were to be taken in á disciplined,
systematic, methodical manner.[2] The same meticulous care
and organizing ability that goes into the manufacture of
a Leica or a Mercedes was then applied to the elimination
of the Jews. *Kristallnacht* was the last occasion that
most German Jews had to fear street violence in Germany.
The hoodlums were banished. The bureaucrats took over.
Himmler was the supreme bureaucrat. Hatred gave way to
planning, organization and method. Only then was it possible to carry out the extermination project with maximum
efficiency and minimum cost to its perpetrators.

One of the gains of the bureaucratization of the extermination project was that German personnel were able to
proceed to their horrendous task unimpeded by feelings of
guilt. They perceived that the sole imperative binding
upon them was the fulfillment of their assigned tasks, regardless of human costs. Again, Weber's 1916 reflections
on bureaucracy are prophetic:

> ...entrance into a bureaucratic office...is con-
> sidered acceptance of a specific duty of fealty
> to the purpose of the office (*Amtstreue*) in return
> for the grant of a secure existence.[3]

During his trial in Jerusalem in 1961, Adolf Eichmann

insisted that he felt neither guilt nor responsibility for
his part in the Holocaust and that *he would have had a bad
conscience only if he had failed to carry out orders.*[4]
Eichmann's statement reflected the SS ideal, *Meine Ehre
heisst Treu,* my honor is my loyalty. His statement was
typical of many made by former SS personnel after the war.
When Nazi officials first defended their wartime actions
on the basis of "superior orders," it was assumed that such
statements were merely self-serving strategies of discredited war criminals. With the passing of time, it has become apparent that the claim of superior orders was more
often than not sincere. The SS code elevated unflinching
obedience to the supreme virtue. Moreover, the code of
total obedience was consistent with the bureaucratic imperative as described by Weber. Admittedly, most bureaucratic organizations are devoted to life-enhancing ends
and our technological civilization would collapse without
them. Nevertheless, the SS at Auschwitz demonstrated that
with adequate planning there is absolutely no limit to the
obedience a well-organized police or military bureaucracy
is capable of exacting from its personnel.

The ability of a bureaucratic organization to exact
compliance from reluctant personnel is enhanced by the
fact that there are few if any officials who cannot easily
be replaced. The interchangeability of personnel and the
division of labor mitigates against any effective moral
protest. Were an official to refuse to carry out an assignment, there is almost always a willing replacement to
assume the task.

Contrary to popular opinion, the Holocaust was not
carried out by a group of irresponsible criminals on the
fringes of society. The personnel who willingly partici-
pated in the actual killing operations included clergymen,

lawyers, physicians, surgeons, university professors and
gymnasium teachers.[5]

Nor was the Holocaust an event which somehow was
wholly at odds with the great traditions of Western civilization. Indeed, we are far more likely to understand the
extermination of Europe's Jews if we regard it as the expression of some of the most profound and deeply-rooted
tendencies of contemporary Western civilization. When
Max Weber wrote about bureaucratic domination, he did not
have the SS in mind nor was he proposing a prescription for
slaughter. His writings on bureaucracy were part of a
large attempt to understand the social structure and the
ethos of modern civilization. According to Weber, modern
bureaucracy can be understood as a structural and organizational outcome of the related processes of *secularization,
disenchantment of the world* and *rationalization*. The secularization process involves the liberation of ever wider areas of human activity from religious domination.[6]
Disenchantment of the world occurs when "there are no mys-
terious forces that come into play, but rather that one can
in principle, master all things by calculation."[7] Rationalization involves "the methodical attainment of a defi-
nitely given and practical end by means of an increasingly precise calculation of adequate means."[8]

The earliest culture systematically to disenchant
the world was the biblical culture of the Israelites. When
the author of Genesis wrote "In the beginning God created
heaven and earth," he was expressing that disenchantment.
In ancient Israel both the natural and the political orders
were progressively desacralized. The domain of the sacred
was relegated to the sphere of the transcendent monotheis-
tic deity. Thus was a beginning made toward that secularization of consciousness that finally culminated in our

times in the most radical forms of secular disenchantment
—the dehumanized, rationalized forms of modern political
and social organization, including bureaucratically-admini-
stered death camps. In the biblical world all human activity stands under the judgment of a righteous, transcendent
deity who has receded into the supramundane sphere. In
the modern world the supramundane deity has disappeared
for all practical purposes. In such a world men and women
are alone. If they have the power, they are free to pursue any end they choose, including mass murder, "by means
of an increasingly precise calculation of adequate means."

    Nevertheless, before persons could acquire the de-
humanized attitudes of fully rational bureaucracy, the
disenchantment process had to become culturally predominant. God and the world had to be so radically disjoined
that it became possible to treat the political and the
natural orders with uncompromisingly dispassionate objectivity. The disjunction occurred with the triumph of
Protestantism, especially Calvinism, and its insistence
upon the radical transcendence of God.[9] Protestantism
brought to full development the secularization of consciousness that was implicit in biblical Judaism. In so doing,
it opened the path to the radical secularization of consciousness of the twentieth century in which the question
of eliminating vast numbers of people who had been rendered
superfluous by bureaucratic definition lost all religious
and moral significance and became only a matter of bureaucratic problem-solving.

    I want to stress that the secularized cultural ethos
which permitted the perfection of rationalized bureaucratic
mass murder was an *unforeseen* and *unintended* consequence of
the Protestant doctrine of God's radical transcendence and
that it is not my intention to "blame" Protestantism for

the institution of the death camps. The doctrine of God's
radical transcendence was an indispensable precondition
of the secularization process, which in turn was, as we
have seen, a precondition of assembly-like mass slaughter,
but the doctrine itself was biblical in origin. This
point is especially important in correcting the view that
regards the Nazi extermination of the Jews as an anti-re-
ligious explosion of alien pagan values in the heart of
the Judaeo-Christian world. Although Nazism had many
roots, some of its most important features were unintended
consequences of the Judaeo-Christian tradition.

In this regard, it is important to distinguish between the *manifest* values proclaimed by a tradition and
the *cultural ethos* generated by the same tradition beyond
the conscious intent of its authors. The Judaeo-Christian
tradition is said to proclaim an ethic in which all persons are regarded as possessing an irreducible element of
dignity as children of the Creator. Nevertheless, beyond
all conscious intent, it has produced a radical secularization of consciousness, involving an abstract, calculating
rationality that can eradicate every vestige of that same
human dignity in all areas of human interchange.

Furthermore, of the two elements that together form
the basis of Western culture—the classical humanism of
Graeco-Roman paganism and the Judaeo-Christian religious
tradition—it is the biblical tradition that led to the
secularization of consciousness, disenchantment of the
world, and, finally, dehumanized bureaucratic objectivity.
*Thus, the culture that made the death camps possible was
not only indigenous to the West but was an outcome, albeit
unforeseen and unintended, of its fundamental Jewish and
Christian traditions.*If there is merit to Max Weber's hy-
pothesis that there exists an "elective affinity" between

the Protestant ethic and the spirit of capitalism, I
would argue that there is also an elective affinity between the rationalizing, secularizing ethos of biblical
religion and the twentieth-century world of systematic,
bureaucratized, mass homicide.

When religious thinkers reflect on the theological
significance of the Holocaust, they tend to focus their
attention too narrowly on the problem of reconciling the
biblical God of covenant and election with the existence
of radical human evil. This is, of course, one of the
most important issues arising out of the Holocaust. I
have attempted to confront it in an earlier work (*After
Auschwitz*). There are, regrettably, other issues of consequence that theologians tend to ignore. As we have
seen, one of them is the question of the possible biblical
origins of the culture that produced the death camps.
Strictly speaking, that question falls within the domain
of the sociology of religion, but it is not without theological relevance. There is also the further question of
whether any law was broken and hence whether any crime
was committed at Auschwitz.[10] To the best of my knowledge no theologian has attempted to deal with this issue.
The natural tendency of theologians is to assert the existence of a natural or God-ordained law binding on all
persons and nations in terms of which the camps can be
judged. Yet, in the aftermath of the war perpetrators of
the Holocaust such as Adolf Eichmann claimed that not only
did they break no law but they were actually carrying out
the laws of the only institution to which they owed their
allegiance, the sovereign German state.[11] It may be argued that there is a law that transcends the law of nations, but even the person with the greatest moral and
spiritual authority in Christendom during World War II,

Pope Pius XII, did not regard the Holocaust as worthy of
even a single public protest. Nor was he alone. At no
time during the war were German Christians told by their
religious leaders, either Protestant or Catholic, that
God's law forbade what the state's law prescribed. Clearly, the Holocaust was not treated as a crime in any mean-
ingful sense by those in Germany with religious authority
during World War II.[12]

Some may argue that the fact that religious leaders
voiced no protest does not exclude the possibility that a
serious crime was committed. Let us grant this and assume that a law transcending the state's law does in fact
exist. Even so, it is difficult to see what practical
difference such a law would make. What would be the penalty for its violation and what impartial agency would
provide the means for its enforcement? It is true that a
few miserable SS camp guards were incarcerated by the
victors after World War II, but the vast majority of the
government and corporate bureaucrats who planned the whole
operation and really made it possible quickly returned to
places of honor and dignity within German society.[13] *If
there is a law that transcends the laws of the sovereign
state, does it have any functional significance if it is
devoid of all penalty when violated?* In an earlier age
most men and women genuinely stood in awe of God and his
law, but is this any longer true, especially among decision-making elites? Even if theologians can demonstrate
the reality of a "higher law," does not the Holocaust demonstrate that it can be safely ignored? We are sadly
forced to conclude that no law that mattered was broken
at Auschiwitz, hence no crime was committed, and that we
live in a world that is *functionally* godless. It may very
well be that something worse than a crime was committed.

Regrettably, our traditional ethical, legal and theological categories fail us when we attempt to apply them to
the Holocaust.

The process of secularization thus ends where it
began. In the beginning secularization involved the de-
mystification and limitation of the sovereign's power.
In the end the secular state has dethroned all mystifica-
tions of power save its own. When unchecked, the modern
state has the power to become the only true god on earth.
It has the capacity to arrogate to itself the ultimate
power of divinity, the power to decide who shall live and
who shall die, as it did under Hitler and Stalin.

Some very distinguished theologians have attempted
to address themselves to the problems arising out of the
Holocaust. Unfortunately, they do not seem to be aware
of the extent to which their own religious traditions,
whether Jewish or Christian, are an intrinsic part of the
problem rather than the therapy. If it is possible to
suggest an imperfect analogy, just as depth psychology was
able to expose the ineradicable shadow side of human personality even in those situations in which persons appear
most loving and altruistic, so the world of the death camps
and the society of total domination it engendered reveals
the night-side of the Judaeo-Christian tradition.

I want to stress that this observation about the
night-side of the Judaeo-Christian tradition implies no
unrealistic proposal for the abolition of that tradition.
There is absolutely no way we can extricate ourselves from
the Judaeo-Christian tradition, for it is only conceptually
distinct from ourselves. Civilization means slavery, wars,
exploitation and, as we have seen, death camps. It also
means medical hygiene, elevated religious ideals, exquisite art and delightful music. It is an error to imagine

that civilization and heartless cruelty are incompatible
antitheses. On the contrary, in every organic process
the antitheses always reflect a unified totality, and
civilization is an organic process. There is only one
way the Judaeo-Christian tradition in either its secular-
ized or its religious form could be overcome: a momumental,
world-wide catastrophe in which hundreds of millions per-
ish and civilization as we know it disappears among the
crazed, surviving remnant. Such a scenario is technically
feasible. We have the weaponry to bring it about. Unfortunately, the traumatic "cure" of the illness we call
Judaeo-Christian civilization would prove infinitely worse
than the disease itself.

The disease we call Judaeo-Christian civilization?
Is the idea really so strange? After all, for all their
limitations biblical men and women understood that, far
from being an achievement, civilization requires a Savior
to extricate mankind from it.

FOOTNOTES

[1]Max Weber, "Bureaucracy" in *From Max Weber: Essays in Sociology,* trans. and ed. Hans Gerth and C. Wright Mills (New York: Oxford University Press, 1946), pp. 215-wl6.

[2]Cf. Raul Hilberg, *The Destruction of European Jews* (Chicago: Quadrangle Books, 1967), pp. 23-30.

[3]Weber, *loc. cit.*

[4]Cf. Hannah Arendt, *Eichmann in Jerusalem: A Report on the Banalty of Evil* (New York: Viking Press, 1964), p. 25.

[5]Cf. Hilberg, *op. cit.,* pp. 187 ff.

[6]Peter Berger, *The Sacred Canopy* (Garden City, N.Y.: Doubleday, 1967), p. 107.

[7]Max Weber, "Science as a Vocation" in Gerth and Mills, *op. cit.,* p. 139.

[8]Max Weber, "The Sociology of the World Religion" in Gerth and Mills, *op. cit.,* p. 293.

[9]For an authoritative discussion of the relationship between Protestantism and the secularization process, cf. Berger, *op. cit.,* pp. 105-125.

[10]For a fuller discussion of this issue, cf. Richard L. Rubenstein, *The Cunning of History: Mass Death and the American Future* (New York: Harper and Row, 1975), pp. 87-91.

[11]Cf. Arendt, *loc. cit.;* a convenient summary of the defenses offered by such Nazi leaders as Goering, Hess, Von Ribbentrop, Kaltenbrunner, Rosenberg, Frank, Streichter and Speer is to be found in G. M. Gilbert, *Nuremberg Diary* (New York: Farrar, Strauss and Girouz, 1947).

[12]The literature on the response of the Chruch to the Holocaust is too numerous to cite. Among the many

studies worthy of serious attention are: John Conway, *The Nazi Persecution of the Church: 1933-45* (New York: Basic Books, 1968); Saul Friedländer, *Pius XII and the Third Reich: A Documentation* (New York: Alfred A. Knopf, 1966); Guenther Levy, *The Catholic Church and Nazi Germany* (New York: McGraw-Hill, 1964); Franklin H. Littell and Herbert C. Locke, eds. *The German Church Struggle and the Holocaust* (Detroit: Wayne State University Press, 1974).

[13]For a resume of the post-war careers of the perpetrators up to 1960, cf. Hilberg, *op. cit.*, pp. 704-715.

FEDERAL REGULATION, THE ADVERSARY SYSTEM, AND MISREPRESENTATION: THE WPIX CASE

FRANK WOLF

INTRODUCTION

The issues of "private and public ethics" have been raised in a provocative way by Professors Weisband and Franck in their recent book, *Resignation in Protest*.[1] Their study concerns government officials who must decide whether to "resign in protest" because of their conscientious objections to government policies. They confined their research to high government officials in Britain and the United States. This case study raises a related issue in the private sector, but in an area of the private sector characterized by a public purpose, namely, news broadcasting on commercial television. This case, then, concerns not so much private ethics in public settings as what might be called public ethics in private settings.

There are two issues which this case raises: (1) What is the relationship between personal and corporate responsibility for behavior?; and (2) how does the regulatory process and its adversarial character influence the context in which the issue of responsibility is judged, and, therefore, the judgments which are likely to be made?

---

[1]Weisband, Edward, and Franck, Thomas M., *Resignation in Protest* (New York: Penguin Books, 1976).

The case involves WPIX, Channel 11, in New York
City. The specific aspect of the case of interest in the
context of a discussion of institutional and personal
ethics involves allegations that the station falsified
and misrepresented news stories broadcast between August
and December 1968. The case still awaits final resolution.

The issue of news misrepresentation only came to
public attention because some writers in the WPIX news
department complained to their superiors about a pattern
of misrepresentation of news stories pursued by a new producer of the evening news program. They first brought
their complaints to the manager of the news department,
the person who had hired the new producer, but their complaint appeared to have no impact. Shortly thereafter,
one of the writers resigned to take up another position.
But one of those remaining, Nancy McCarthy, refused to
acquiesce in the practices she questioned. She made several further attempts to persuade the news department manager that the new producer's policies were wrong and that
he should be dismissed. Ultimately, she took her complaints to the president of the station. The immediate
outcome as far as Nancy McCarthy was concerned was that
she was fired. In this case, then, Nancy McCarthy did not
"resign in protest." She was fired because she protested.

Three developments after Ms. McCarthy's firing made
the issue visible outside the station organization: (1) a
story in *Variety* about staff dissatisfaction and allegations of news misrepresentation culminating in McCarthy's
firing; (2) the fact that a personal letter written by
Nancy McCarthy to a friend found its way to then FCC Commissioner Nicholas Johnson, a letter in which she outlined
her allegations against WPIX; and (3) a competing application by Forum Communications,Inc. for the WPIX television

license whose triennial renewal date was upcoming. Had
it not been for these developments, especially the competing application of Forum, there is no reason to think
that McCarthy's efforts would have had any impact on the
station's news policies or on its license renewal.

There is a very good chance for reasons unconnected
with the alleged misrepresentations that the WPIX license
will be renewed. But whatever the outcome of the license
renewal, Nancy McCarthy lost her job because she was, it
appears, more loyal to the professional ethics of her
craft—and perhaps to her private ethics—than she was to
her immediate superiors.

The claim of this paper is that this case provides
a useful setting in which to consider the relationship
between personal and corporate responsibility for behavior,
and that the regulatory process and context in which the
judgment is being made is likely to mute, if not obscure,
this very important issue. Before these claims can be
demonstrated, a recounting of the story of Nancy McCarthy
and of the incidents in which the alleged misrepresentations took place is first required.

1. *THE BACKGROUND OF THE WPIX CASE**. WPIX is one
of three non-network commercial VHF television stations
serving New York, the most competitive television market
in the United States. From 1949 to 1966 the Consolidated
Edison Company sponsored WPIX's evening news program with
anchorman John Tillman. This news program enjoyed good
audience ratings until the network affiliates expanded
and developed their early evening news broadcasts beginning in the early sixties. The result was that the

---

      *I am indebted to five of my students (Paul Boren,
Charles Gertzog, Joel Gininger, Stella Leo, and Walter
Shellman) who gathered much of the data on which this paper
is based.

audience for WPIX's news program began to shrink. As a
result, it was decided to move the program to the late
evening time slot. At just about that time the leading
attraction of the program, anchorman John Tillman, left
WPIX for another position. The move to the 11:00 pm time
period did little to restore the audience to WPIX since
the network stations were broadcasting their late evening
news broadcasts in competition with WPIX.

          With the loss of Tillman and the altered time per-
iod and the declining size of the audience, Con Edison
withdrew its sponsorship. At this point, the station renewed its efforts to make the news program more lively
through expanding its staff, shifting the time period of
the program to 10:00 pm and using Lee Nelson as anchorman.
These changes took place in December 1967. Now in competition with WNEW (Channel 5) and its 10:00 pm news program,
the WPIX show still failed to win a substantially expanded
audience. In July 1968 the manager of the news department, Walter Engels, proposed a revamped and expanded news
department to the president and general manager of the
station, Fred Thrower. Engels recommended that a recently
hired temporary writer named Ted Kamp be made the producer
of the new evening news program which should be broadcast
at 9:00 pm rather than 10:00. Also involved in Engels'
plan was the hiring of free lance specialists, a street
camera crew, and a number of other new employees. In short,
a new news program with a new producer and many new persons
was begun in August 1968 was a view to recapturing the
audience for WPIX.

          It was only a week after she began working on a team
of writers for the new program that Nancy McCarthy first
complained to news department manager, Walter Engels, about
what she regarded as dubious practices on the part of Ted

Kamp. When the falsifications continued, several writers
including Nancy McCarthy met together to develop
a formal complaint to Engels about the on-going pattern
of falsifications in the news program. In preparation
for this meeting they prepared a memorandum in which they
identified the specific episodes which exemplified the
pattern of which they were complaining. After the meeting
with Engels the group agreed to prepare proposals for im-
proving the conditions of which they complained. This
they did in a memorandum several weeks later. This memorandum of early November 1968 spoke of the need for an improvement of the news program, made proposals for eliminating the use of stale and out-of-date film which Kamp
was misrepresenting as fresh film, and included as well
the suggestion that Kamp be instructed to stop the misrepresentations and distortions. It was a month after Engels
received this memorandum that he forwarded a copy to Fred
Thrower, President and General Manager, for his reaction.

    At about the same time that Engels received the memo,
Nancy McCarthy had a second meeting with him to outline
her notions of how the news operation could be improved.
She began by suggesting that Ted Kamp be fired. Engels
appears to have viewed the original complaints of the
writers, especially Nancy McCarthy's, as evidencing a personality clash. At least, that is what he later claimed.
Not only had McCarthy insisted that Kamp be excluded from
the first and second meeting, and suggested he be fired;
Kamp had asked that McCarthy be fired because of her refusal to do a story precisely as he had asked.

    After her second meeting with Engels, McCarthy sought
to enlist the news director's help in fighting the news
distortion issue. Nelson, the news director, was aware of
her meetings with Engels and suggested that the root of

the problem was Kamp's abrasive personality. He further
suggested that the solution should be worked out directly
between McCarthy and Kamp and that McCarthy was making a
mistake in going over his head. As had Engels, he rejected McCarthy's recommendation that Fred Thrower, the President, be confronted with her complaints. Meanwhile,
Engels informed McCarthy that he saw some of her recom-
mendations as having merit and that he was turning them
over to Kamp for implementation!

Shortly thereafter McCarthy sought a meeting with
Fred Thrower. In fact, two meetings took place, a short
meeting on December 4th in which she outlined the problem
in brief, and a longer meeting the following day where the
allegations were laid out in detail. In the course of the
second meeting, on December 5th, Thrower told McCarthy
that both Nelson and Engels had characterized her as a
disruptive person whose charges were untrue, and that they
both recommended her firing. On December 6, 1968 Engels
informed Nancy McCarthy that her employment was terminated.

In a memorandum dated December 9, 1968, President
Thrower recounted the specific incidents recited by McCarthy and noted to Engels that he would never want to be
accused of misrepresentation and that WPIX could never be
a party to such practices. At a meeting with Engels on
December 10, as recounted by Engels and Thrower months
later, Thrower asked Engels to "get at the facts" and give
him a report. Engels chose not to involve or approach any
other members of the news department in his "investigation"
because he disagreed with McCarthy's charges, he later said.

About two weeks later, which must have been just
about Christmas day, it was learned at WPIX that *Variety*
was preparing an article about the McCarthy allegations.
At a hastily called meeting Engels reported slow progress

to Thrower, explaining that his investigation had to compete with his regular day-to-day schedule. On January 1,
1969 the feared article appeared in *Variety*. As a result,
Francis Flynn, Chief Executive of WPIX's parent company
(which was affiliated with the *Daily News*), instructed
Thrower to investigate the matter thoroughly despite
Thrower's characterization of the McCarthy allegations
as "baseless."

   According to WPIX's later claims, Engels gave three
oral reports to Thrower between early January and late
March 1969. Reviewing only script material, Engels said
he reported a few "mistakes," but nothing which concerned
him very much. Thrower was to testify that only much
later did they realize that some of the complaints and
allegations referred to practices they could not really
defend.

   The WPIX license was due for renewal on June 1, 1969.
In May, Forum Communications, Inc. informed the Federal
Communications Commission that it intended to file a competing application and asked that the Commission not act
on the renewal before June 1, the license anniversary, to
give it time to assemble a complete competing application.
In asking the FCC to hold off action, Forum was seeking
an exception to a technical rule of the Commission according to which the FCC can act up to thirty days before the
actual anniversary of a license, requiring therefore that
any contesting of license renewals must be made before the
thirty day period. Despite the request of Forum, therefore, the FCC decided on May 22, 1969 to renew the WPIX
license. Nicholas Johnson, then an FCC commissioner,
filed an angry dissent to this decision. As an avowed
sympathizer to license challenges, Johnson saw the FCC action as a deliberate attempt to preclude such a challenge.

The following day he forwarded to the FCC's Broadcast
Bureau a copy of the letter written by Nancy McCarthy to
a friend.   In this letter, it will be recalled, McCarthy
outlined her charges of news fraud.

On June 20, 1969, on the recommendation of the
Broadcast Bureau, the Commission decided to set aside the
recently granted license until the Broadcast Bureau could
complete an investigation into the McCarthy allegations.
In so doing the Commission had to permit Forum's competing
application to go forward, as Johnson, no doubt, had hoped.
As a result of the Broadcast Bureau investigation, the
Commission decided on October 28, 1969 to designate for
consolidated comparative hearings the application of WPIX
for license renewal and the application of Forum Communications for a construction permit for a station on the same
frequency, i.e., a competing application.   *Therefore, it
is in the context of Forum's efforts to secure the WPIX
license that the allegations of news fraud have been scrutinized.*   And the final decision by the Commission as between the two applicants had not been made by early 1977.

2.   *THE ALLEGATIONS DESCRIBED.*   In its October 1969
order the FCC identified the "news practice" issue and
stated that in the comparative proceeding it would have to
be determined in respect to the application of WPIX, Inc.

> (a) Whether the licensee or any of its
>   employees distorted, falsified or
>   misrepresented news;
>
> (b) In view of the facts ascertained under
>   issue (a) whether WPIX, Inc. has demon-
>   strated sufficient knowledge, control,
>   or supervision of its news operation;
>
> (c) What actions WPIX, Inc. took to exercise
>   control or supervision of its news opera-
>   tion subsequent to the disclosure of the
>   facts ascertained and relevant to issue
>   (a); and

(d)   Whether in the light of the evidence adduced
      pursuant to the foregoing issues, WPIX, Inc.
      is disqualified to remain a licensee of the
      Commission or, if not so, whether a comparative
      demerit or demerits should be assessed against
      it in this proceeding.[2]

In its order the FCC placed the burden of introducing evidence with respect to items (a), (b), and (c) upon the
Broadcast Bureau. Upon WPIX, Inc. was placed the burden
of proof with respect to all the issues.

There were a number of specific incidents of news
misrepresentation and falsification originally complained
of by Nancy McCarthy which the Broadcast Bureau was able
to corroborate.   The major ones will be summarized below.

The Maine Driver

Colin Gibson, one of the three temporary writers who
originally complained to Engels, was asked by Kamp to
write a story about a man in the state of Maine who
was stopped by the police for driving too slowly.
The man explained to the policemen that his car was
unable to go faster. Someone, apparently Kamp, added
to the script that the man had been put in jail, a
fact unmentioned in any of the wire copy sources from
which WPIX had gotten the item.

The Scissors Bridge Incident

Kamp gave Colin Gibson a piece of film and a "spot
sheet" with instructions to write a thirty-second
item "with a South Vietnam angle." The film concerned a new piece of U.S. Army equipment being
tested at Fort Belvoir, Virginia. Gibson completed
his task and then reported overhearing Kamp order a
"super" (words superimposed on a TV picture) of
"Central Highlands" for the film. Gibson pointed
out to Kamp that the film had not been shot in Vietnam but in Virginia. Gibson says Kamp replied that
he had been in the Central Highlands and knew how
they looked. The next day the film appeared with
the "super" "Central Highlands." The "spot sheet" re-
leased with the film by UPITN (United Press Inter-

---

[2]Designation and Order, 20 FCC 2d, 298.

national Television News) from whom WPIX had gotten
the film made it unmistakably clear that the film
had been taken in Virginia.

The Nixon Motorcade, Houston

Film shot by UPITN in San Francisco on September 5,
1968 showing candidate Richard Nixon arriving at the
airport was shown on September 6 on WPIX while its
anchorman said that Mr. Nixon was arriving at the
airport in Houston, Texas on September 6.

The Bucharest-Braley Incident

On August 20, 1968 the USSR invaded Czechoslovakia.
In the following period WPIX sought correspondents in
that   country and surrounding countries for telephone
reports to the U.S. on tape for use in its news programs. On August 26 WPIX had two such tapes available, one from reporter Russ Braley in Prague, another
from an unidentified reporter in Vienna. Both Ted
Kamp and Nancy McCarthy agreed that the Vienna account was more dramatic and newsworthy than the dry
account by Braley. Kamp ordered the Vienna report
used after a short excerpt from the Braley report
which was identified as coming from Prague. The effect was to leave the impression that the entire
report had come from Braley in Prague. McCarthy also
said Kamp asked for a "via satellite" "super" for the
film. Though she never claimed to know where the film
came from, she knew that no satellite feed had been
organized by WPIX.

In a related incident a Braley report was combined
with crowd film from Bucharest since WPIX had no
such Prague crowd footage available. Two "supers,"
"Prague" and "Russ Braley Reporting," were typed in,
and the word "sat" (by satellite, presumably) was
also included. No party ever claimed that WPIX did
indeed receive either live or film coverage from
Prague by satellite during 1968.

The Putzel Incident

On August 26, 1968 as part of its coverage of the
invasion of Czechoslovakia, WPIX broadcast the reactions of the "man-in-the-street" in the Soviet Union
to the news of the invasion of Czechoslovakia, as observed by one Professor Max Putzel. In fact, the
conversation with Putzel, who was Ted Kamp's brother-
in-law, came by telephone from Gary, Indiana some days

after Putzel's return from a nine-week trip to the
USSR. Kamp ordered the use of several "supers" including "Professor Max Putzel," "eye witness account,"
and "from Moscow." Putzel was described as an authority on Russian affairs when he was in fact a professor of German literature.

The Misidentification of Audio Tapes

In addition to the above incidents involving Braley
and Putzel, there was a series of similar episodes
where WPIX reports were attributed to places other
than their exact places of origination, presumably
to give the impression that the journalists' reports
were from places where fast breaking stories were in
progress. Among these was a report identified as
coming from "on the Czech border" which came in fact
from Vienna, two reports from Vienna identified as
coming from Prague, the use of background film purporting to be actual film of events then in motion,
and a reporter in Paris assuming a name other than
his own.

The Herman Ferguson News Item

Herman Ferguson, a black candidate for the Senate,
was sentenced on October 3, 1968 to $3\frac{1}{2}$ to 7 years
in the state penitentiary at Sing Sing. On October
4 he was lodged in the Queens County jail while bail
was filed for. On that evening's news program, Kamp's
script read, "So, if you want to vote for Herman Ferguson, peace-candidate for the Senate, you'll have
to prepare yourself to send all cards and letters to
the prospective Senator at Sing Sing—that is where
he'll be, at least for the first half of his term in
office." Later that day, Ferguson did file for bail
and he did not reach Sing Sing for almost a year
after the broadcast.

Student Disturbances in Paris or Berlin?

Nancy McCarthy alleged that film used in September
1968 purporting to show student disturbances in Berlin that month was in fact film previously acquired
by UPITN (in April) showing similar disturbances in
Paris.

Stale Film of Boston, San Francisco, and Ohio

Nancy McCarthy alleged that in its coverage of a Boston high school demonstration of black students in

September 1968, film from the day before was misrepresented as being "today." The same charge was made
in regard to student disturbances at San Francisco in
December 1968 and to coverage the previous summer of
floods in Ohio.

Lady Professor Wears "See-Through" Blouses

In a feature on a young university teacher and her efforts
to relate to her students, it was charged that Kamp
changed the text to suggest she was wearing "see-through"
blouses when the story was that she was wearing "mod
clothes."

Most of these allegations made by Nancy McCarthy
were in fact corroborated by the FCC's Broadcast Bureau
investigation in the summer of 1969. And other comparable
incidents were also brought to light. In the view of the
Broadcast Bureau, at least, WPIX did indeed engage in a
pattern of news misrepresentation as Nancy McCarthy had
in fact originally charged.

Despite the formidable evidence gathered by the
Broadcast Bureau, Administrative Law Judge James F. Tierney, after conducting hearings and examining briefs,
counter briefs, and examining transcripts of testimony
taken by investigators, concluded that WPIX, despite some
errors, had not engaged in a deliberate policy of news
falsification and that, to the extent that there were such
incidents, they had been the work of a single over-zealous
producer who was no longer with the station. (Both Kamp
and Engels left WPIX in early 1970.) Both the Broadcast
Bureau of the FCC and Forum Communications, Inc. have
filed briefs in support of exceptions to Judge Tierney's
initial decision, which decision was in favor of WPIX's
license renewal. These appeals are what the FCC had yet
to act upon by early 1977. When the Commission does decide
the matter there will still be the possibility that either

party may appeal the decision to the U.S. Court of Appeals
for the District of Columbia, and from there to the U.S.
Supreme Court. There were many other factors contributing
to the case not discussed here which in part explain the
great delay.

    3. *THE ETHICAL ISSUES RAISED BY THIS CASE.* Judge
Tierney, in his own most unusual writing style, refers to
the ethical issues raised by the case as follows:

> That the few incidents disclosed in the record are
> little more than singular lapses in poor, even
> reckless judgment, perhaps mindless taste, is echoed
> in the testimony of the principal complaining wit-
> ness, Mary [*sic*] McCarthy. Besides expressing sur-
> prise, if not chagrin, on learning that the contents
> of her private and personal letter to a friend had
> worked its way through to the launching of this pro-
> ceeding, Miss McCarthy summed up her thesis and that
> of her fellow journalists of these events, that the
> program producer, Kamp, and his liberty-taming tac-
> tics were in her mind clear incidents of 'unethical'
> news practices. The thrust of the evidence in this
> area disclosed the personal concern of Miss McCarthy
> for journalistic ethics or integrity directed at
> Kamp's sacrificing good journalistic values for show
> business values. This is borne out in the supporting
> testimony of her fellow writers at WPIX, *'Ethics'*
> *like 'taste,' especially 'journalistic ethics,' would*
> *not only entail an ambush-prone foray into the 'im-*
> *penetrable thicket' the Commission imperatively*
> *shuns; worse, it would be a plunge into an abysmal*
> *abyss.*[3]

    The facts in this case have been briefly presented
to provide a concrete context in which two issues can be
raised: (1) Who is and should be responsible for behavior
in corporate settings—the individuals specifically involved, or the corporation itself? and (2) How does the
regulatory process and its adversarial character influence
the context in which such issues are judged, and, there-

---

[3]Initial decision of Administrative Law Judge James
F. Tierney, issued November 27, 1974, paragraph 472.
(Emphasis added.)

fore, the judgments which are likely to be made?

CORPORATE AND INDIVIDUAL RESPONSIBILITY

Though WPIX questions how much misrepresentation was really entailed in the incidents recounted here, and though WPIX denies that together they make a showing that WPIX is unfit to hold a television license, the corporation additionally claims in its briefs that any wrongdoing that may have occurred was not the behavior of WPIX, Inc., the licensee whose license renewal is at issue. Rather, WPIX claims, not surprisingly, that the behaviors in question were isolated instances evidencing bad judgment of an over-zealous producer who has since resigned, and *not* news misrepresentation on the part of an FCC licensee. Judge Tierney agreed with this claim.

Though my reading of the record would lead me to an opposite conclusion, what is important is not whether the WPIX argument is persuasive, at least not in the context of a discussion of private and public ethics. The concern here is how such judgments, generally speaking, should be made. If anything emerges clearly from this account, it surely is that such judgments are terribly difficult to make. And it seems certain that no set of abstract principles will provide absolute guidance about how to make a determination as to who is responsible in any particular case. And my concern is not so much with what the law currently requires, but what, as a matter of prudent social policy, should inform judgments of this kind.

The WPIX case raises a number of questions which should be asked in arriving at judgments about whether responsibility for behavior in corporate settings should be placed on the individual, on the corporation, on both, or on neither. First, there are a number of questions

about the behavior itself. Is the behavior clearly unethical? Does it absolutely and clearly violate professional
norms and corporate practices as they are understood within the corporate world? Or, is the behavior one where
reasonable and responsible persons would be likely to disagree about what appropriate behavior would be? Furthermore, was the behavior in question an isolated instance,
or was it reflective of a wider pattern of such behaviors?

Nancy McCarthy and the Broadcast Bureau argue that
the behaviors in question clearly violated the ethical,
legal, and professional responsibilities of an FCC licensee.
In the view of the Broadcast Bureau the FCC ought not to
renew the WPIX license because the FCC is charged by the
Federal Communications Act of 1934 to serve the "public
interest, convenience, and necessity." Clearly, if the
Commission or the courts accept their argument, WPIX will
lose its license. On the other hand, Judge Tierney takes
quite a different approach when he argues that the practices in question involved matters of news judgments,
questions about how best to present the news. These matters, argued Tierney, are properly the responsibility of
the licensee, not the FCC or the courts. For, according
to Tierney, the First Amendment protects freedom of the
press, and no government agency should substitute its
judgment for that of the press itself.

There are also questions which go beyond the behaviors themselves. Does not the nature of the organization
in which the behaviors arose influence whether the corporation or the individual should be held responsible for behavior? Were the principal officials of the corporation
unaware that the behaviors were taking place? Did they

leave the individual engaged in the behavior in a position
to infer that what he was doing was understood, known,
and condoned, albeit implicitly, by his superiors? Did
the organization have established organizational routines
to ferret out behavior which it claims is inconsistent
with its general policies? And does the fact that the organization operates because of a license granted by a public agency impose special responsibilities on a licensee
which might not be imposed on an ordinary private corporation? Though it is difficult to draw an exact analogy
to the newspapers, if a paper were to publish a photograph
of Gary, Indiana with a caption suggesting the photograph
was taken in Moscow, it is not clear that such a practice
should be illegal, though it seems certain that most would
agree that the practice would be unprofessional, if not
unethical.

There are further organizational questions. When
evidence was presented to suggest that improper behavior
was taking place, did the officials evidence an unambiguous
interest in discovering the facts and removing the abuses?
Should the fact that the person complaining rather than
the person whose behavior was complained about was fired
be taken as germane to this question?

And of what of motivation? If Kamp was engaged in
"news misrepresentation" to advance his own personal interest at the expense of corporate goals, would the case for
his personal responsibility be more compelling? In this
case, he was probably purusing a course of action he believed would advance a corporate goal—increasing the
audience for the evening news show—a goal not inconsistent, presumably, with his own personal advancement both
within the organization and his profession. Does the fact
that Kamp was hired as producer of the evening news program

specifically to revive and recapture an unenthusiastic
and diminishing audience permit us to infer that the corporate motives explain what might be described as WPIX's
studied indifference to the charges made by Nancy McCarthy?

So too, if Engels was right that Nancy McCarthy's
interest in the abuses she attributed to Kamp was generated
not by a concern for high professional and ethical principles, but by personal animosity, does that make the case
for corporate indifference to Kamp's misbehavior weaker?
Or, if Kamp, Engels, and Nelson, knowing that Thrower, the
President, could not be a party to such practices, at least
not explicitly, colluded in keeping such information from
him, does that make more or less compelling the case for
holding the corporation itself responsible for the behaviors in question? Should not Thrower as the chief executive officer be held responsible for the behavior of his
principal assistants in any case? And if so, does that not
mean that the behaviors in question should properly be regarded as corporate acts?

This series of questions by no means exhausts those
that could reasonably be raised. They are all germane to
assigning moral, ethical, and legal responsibility for behavior in corporate settings. But more important than any
particular question raised here is the fact well illustrated
by this case—that such questions cannot be detached from
the organizational settings in which they arise without
robbing them of some of their ambiguity. On these grounds,
then, this case would lead me to take issue with David
Little's treatment of "conscientiousness" because his description implies that conscientious decision-making is a
kind of disembodied, abstract process. In fact, such dilemmas typically arise within the webbing of social and
organizational networks which to a great extent define the

meaning of the choices that must be made.

And it should be noted that Nancy McCarthy is a woman who, in Elizabeth Janeway's words, saw power relationships at WPIX from below, who "spoke from another part of
the forest." The men in positions of power within WPIX
might have acted unwisely and even unethically in part
because they did not listen to or really hear Nancy McCarthy. That Nancy McCarthy was seen as a disloyal member of
the "team," the kind of male metaphor of which Karen Brown
complains, is, presumably, illustrative of the way in which
typically male terminology gives contextual meaning to her
behavior.

Finally, since judgments about responsibility in
this case will inevitably be shaped by the setting in which
they are made—the regulatory context, it becomes important
to examine that context, not only to predict the outcome,
but to establish the moral valences which are likely to be
assigned to the questions raised here.

THE REGULATORY PROCESS AND JUDGMENT

In television license renewal actions the Federal
Communications Commission has long exhibited an ingenious
capacity for justifying the renewal of incumbents' licenses.
The process itself is well-designed to assure that result.
Until 1969, no party without a pecuniary interest in the
outcome of a license renewal had standing to make repre-
sentations to the Commission in the administrative process.
Since the Jackson, Mississippi case brought by the United
Church of Christ,[4] groups with an interest in programming,
or employment policies, or violence, or any such matter

---

[4]Office of Communication of the United Church v.
FCC, 359 F2d, 994 (DC Cir. 1966).

have been granted standing.

There are two major ways a party may contest the
renewal of a license: (a) through petitions to deny renewals; and (b) through a competing application (so-called
"strike applications") of the kind made by Forum Communications in the case described here. In either case, it is
incumbent upon the party seeking to contest the renewal,
not the FCC or any other governmental body, to marshall
resources—both money and information—sufficient to persuade a reluctant FCC that non-renewal would serve the
"public interest, convenience, and necessity." The record
to date makes it clear that the chances of a successful
petition to deny or a successful strike application are
tiny. The FCC has largely neutralized the movement for
citizen group intervention in license renewals, and the
broadcasting industry has enthusiastically colluded with
the Commission.

It goes without saying that to deprive a licensee of
a renewal is no trivial matter. Licensees have substant-
ial financial investments in their stations and enormous
stakes in the often lucrative profits they produce. Because the value of holding a license is great, a decision
to withhold renewal is a great punishment. But the FCC
has no other punishment, practically speaking, which it
can mete out when licensees fail to meet their obligations,
at least not the sort of abuse involved in the WPIX case.

And the way in which such matters come before the
Commission almost inevitably implies that the judgments
made will be in favor of the incumbent licensee. In this
case the FCC must decide not whether the news misrepresentation engaged in by WPIX or its employee was wrong, but
whether WPIX, Inc. or Forum Communication would be the
licensee most likely to serve the public interest. *There-*

fore, in this context Forum's deficiencies become WPIX's strengths. If Forum Communications is judged to lack the requisite financial qualifications, or the requisite broadcasting experience, or a plan for programming clearly superior to what WPIX has planned, then the news misrepresentation issue will be but one of many issues shaping a comparative judgment between the applicants.

It is important to remember at this point that the only reason the FCC ever became involved with the news misrepresentation issue was because of Forum's competing application. And the only reason Forum succeeded in having its competing application considered, despite its untimely filing, was because Commissioner Johnson referred the complaint he had received against WPIX to the Broadcast Bureau precisely because he was anxious to create the possibility that Forum might make a challenge.

There is only one other plausible scenario which might have resulted in the charges against WPIX coming to the attention of the FCC. This other course of events would have arisen had a citizen group filed a petition to deny and based its petition in part on allegations of news misrepresentation. This situation would have produced a *slightly* different context for judgment. The burden of proof that misrepresentations actually took place would have been on the petitioning group, typically, a group without much money. And the petitioners would have had to prove to the FCC's satisfaction that the misrepresentations were sufficient to disqualify WPIX as a licensee. That case might have been easier to make.

But even in the case of a petition to deny, the question still becomes whether the license should not be renewed, not whether the deeds in question were wrong, or, whether the station or the individual should be held

responsible. That is, *in any case,* the regulatory process mutes and obscures the ethical dimension involved
because it is primarily a licensing decision which is at
stake.

WPIX says in its case that the question is as follows: Should its 25-year-long history of service to New
York when laid aside a four month period of small excesses
by one producer no longer with the station lead one to
conclude that, on balance, Forum Communications with all
its inadequacies would be a licensee more likely to serve
the public interest than WPIX? This is the context in
which the behavior at issue here will be judged. The context is one where adversaries are seeking a television
license, and it will be in that context that the judgment
will be made.

Whatever the outcome, the judgment will not be about
the misrepresentation of news but about license renewal.
And, perversely, were it not for the question of license
renewal, the complaints and charges made by Nancy McCarthy
would have remained largely unknown.

And we can wonder what happened to Nancy McCarthy.

PART IV

MINORITY ETHICS AND THE
PRIVATE AND PUBLIC SECTORS

FEMINIST PERSPECTIVES

HERETICS AND PAGANS: WOMEN IN
THE ACADEMIC WORLD

> *Karen McCarthy Brown*

THE POWER RELATIONSHIP: THE VIEW
FROM BELOW

> *Elizabeth Janeway*

HERETICS AND PAGANS:
WOMEN IN THE ACADEMIC WORLD

KAREN McCARTHY BROWN

The debate over public and private ethics begins
with the suggestion that individual persons and public
institutions do not share the same moral universe, that
the values appropriate to the first are inoperative, or
at least necessarily compromised in relation to the second.
More than one paper in this volume denies that as a necessary condition of life and calls for a closer relationship
between private conscience and public action. Insofar as the
claim that there is a special morality appropriate to
public spheres of action has been used in bad faith, to
disguise power or profit motives, for instance, we are
clearly better off without the idea. Are we then rid of
the distinction between public and private ethics? I
think not, for it reasserts itself in another light where
questions are raised about minority worldviews, and so
minority ethics, and their carry-over into the public realm.

There is a series of assumptions about the nature of
culture that lies at the root of my thinking on this issue.
While they cannot be fully defended in this short essay,
they should be stated at the very least. All ethical
values are culture relative; they are in some sense derived from the worldview of a particular people. It should
be added that it is equally true to say that the worldview
derives from the ethos.[1] Worldview and ethos are co-

266

creators, throughout history, of human experience, just
as they were (and are being) created by that experience.
Within a culture, subgroups may, for one reason or another,
have certain experiences of the world consistently different from the "official" version of reality, the official
version being made up of the experiences of those who hold
power in that group. Now, since different experiences
alter the worldview and the ethos, the result is what I
referred to above as a minority worldview and a minority
ethic. This understanding is especially important to set
the stage for a discussion of women and morality. In relation to women, of course, the word "minority" indicates
status rather than numbers.

Very early in the socialization process of a person,
gender roles became significant; in fact the first question
asked about a newly-arrived human being deals with gender:
Is it a boy or a girl? The answer to this question not
only provides biological information, but also determines
social response, which in turn shapes the experience of the
subject. In this way sex roles become primary structuring
principles in the creation of a world-taken-for-granted.[2]
The important thing here is the insight that from the very
beginning of the socialization process the female child
has a quite different experience of the world from that of
the male child. By the time sexual maturity and moral maturity are achieved, the experiential worlds of men and
women have diverged significantly. Oh, certainly the
worlds of men and women are not entirely different; no one
would argue that. We do share a common culture language.
Yet it is my belief that we underestimate the degree to
which fundamentally different experiences underlie our
speaking in the world. The complicating factor here is
that the institutions of our society without exception

are constructed out of the world-as-taken-for-granted by
men. I say without exception, and I mean without exception, for even the family is dependent on the male worldview internalized (although never completely so) and en-
acted by the female.

This general point about social institutions is important for any discussion of public and private ethics.
For most men,[3] the flow from individual conscience to the
performance of a specific public role is facilitated by
the fact that the individual and the institution share
the same experiential base—that is to say, the same general assumptions about "what is so" in this world, and
thus about what "ought to be so." Women, whose special
experience is the topic of my paper, are not in that position. Although we are occupying more and more positions
of responsibility in the public sector, many of us continue not to feel at home there. I attribute this feeling
of dislocation to the psychic dissonance arising from the
difference between the way we experience the world and the
view of the world existing at the level of assumption in
public institutions. This is where the neat picture presented above of different experiences producing different
worldviews and different ethics becomes more complex. For
those who have a minority view must nevertheless operate
in institutions defined by others.

Those of us who share the "view from below", to bor-
row Elizabeth Janeway's phrase, may be more or less conscious of the gap that separates our own from the official
view of reality, but all of us, I dare say, feel the dislocation more acutely when caught in a moral dilemma.
Ethical decision-making within the institution serves to
point up clearly the difference between personal integrity
and the public good, where the content of the latter is

defined by an experience alien to one's own. Women and
other low-status groups who seek positions in government,
in business or in the universities thus experience the
difference between public and private ethics in a new way.
In other words, the dislocation mentioned above is endemic
to the situation of acting in the world for all minority
groups. This chapter is an attempt to present a phenomenology of women's experience of dislocation and to do so
specifically in relation to the academic world. While
some possibilities for a feminist ethic will be mentioned
in passing and some particular ethical dilemmas alluded to
from time to time, the point of the chapter is neither to
outline an ethic for women in academe nor to analyze particular ethical issues.

The answer to our dilemma does not lie in the victory of the underdog. The goal is not for women's point
of view as it now stands to prevail; for as this section
will try to show, it is not so much that most women have a
different ethic as it is that being denied access to action, most women also have been systematically denied the
psychic and social space to become fully mature ethical
beings. Similarly it is not the answer for women to "grow
up" to assimilate the moral universe of those in power.
The act of bad faith involved in preserving their own
sense of well being at the expense of others, has left the
powerful with a crippled moral sense as well. The answer
lies in a radical redefinition of the basis of all moral
thought, that is community, and especially community in its
most rudimentary form, the intimate relationship between
two persons. While I recognize that this is finally what
must be done, this chapter does not have goals so large as
that. The aims of this essay as I indicated above are more
humble. I want to illuminate the problem, and, for now,

nothing more. At any rate, the conclusion is that we cannot do away with some kind of distinction between public and private ethics as long as the public institutions reflect the experience and values of only one segment of the people they are supposedly designed to serve.

A large part of the research for this paper has consisted of reflection on my own experience. I have consulted with other professional women from time to time to check my conclusions, however. One thing we have all agreed upon is that while women in the universities do have special problems, these problems are inseparable from the larger issue of women's oppression. This will be reflected here, pausing from time to analyze certain elements in women's common experience before moving on to show how these manifest themselves in the particular context of women working in higher education.

The title of this chapter refers to women as heretics and pagans. Now, originally a heretic was anyone who held opinions against church dogma, but these days the term is used more frequently to refer to a person who disagrees with any "official" point of view regardless of the institution. In relation to the institutions of higher learning, women's heresy is just beginning. There *is* an aliveness to some of the work being done by women scholars these days. Witness the well-attended women's sessions at the annual conventions of various scholarly groups. Yet, too often this work is praised for its freshness and insight while the fundamental challenge it poses to the academic way of things goes unnoticed. It is my belief that the domination of the woman by the man is the primary metaphor for all other forms of human oppression, and so the feminist consciousness that would challenge that most basic of heirarchies, also inevitably challenges the very root

system of one of the most rigidly hierarchical institutions
in our culture——the university. But most of us do not
know that yet, and if we know it with our heads it is
still difficult to imagine with our hearts that there
really could be another way. Women's potential for heresy
is the optimistic note in this section.

Now, to call an academic woman a pagan is to make
another point, one quite different from noting that she
can be heretical. My dictionary tells me that while "pagan" formerly meant a person who was not a Christian, the
word today is used to indicate anyone who is not either a
Christian, a Muslim or a Jew, or it can mean quite simply
someone who has no religion at all. This definition is
an illustration of a devastating technique used by those
who have power over others to avoid a challenge to that
power. Let us call this the "paganizing technique." It
consists of defining ideas that oppose one's own as non-
existent. If you operate on principles other than their
principles, you are said to be *un*principled; having values
other than the official ones makes you *un*ethical; reasoning
in a way other than the accepted way, makes you *ir*rational,
and not being a Christian, a Muslim or a Jew, means that
you have no religion at all.

When I say that women in the academic world are experienced as pagans (both senses of the phrase intended),
I am making a point similar to one Simone de Beauvoir made
when she said of women in general, it is not so much that
we are seen as the second sex, but that we are seen as the
other sex.[4] In the otherness of our sex, women are like
blank screens on which men project their best and their
worst fantasies. Yet, whether perceived as goddess or man-
eater, woman remains essentially unknown. The same is
true of those peoples who, in the past, were called pagans.

Whether caricatured as noble savages or as cannibals very
little was actually known about them. So, when I say that
there is something of the pagan in the image of women in
the academic world, I intend to say several things. First,
she is an outsider. Her interests and her activities have
no prestige and in fact are often maligned. Furthermore,
like the noble savages of former days, the adulation a
woman in academe gets is often condescending and controlling; more frequently, she engenders fear and upset. I
also intend to include in the idea of her pagan image,
that very little is actually known about this academic woman and what she thinks and how she views the world.

    One of the major ways in which women in general have
been paganized is through a claim that we simply are not
as ethical as men are. Freud, while not the inventer, was
certainly one of the leading proponents of this position.
I quote from the 1925 essay wherein he argues that since
women cannot be shaken out of their version of the Oedipus
complex by fear of castration (alas, we have already been
castrated!) and since there is no similar threat for their
sex (we presumably have *nothing* to lose!) the resulting
superego, rooted as it is in the fear-inspired incest prohibition, is less firmly planted in female hearts.

> I cannot escape the notion (though I hesitate
> to give it expression) that for women the level
> of what is ethically normal is different from
> what it is in men. Their superego is never so
> inexorable, so impersonal, so independent of its
> emotional origins as we require it to be in men.
> Character-traits which critics of every epoch have
> brought up against women—that they show less sense
> of justice than man, that they are less ready to
> submit to the great necessities of life, that they
> are more often influenced in their judgements by
> feelings of affection or hostility—all these would
> be amply accounted for by the modification in the
> formation of their superego which we have already
> inferred. We must not allow ourselves to be

> deflected from such conclusions by the denials
> of the feminists, who are anxious to force us
> to regard the two sexes as completely equal in
> position and worth.[5]

Feminists have been complaining about Freud's own
defective sense of justice since he wrote these lines.
Unfortunately the outrage that women feel at such misogy-
ny has kept us from seeing what there is of truth in the
idea. The portrait of woman with which Freud begins—
that she has a less well-developed sense of justice and
tends more to emotionalism—is a stereotype, the material
of which cutting remarks are made. But a remark could
not cut unless there were some truth in it. What is the
truth in this stereotype of women? It seems to me that
there *is* a sense in which I might feel comfortable with
the proposition that women have a less-strongly internalized ethical sense. A word of caution though: to agree
that women may have weaker superegos is to agree to nothing whatsoever about women's behavior. Women do not
therefore act less ethically. As a matter of fact the
reverse is probably true. Freud was an acute observer of
the individual psyche but he was not particularly good
when it came to the social process, and this is what makes
women careful followers of the rules. More on that later.
Freud's other problem was that he saw women's weaker superegos as arising from their biological make-up. The
title of his article, "Some Psychological Consequences of
the Anatomical Distinction Between the Sexes," clearly
indicates that. In fact it is in women's cultural situation that we find the reasons for this state of affairs.

As Simone de Beauvoir pointed out in *The Second Sex*,
women are reared to be objects, men to be subjects; men *do*
things, women *are* things.[6] A young boy is praised for
catching a ball, for running fast; girls are praised for

looking pretty, being sweet tempered. Active virtues—
such as bravery—are not even appropriate to the female
animal. As a matter of fact people tend to think something is wrong with her if she does exhibit them. Why
was Joan of Arc burned at the stake? As for other sorts
of qualities valued in our Judeo-Christian culture—pa-
tience, forebearance, willingness to forgive—these do
not curb the natural instincts of women, but rather exacerbate her culturally determined condition. Women do not
need to be exhorted to be patient; culture dictates that
we play a passive role in the majority of life situations.
Women do not need a conscience to tell us to turn the
other cheek, we are well schooled in the role of victim
and can play the part without a hitch. What I am saying
is that for women the ethical values of our culture are
often counter-productive. They do not challenge us; *they
have no transformative power.* When the "passive" virtues
are forced on women by the society, to the point that supreme effort is required to do otherwise, why would there
be any need for an internal enforcer, a strong superego?

There is another thing to be said here. Women are
not allowed to participate as actively as men in our culture. Not being full participants in the game women are,
of course, less likely to accept the rules unquestioningly.
A woman is more inclined to be situational in her ethic
and to have an ironic sense about the whole. This aspect
of women's character Elizabeth Janway has called the Crazy
Jane in each of us, after Yeat's anti-heroine.[7]

So it seems there is something to the claim that
women have a less strong superego than men. Of course,
the same thing could be said of any oppressed group within
a society, although the manifestations of the condition
are bound to be as different as the forms of oppression

that brought it about. This thesis needs to be qualified
in at least two ways to be fully descriptive of the situation. First, from my observation, I would say that while
most women seem not to internalize the "official" ethic
in as complete and unquestioning a way as men, we generally do have a strong set of "shoulds" and "oughts" in our
lives. However, these are different from a superego because they are concerned mainly with appearances. Women
do not want to *appear* unethical, just as we do not want to
appear ugly. A lifetime of being the object, the other,
has prepared us for this.

The phenomenology of our experience emerges. We are
caught between Crazy Jane and the Bishop,[8] between the ir-
reverant iconoclast in each of us and the habituated fol-
lower of rules, the professional pleaser of others. The
sad thing is that neither posture touches our core. And
this leads me to my second qualification.

When I first spoke of the technique of paganizing,
and referred to the charge of women being unethical as an
instance of it, I implied, if I did not say outright, that
this was a false charge. Yet the analysis since then has
led only to uncovering the truth in the stereotype. What
of the other side? The question that remains has to do
with the visibility and power of a minority ethic. *Some*
women, out of their experience as women, have developed
an ethic appropriate to themselves. I should add, however,
that the strength of this ethic is contingent upon the
growth of a woman's social, political and psychological
consciousness about herself as a woman. It is necessary
that she realize that others have appropriated the power
of the word, and that women are being defined from a point
of view outside of their own experience. It is further
necessary that she be willing to risk a great deal to

reappropriate the naming power for herself. In spite of
the difficulty of this enterprise, I find an ethical voice
in growing numbers of women. In spite of the fact that
what they value is not valued by those who have power in
society, they have internalized this ethic to the point
that they too have an inner voice that cries "foul" when
the rules are violated, an internal voice that speaks with
such authority that they are driven to act upon it in
spite of the pressures of the moment. This voice demands
only two things: (1) stay in touch with yourself; know
how you feel about things; (2) tell the truth about how
you feel. This ethic, of course, is not the exclusive
property of women,[9] yet it probably does have a special
flavor for us because we arrived at it through women's
experience.

What is distinctive about this ethic is the view of
human relationship that underlies it. It is not a do-for-
others ethic. Women have had enough of that and we know
better than men that "helping" other people can be a way
of controlling them. It is rather an ethic that assumes
the connection—no, the identity—of love for self and
love for others, and furthermore assumes that love grows
naturally from awareness. This obviously remains more of
an ideal than a reality for most of us, and most of us remain somewhere between Crazy Jane and the Bishop, without
real respect for the system, and yet needing, for practical
and personal reasons, to be accepted by those who run it.
Caught between two such antithetical points of view, unable
to express either without qualifying it by the other, we
cannot escape a certain degree of hypocrisy. Perhaps hypocrisy is too strong a word; let us say that the situation
is such that women's communications in the world can never
be unmixed.

Let me illustrate this with specific reference to
academe. The hierarchical structure of the universities,
their competitiveness, the endless testing of power and
authority—these are not familiar ways of being for a woman, especially when she is in the professional role and
is supposed to wield some of this power. She is more ac-
customed to being on the other end of relationships defined by relative power. (The experience of being on the
wrong side of an oppressive relationship is an invaluable
asset, although we seldom include it on our resumes!) All
women in the academic world whether or not they have reflected on it, have had that experience many times over.
Those women who have given it some thought have trouble
mustering full enthusiasm for the various practices that
are pursued in the name of academic excellence, for instance. Such women are more likely to be changed by the
realization that grading is often punitive, arguments
often *ad hominem*, data often manipulated to enhance one
person's reputation over against another's. After a particularly grueling experience with one of these as a student
a woman may be profoundly changed and she will still be affected as a teacher. The next time someone holds up the
standard of academic excellence only half of the woman
salutes. This sense of dislocation—of being only half
saluting—is endemic to women in higher education. We
will not let go of our realizations, even though as yet
we do not have the will or the way to wage a revolution.

There is another facet of this condition that needs
to be explored. This is the constraint women in academe
feel to hide any part of our lives which would cast us in
a specifically female role, and we fear, at the same time,
make us appear less competent academically. The irony is
that in concealing our domestic efforts, women conform to

an old and extremely oppressive stereotype. Let me explain this.

I have two strong visual images in mind. One is a
weightlifter, huge bulging muscles, his face contorted
with effort, sweat streaming off his body. He grasps the
bar of the weight, flexes his fingers two or three times
and lifts it up to shoulder height. Then all the way up
in the air. He totters for just a second under it, before
finding his equilibrium. The crowd roars approval and on
his face pain is mixed with triumph. The contrasting
image is this: a slim young woman, wearing a quite bare
evening dress, is lighting the candles on her dining room
table. The table sparkles with china and silver and crys-
tal. She glitters with gold and red nail lacquer. The
voice of a male announcer is heard: "Mrs. X you have such
lovely hands! No one would ever know that you are a 35-
year-old housewife."

Now, Mrs. X has probably had a hell of a day clean-
ing, baking, running errands, and acting as family chauf-
feur. By the time she gets around to jobs such as candle
lighting she is in all likelihood exhausted and distracted.
At the very least, her mind is full of all the details
necessary for the successful completion of the evening's
dinner party. Yet this woman is held up to us as a winner
precisely because all of her effort has been disguised.
While she has worked like a trojan all day, she appears
to have done nothing more strenuous than strike a match.
She is a model woman because her hands are so smooth that
no one would ever know that she does what she does. Apparently women are to be effortlessly efficient and secretly productive. Interestingly enough, both the weightlifter
and the sophisticated hostess expose their bodies, yet for
very different reasons. The weightlifter would show us how

admirably his is suited to its task. The woman would
defy us to find any sign on her body that would connect
her to her tasks.

     Actually both the weightlifter and the housewife ex-
pend tremendous amounts of energy in doing their jobs. But
the effort of the weightlifter is up-front, and public. He
is heroic in his effort and earns applause for it, while
the woman must conceal her effort to earn the discrete applause allowed her. The best sort of compliment for Mrs.
X is to murmur: "I don't know how you do it." Why? Because, although our society is clearly dependent on the
efforts of women in the homes, factories, offices and
classrooms ot this country, women are not officially acknowledged as productive. Men do; women are. So a woman
can *be* lovely; she can even *have* a lovely home, but there
is no heroism involved in the actual effort she expends
to bring these things about. As a matter of fact she is
embarrassed about her effort. A woman hides her hair
curlers and her work clothes, because both are signs of
the effort she puts out. Even her best friend is an in-
truder when she is washing the kitchen floor. She apologizes for being caught in the act. Of all things, she
apologizes! Can you imagine a man apologizing for being
"caught" driving a truck or wielding an axe? Even so free
a woman as Margaret Mead let herself get caught in the demand to be effortlessly efficient and secretly productive.
I quote from *Blackberry Winter,* an autobiographical work:

> Reo did not like to see me doing the housework,
> which he did not intend to help me with; yet he
> felt it was a reproach to him that I had to do
> it at all. As a result, I became expert at
> tidying up on Sunday morning while appearing
> to give complete attention to what he was saying.
> I would wait for a pause in the conversation to
> slip out and spread one sheet or wash one cup and
> then appear again. In this way I managed to get

> the necessary things done so unobtrusively that
> later, when Gregory Bateson visited our camp on
> the Sepik, he remarked that he had never seen
> me perform a domestic task.[10]

Obviously with any point such as this one can think
of exceptions. Women who are dancers, gymnasts or tennis
players are watched and admired "in-the-act" so to speak.
The point still stands. The weightlifter and the housewife with lovely hands are simply unusually direct images
of what is generally more covert, but still just as determinative in our expectations for men's and women's work.

This attitude toward public effort puts women in a
special bind in the academic world, one of the most competitive of work arenas. The feeling that it is somehow
not right for women to display their efforts may manifest
itself in a deeply-felt reluctance on the part of women
to openly compete, to spread out their accomplishments before male colleagues. We go about our business being effortlessly efficient and secretly productive. Of course
the danger is always that we may be perceived as simply
ineffective.

Naturally the demand that women disguise the effort
behind their work takes a particularly insidious form for
married women and/or women with families who also have
careers in academe. Here the work that must be hidden is
specifically anything that would connect her with traditionally female occupations—housework, childbearing and
so forth. In the nineteenth century women who were pregnant, or nervous, or depressed or simply tired were often
given prescriptions that included bedrest and the strict
avoidance of any use of the mind. According to the then-
current theory of energy conservation in the body, any
activity in the head drained energy from the womb, and
since womb activity was seen as women's principal function,

all efforts were to be made to conserve the energy there.[11]
The same pitting of the womb against the head still seems
to be going on, although women in the academic world feel
it in reverse form. An academic woman is an honorary male
with visiting privileges in a male world and consequently
she must conceal anything that would give away her womb
identity.

When a woman has children in this culture it is still
assumed that the primary responsibility for rearing the
children lies with her. A woman who works is felt to be
abandoning that responsibility and is therefore immediately suspect. A man goes to work also, but this is never
construed as leaving his children. The working woman is
further suspect since, even though she supposedly left the
children, she is perceived by her colleagues as trying to
do two things at once, two full-time jobs. (Most of them,
of course, have full-time wives.) So, any indication on
her part that dealing with the children requires time and
effort is in danger of being perceived as evidence that
she cannot handle her job. The colleges and universities
of course do little to help. Specifically they rarely
provide daycare facilities for faculty families. The
pressure is sometimes more subtle. Women are made to feel
guilty for having children. Somehow their dedication to
their careers is not what it should be. No man is thought
to be less dedicated for wanting to combine career and
children. This obvious inequity is handled by referring
to the great myth of motherhood, spun out in new and more
subtly entrapping forms recently by men who are professors
of child psychology. All of this leaves professional women wary of revealing too much about their involvement with
home and children.

Married women without children have some entangle-

of their own arising out of the requirement that we act
like honorary males. It is a good idea to remember that
an academic woman, no matter how liberated her marriage,
has no wife. Chances are that if anyone does her laundry,
she pays that person to do it. And hiring people to do
these chores is not the same as having a companion who
knows your life well enough to be able to take responsibility for its trivia. A woman's mind whether or not she
has a PhD is full of trivia. She not only knows Shakespeare sonnets by heart, but also knows at any given time
just how much milk there is in the refrigerator. It is
often the case even in a "liberated" marriage that the man
is willing to help only when he is told exactly what to
do. This leaves the woman with all of the details in her
head and the responsibility for day-to-day maintenance
still on her shoulders. Professional women thus have
multiple responsibilities, but they must carefully isolate
the domestic ones from the professional ones. The children
also must not be made to feel that they have less than a
full-time mother.

Obviously it is not a question of the amount of time
one spends at a job, or even of the amount of energy put
into it. And it is certainly not a question of how well
one does the job. The situation that makes women conceal
work related to the home, and that makes men suspect the
professionalism of women who do not, is a classic situation of role conflict. Women in the universities are sex-
ually anomalous because they are doers; they have given
up object status. They therefore are to be treated as
honorary males. When they inadvertently reveal a domestic
world, and one that might brand them as unmistakably female, all the traditional signals are thrown into confusion. So women hide the effort they put out in their

private lives.

   There is a funny quirk in the process here for women who have this honorary male status are still expected
to *look* like women. That is to say they are expected to
be attractive and any woman who is not is fair game for
joksters. The usual assumption is that the books are a
second choice for a woman who could not "get a man". Apparently there is one thing innately satisfying in the
image of a beautiful woman who is also brainy. What satis-
fies, or course, is the element of contradiction as in
talking dogs and crickets who wear top hats. The message
is clear that what our society calls femininity and what
our society calls intellect are antithetical qualities.

   There is a further way in which the prohibition on
public effort complicates the lives of women in the universities. The language of academe is violent and assertive and women are inevitably disadvantaged in speaking
it. Of course the violence in academic life is covert.
It simply would not do for the good professors to actually
come to blows! There are two situations in which violence
is allowed, even expected, by our society: sports and war;
and we should not be surprised to note that these two
systems of approved violence provide the metaphoric base
for much of academic language. We try to *make a point*
against our opponent; to win an argument. (The language
of making points and winning arguments is so frequent
among us its violence goes unnoticed, yet some young people not yet inured to the system wonder aloud why thinking
and arguing get so easily confused.) When faced with a
theory opposing our own, we attack. We try to tear down
the system, to destroy the argument of the other side.
We shoot down those who disagree with us; we slash their
work to pieces. We even wrestle with our own ideas. Re-

search designs are game plans as are our approaches to
the tenure and promotion committees. We have tactics and
plays and turns and above all we *maneuver.*

The covert violence of the language of the professional academic is disturbing in itself, but it becomes
more so when we realize the degree to which it automatically excludes women. In the larger social context sports
and war are almost the exclusive province of men. Women
have no social credibility in these areas. Men go to war
to protect the women and children. Women are hardly considered peers and co-equal competitors when it comes to
things military. Women do compete in sports but as a rule
neither with nor against men. When Billie Jean King and
Bobby Riggs met on the tennis courts, many people considered it something of a joke. In the academic world when
women enter the fray with men, when they try to make a
point or win an argument, they are often treated with the
same assumption of inferiority. However, in academe the
winners and the losers are not so clear cut as in tennis,
so the academic woman is not often as fortunate as Billie
Jean King.

One of the most vexing problems for women competing
in the academic world is the mercurial nature of academic
language. It is a stunning blow when we realize that
the tools of the trade—this language loaded with metaphors
of sports and war—changes fairytale-fashion from singing
sword to witch's pointed hat when a woman appropriates it.
This was brought home to me with great clarity when, as a
graduate sutdent, I heard two men professors debate in a
department colloquium. One began his response to the
other's presentation with: "Now, if my learned opponent
had actually read any of the books we are discussing today...." The rules of male bonding allow for that message

to be sent out and received with at least the appearance
of great good humor among men, but when I tried to think
how that line would sound if delivered by me or any other
woman, I knew it kept coming out somewhere between a bitch
and a whine. I knew then that there was no way I could
play that game. In fact I have learned that this realization of my incompatibility with the system applies to general behavior as well as language. Where a man exhibits
healthy assertiveness, the woman is seen as letting her
bitchiness slip out. Where the man has ambition, the woman is insecure. Where the man is full of energy and
drive, the woman is simply in a frenzy; she is nervous.
The man is spontaneous, the woman disorganized; the man
creative, the woman soft-headed.

When women are aware of this double-bind, they are
left with a sense of being humorless. (If you do not
speak the language, you cannot make jokes and ones made
by others are not particularly funny.) And we are always
on guard. This is part of the larger experience of dislocation I spoke of earlier. Because academic women are
workers in a system that, not only is not designed for us,
but at times is positively antagonistic to us, we cannot
operate in that system in a simple and direct way. All
our communications, like all our perceptions are mixed.
Understood sympathetically, this can be seen as the inevitable result of having to speak in an idiom unsuited to
what we have to say.

One of the ways in which women have responded to the
experience of being marginal in the academic world is by
gravitating to the marginal areas in our disciplines. We
have become interpreters of heresy and exegetes of the
pagan point of view. A friend began her PhD in New Testament studies working on Paul, and ended up writing about

Gnostics. I began my graduate work in philosophy of
relition——I was interested in Kant——and ended up writing
my doctoral dissertation on Haitian Vodou. I have heard
so many women describe similar shifts in their work emphasis. It is a matter, for one thing, of finding a
field in which it is possible to speak with authority and,
more important, to be perceived as authoritative. I find
people much more willing to acknowledge my expertise in
Vodou than they were my expertise in Kant. It used to
puzzle me that there have been so many more women anthro-
pologists than women philosophers. Perhaps one of the
reasons is that women feel a stronger need to escape the
system, that is to find a radically different point of
view from which to critique their culture, than they do to
order and explain that system.

It is the critical distance that women as outsiders
in the academic world are achieving as they become aware
of their situation that sounds the note of promise in all
of this. Women are the heretics and pagans in the academic world, both in relation to tis basic methods and
styles and in relation to its specific subject matters,
and as such we are in a better position than most to be
trenchant critics of the academic system.

FOOTNOTES

[1]See Clifford Geertz, "Religion as a Cultural System," in *Reader in Comparative Religion: An Anthropolo-
gical Approach,* 2d ed., rev., pp. 204-216, edited by William A. Lessa and Evon Z. Vogt (New York: Harper and Row,
1958). In this essay Geertz identifies the symbol system
of religion as the mechanism by which worldview is translated into ethos and ethos into worldview.

[2]See Kate Millett, *Sexual Politics* (New York: Avon
Books, 1970), pp. 298-312, for a lengthy discussion of
sex role learning.

[3]It seems obvious that minority males will, to some
degree, be an exception to this.

[4]Simone de Beauvoir, *The Second Sex,* translated and
edited by H. M. Parshley (New York: Alfred A. Knopf, 1957).
The theme of the "other" can be found throughout the work.
For an introductory definition of the term see pp. xvi-xvii.

[5]Sigmund Freud, "Some Psychological Consequences of
the Anatomical Distinction Between the Sexes," in *Sigmund
Freud: Collected Papers,* vol. v, *Miscellaneous Papers 1888-
1938,* edited by James Strachey (New York: Basic Books, Inc.,
1959), pp. 196-197.

[6]Simone de Beauvoir, *The Second Sex.* An especially
interesting treatment of this theme is found in Chapter
XII, "Childhood," pp. 267-327.

[7]Elizabeth Janeway, "Images of Woman," in *Between
Myth and Morning: Women Awakening* (New York: William
Morrow and Co., Inc., 1975), p. 169.

[8]In one of the Crazy Jane poems of William Butler
Yeats, Jane talks in counterpoint to "the Bishop" who
condemns her life and defends moral rectitude.

[9]This ethical model owes a great deal to the insights of psychotherapy, and shares certain general attitudes with segments of the human potential movement.

[10]Margaret Mead, *Blackberry Winter* (New York: Simon

and Schuster, 1973), p. 182.

[11]Barbara Ehrenreich and Deidre English, *Complaints and Disorders*, Glass Mountain Pamphlet No. 2 (Old Westbury, New York: The Feminist Press, 1973), p. 27.

THE POWER RELATIONSHIP: A VIEW FROM BELOW

ELIZABETH JANEWAY

As my title indicates, I am approaching our discussion with an eye on both members of the power relationship: the powerful, or the governors, at one end and the weak and governed at the other. The subject for this colloquim seems to me—as stated, anyway—to confine itself to the ethics of the governors; and the aims appear to be an exploration of how they will best deal with tensions between personal integrity and the demands of institutional responsibility. To my mind, this concentration produces a surrealistic effect for it confines us to a survey of the inside of the heads of the powerful and a consideration of power as an instrument in the possession of the powerful, usable as they choose and directed solely by their will; in fact, things don't quite work out that way and they haven't quite worked out that way here. One can, like Owen Glendower, call spirits from the vasty deep; but one must also consider the question raised in reply by Hotspur: whether or not the spirits come when summoned. Or, to put it in terms of our topic, any decision taken by a governor or by a powerful elite, on the inside of the head, has to be actuated in the world of reality by others it it is to have a perceptible effect on the course of history. These others must be persuaded to act, or they must accept an order to do so. Even in the latter case, where a government can enforce its fiats, those who carry them out are not automata. I do not wish to belittle the value of personal integrity, nor the need for a code of

ethics to guide the actions of those who sit in the seats
of the mighty. What I am saying is that whatever sort of
decision is made, it is only a first step; and that a code
ot ethics which ignores the context of reality in which it
must operate is useless.

You can put in another way, if you like: "Yes, Virginia, there is a social contract." And I am introducing
the concept for our consideration not only because I'm a
functionalist and a pragmatist, a condition that overtook
me first looking into William James, but also because it
is relevant to our discussion. Indeed, with a little effort I can be fitted under the tent of our title which
includes the words "Institutional Responsibility". What
is the institution to which the powerful must be responsible in American society? Answer: the Constitution, democracy, the will of the people, the social contract with
the governed.

But if we consider this contract, or compact as
Locke preferred to call it, only from the side of the
powerful, we shall be deceiving ourselves, for what the
powerful feel and do is not the whole story. Any relationship is in fact a working partnership aimed at achieving
some goal even if the goal is simply the maintenance of
the status quo. In a partnership each member has effective
influence over the other, though usually the influence is
neither equal nor exactly similar. Each member supplies
input, each member controls something that the other member
needs and knows that he or she needs. The relationship
between governors and governed accords with this description: each needs something from the other, each can therefore be influenced by the other. And because this is so
we cannot talk realistically about the moral and ethical
problems of the governors without paying attention to the

context. Governance is a process of interaction between
governors and governed. Ethical decisions are not made
in a vacuum.

It may be dangerous to say this at a time when it
is all too easy to recall the Watergate question: "But
will it play in Peoria?" Well, I am willing to accept
the risk. I believe that government had better be responsible to its constituents. Of course the real trouble
with the Watergate question is that it did not have to do
with action, but with deception. Erlichman's Peorian was
not being asked to actuate a decision, but to allow the
wool to be pulled over his eyes—(her eyes, too, let's not
be sexist about dupery). When the Nixon Administration
thought about its general public it did so in the same
fashion that P. T. Barnum thought about his. And if we
had had to rely on its sense of ethics and the personal
integrity ot its functionaries, we would be in a bad way.
Fortunately, we didn't. Another factor came into play.
The governed withdrew their consent from these rulers and
the administration fell. That is an example of the powers
of the weak.

Step back in your minds to the preceding administration which was, at this distance anyway, a good deal more
sympathetic. In George Reedy's fine little book *The Twi-
light of the Presidency,* he speaks vividly of the tendency
for presidents to float off into a euphoric empyrean in
which they cease to question the correctness of their own
judgments of things and people and processes; a tendency
which, he goes on to say, is encouraged by the correspond-
ing reluctance of their advisors to challenge this view.

"To put it simply," he writes, "no one is going to
interfere with the presidential exercise of authority

unless the president drools in public or announces on
television that he is Alexander the Great. This reluctance, of course, does not spring merely from awe of high
office or fear of retaliation. At bottom it is a reflection of the ultimate nature of the presidential office—
an environment in which for all practical purposes the
standards of normal conduct are set by the president himself." As Reedy's particular chief executive used to remark, "I'm the only President you've got"; but in fact
extrapolation from a sequence of one is not a useful endeavor, especially for determining standards of normal
conduct. Johnson was indeed the only president we had;
but I think we would do well to reflect on the fact that
we ceased to have him—and by his own decision. He was
by no means a stupid man and over the months of 1967 and
'68, the progressive withdrawal of the consent of the
governed to his actions in Vietnam got home to him. Because he did understand the operation of the power-relationship, he retreated in better order than did his suc-
cessor; but his decision to retire from contention for
another term cannot be said to have been based on ethical
grounds. He went on believing he was right. He had no
doubts about his personal integrity; he just didn't think
he could get elected again.

I want to be very clear about this. Am I suggesting
that it's useless, or irrelevant, to raise the matter of
ethics and personal integrity in a political context, and
that instead we should retreat to a view of politics as
simply "the art of the possible"? That a vulgar sort of
pragmatism which asks first, "but can you get elected?"
is the only proper question. Not at all. But if we are
going to talk about ethics, we have got to accept the
fact that an ethical code is a social, a public, matter.

Personal integrity, tormenting decisions as to what is
right, are tense and difficult because any code—public
or private—is based on social determinants. This is an
axiom. Human creatures are social beings. They are
formed and reared and created as adults by a long, slow
process of socialization, In which they absorb and internalize the values of their cultures, whatever these
may be. I think the formulation that Durkheim made two
generations ago, in *Elementary Forms of the Religious
Life,* is valid—that our sense of the sacred and, descend-
ing from that, our sense of ethics and morality, is an
internalized sense of the power and authority of the social group. I believe that there is no way to extract
oneself from the group—though one may certainly disagree
with a whole range of social myths and behaviors—without
diminishing one's humanity. And, coming back now to the
power-relationship, I believe that its proper operation
depends on the full acceptance of the human value of both
members to it by both members to it—the governors and
the governed. In short, I cannot conceive of a personal
integrity which is not rooted in a sense of one's own
human membership of a larger community, and the full participation in that community of others; including the
weak.

       Let me come back once more to our subject—"Private
and Public Ethics: Tensions Between Personal Integrity
and Institutional Responsibility in American Life." In
the course of ten years or so of writing and thinking
about social mythology, I have grown a bit wary of accepted
definitions. One description of social mythology that I
like (it is a limited one, of course), stems from Josh
Billings' remark that it's better to know nothing than to
know what ain't so. I have found that looking hard at

what we take for granted is a good way to trace out the
structure of our own great network of beliefs. What we
feel we do not have to explain is what we take for granted,
and what we take for granted is the truth of the premises
on which our culture rests: and many of these premises can
be described as things we know that ain't so.

So let me look at our subject, and inquire whether
we are not forcing a dichotomy that is really unproductive.
Perhaps not; but if not, I think we must try to define
what we mean more clearly. *How* do public ethics differ
from private ethics? Must personal integrity *oppose per
se* the obligation of responsibility to the institutions
of government? Where does personal integrity, where do
private ethics come from? I cannot, myself, see any possible source for them except the human relationships which
make up our community of living creatures. The fact that
we have internalized them, so that they feel like instincts,
so that the super-ego has become an organ of mind—well,
that's a very interesting psychological fact; the result,
it would appear, of a long process of evolution in the
species and of maturation in the individual. It is certainly one to be applauded. All I am saying is that I
find it extremely hard to draw a line and say that personal integrity lies on one side and that openness to public
pressures lies on the other. Or might we still call such
public pressure "the consent of the governed"?

Can we take for granted that personal integrity is
always right—always a good thing in the immortal words
of *1066 and All That*? May it not sometimes degenerate
into stubborn insistence on one's own willed, and possibly
quirky, imperatives? When does a refusal to pander to
public opinion become a refusal to respond to the will of
a democratic majority?

In times like ours, times of very rapid social
change, it is easier to raise questions like these than
in periods when a coherent ethical code and its required
behavior has endured long enough to take on an aura of
sanctity. But it is possible for us, today, to compare
the bitter opposition to the war in Vietnam, which convinced Johnson to bow out, with the bitter opposition to
the Second World War which Roosevelt overcame, and which
was seen at the time and pretty generally thereafter to
be a bad thing, selfish, malicious, and irresponsibly
isolationist. Personally I can see the difference between
the two. But believe me, I don't see it as an internal
element—I see it in terms of the ongoing context of history. In my opinion, Roosevelt was right and Johnson was
wrong. But my opinion is based on my perception of what
was going on in the world, and therefore on what a proper
response to these realities demanded of the government of
the United States. That is, my judgment is based on human
estimates of events, not on principles; or rather, not on
principles *alone*. Let me put it this way: the most noble
principle in the world will not provide a solution to a
problem of governance if it is not the relevant, appropriate and overridingly significant principle to apply to the
circumstances.

It seems to me that this leaves us in something of
a box if we try to sort out rules for action by means of
the terms laid down in our subject for discussion. I do
not want to get rid of them I repeat, but I do want to
transcend them. I want to get *outside* the heads of the
powerful and introduce the action process of the power-
relationship into our conversation. What does this relationship consist of? To put it at its simplest, governance is a chore confided to the governors by members of

the body politic because—as Locke described it—man in
a state of nature does not have time to do everything himself. There must be some division of labor. However,
again in Lockean terms, if the governors put their own
interests first, they divide themselves off from the community and forfeit the right to govern. At this point,
the governed should properly withdraw their consent and
declare the social contract null and void.

Leave aside how they do that for the time being.
The point is that *they*, not the powerful, are the proper
judges of public ethics. As far as morality and ethics
go, that should surely be a great relief from tension for
the powerful. It is not their strained nerves which must,
alone, decide the issue and separate right from wrong.
Indeed, this seems to me a much more satisfactory image
of governance than one in which the actions of the powerful are judged solely by their adherence to an ethical
code, as they see it. Unless we have angels with flaming
swords standing around to direct traffic, we are leaving
the interpretation of right and wrong in public action up
to the powerful, if we have no other sanction to apply
beyond their own ethical standards. Frankly, I think we
would be nutty to rely on their moral sense. But there
is another sanction present and operative; the consent of
the governed. It may not always work as well as it should,
but I suspect that that is partly the result of our inattention to its workings and our undervaluation of its effectiveness.

At this point it seems proper to remind you that I
am a woman. Those of us who are members of this central
and ancient group among the category of the weak have had
a different experience of governance from members of the
other sex, from which our rulers are exclusively drawn.

Now, of course, the statement that the powerful in our
society are all male can't be reversed to read all males
are powerful. Many certainly are not. And there are
those who are debarred by a stigma of race or some other
stamp from ever attaining high status and great power in
our society, just as effectively as women are still debarred from the heights. However, it is fair to say that
norms of our society hold out to men the potentiality of
attaining power if they do not exhibit such specific stigma; these norms being based on the idealized experience
of the white middle class, which is the normal and normative rank and status among us. By definition, women cannot attain this status and so do not internalize the potentiality of wielding power as a realistic goal, other
things being equal. It is not a realistic goal for us
under any circumstances. A few women can now expect to
reach levels in industry, the professions and government
where they can exercise some measure of power, but they
are still anomalies.

        I bring this up because it is important to make
clear that my experience comes from a different part of
the forest than does the experience of the other speakers.
I believe that my part of the forest is a fine and fascinating place, and my hope is that, over the course of time—
optimistically, over a short course of time—these woods
and groves and clearings will become as familiar to all as
is the place where men have dwelt.

        At present, however, my understanding of power de-
rives from an existence in which I have to see myself as
one of the governed. I do have access to people in power,
and I can from time to time exercise some influence on a
particular point. If I want to lobby a Senator, he will
usually give me an appointment. I am personally acquainted

with several members of the present Cabinet and that has
also been true a fair number of times in the past. Moreover, I am successful enough at my profession to have some
access to the press. I get interviewed from time to time.
And of course, I write and speak publicly, so my ideas can
get a hearing.

Is that power? Not in male terms. That is, not according to the regular dictionary definition, in which
power is an attribute of the powerful, the capacity to act
independently and to compel obedience. It is power in my
terms, though—in terms of the power-relationship in which
the governed interact with the governors. The ability to
influence the decisions of the powerful without, oneself,
being able to make a controlling decision is one of the
powers of the weak; and it is very familiar to women. Nor
is it one that we will abdicate, in favor of depending on
the ethical code of those more powerful than ourselves.
Why not? Because we know more than they do. Because our
experience takes in territory that is overlooked or obscured by a mist of mythology for them. Because we are
capable human creatures who have much to contribute to the
running of the world, if our contribution can be heard.

Please take my words as a parable. Women, I repeat,
occupy a central position among the governed. Survival
requires us to think about the power relationship as a relationship. We cannot think of exercising power in an un-
inhibited fashion as our wishes may dictate. We are pretty
generally in a negotiating stance. Also, there is for us
very little difference between public and private ethics.
We have not had much opportunity to think and act publicly;
except, of course, as members of the group of the governed.
What we do know, and know very well, is that—as I said at
the beginning—no decision becomes effective unless and un-

til it is made actual by the work of others than the decision-maker. These others may be staff who follow orders; but there must also be a general public acceptance
which validates the decision. And the latter of these
is the most significant.

I described the power-relationship as being one in
which each member wanted something from the other, and,
following Locke, characterized the requirement of the
governed as being governance—taking care of public matters, deciding disputes, providing for public safety, and
so on. That's easy to see. But what do the powerful
want from the governed? Perhaps my parable illustrates
that. They want validation—the validation that turns
power into legitimate authority. This is a very valuable
quality. It means that the governed will agree easily to
the decisions of the governors, that public order is maintained without excessive cost for policing and that a
good deal of lee-way exists for the powerful to move in
directions that may not be immediately popular, but are
required (in their view) by social or economic circumstances. The rulers are trusted by the ruled, and this
trust is something that all rulers very much desire, even
tyrants.

But in order to get it, and here I come round again
to my thesis, the relationship between governors and governed must be a real interaction, trust must flow both
ways, an understanding of the human value of each partner
must be present. And, finally, to get back to our title,
personal integrity has got to be understood in the light
of public responsibility. It cannot be set off from it,
for the guardians of the rights of the people can only
be the people.

I realize that ahead of me, at this point in my argu-

ment, looms the swamp of Rousseauvian belief in the right
responses of natural man. Though I am an optimist, I am
not that much of an optimist. Certainly natural man can
make terrible mistakes, the people can be, and frequently
have been, misled and horrors have resulted. Our modera-
tor might very well put to me the question: is it not a
matter of personal integrity and private ethics to refrain
from misleading the people, to refuse to pander to the
urges of the mob? And I have to answer that, yes, it is
indeed so. I must praise the honor and courage of the
men and women who condemned lynching when that was a mob
recreation; who stood out against fascist repression; who
face arrest in South Africa today for speaking against the
race laws. I do not want to detract from the high values
of these actions.

But I want to go on from them. What happens next,
beyond testament and prophecy? How do we change the world?
There must be leadership—but leadership is not enough.
The leader must reach and activate a group; and that is,
again, a process of interaction and of communal effort.
An emphasis on private ethics and personal integrity would
lead us to describe the role of leader as "speaking for the
group." I want to change that phrase. I ask you to think
of such a leader as speaking with, acting with, the group,
not for them. Ideally, it seems to me, such a leader is
known for the openness and receptivity that he or she
brings to this role, for representation that is also participation in the experience of the group. And though we
may never achieve the ideal, I believe that keeping this
difference in mind is valuable in itself—"with, not for."

An illustration: I will take it this time not from
the woman's movement, but from the interesting book by two
of those present, *Resignation and Protest*, that was sent

to all of us for consideration as we prepared our remarks
for this discussion. I want to look at the case of Cabinet officer who did resign in protest, and did make a
campaign against the administration he left, William
Jennings Bryan. Bryan resigned as Secretary of State
over the issue of a note to be sent to the German government protesting the sinking of the British liner. Lusi-
tania, or, to be exact, the proper response to a German
reply to this note, maintaining that the liner had been
carrying troops and munitions, unknown to the passengers
aboard, and that the act of torpedoing her was undertaken
in self-defense. Pressure was put on Bryan to follow a
tough line. He refused, he resigned, and at once began a
campaign to alert the country to the danger of war. "Every
day for a week after his resignation," write the authors,
Drs. Weisband and Franck (p. 29), "Bryan produced a major
essay on the issues facing the nation.... Most newspapers
vilified or tried to ignore Bryan's arguments, but his
messages continued to pour forth and to command national
attention."

       He would seem to be a hero after the hearts of the
authors of this interesting book. But his campaign failed.
Now, I know we cannot win them all; but it is worth considering the reasons for this failure. And it appears to
me that Bryan failed because he was not able to reach a
group of believers and activate them for an effective
campaign. It is unfortunate, the authors point out, that
an existing group expressing anti-war sentiments did take
him up——and tar him with the brush of bias in the eyes of
the country, for they were German-Americans who were presumed to be acting not as pacifists, but as the descend-
ents of their ancestors. Well, nature abhors a vacuum.
There was no way to stop the German-Americans from coopting

Bryan and selling his words——as they had every right to.
His problem was that there was no other group for him to
work with. He had no constituency. Personal integrity,
private ethics, got him out of office; and his effectiveness stopped right there. ' When he ran in the Nebraska
primary for a place at the next Democratic National Convention, he was beaten.

Weisband and Franck are aware of this question.
"All resigners who choose to carry their campaigns to the
public, and do so over a long haul," they write, "must
calculate whether they can sustain their effort without
the aid of an organized political party." I suggest to
you that they cannot do so effectively without some kind
of organization, party or not; but I repeat that their
relation to this organization can't just be one of demanding support and acting as spokesperson. In 1948, as
our authors go on to remind us, Henry Wallace ran for
president on a third party ticket, which might be seen as
a sort of bastard step-grandchild of Bryan's campaign for
peace. Wallace opposed the cold war as Bryan had opposed
the shooting war, and was vilified as being a power of the
totalitarian forces of Communism as Bryan was for being
a tool of the Kaiser. In the face of these attacks (and
I might say from personal experience in the face of a
great measure of political ineptitude), Wallace got a million popular votes. What happened next was the McCarthy
era.

I did not vote for Wallace myself, I voted for Truman. But not because I was opposed to the public stands
that Wallace was taking or because I doubted his integrity
or his sincerity. I voted against him because I judged
that he was fundamentally a silly man and that he would
not be able to carry out his program effectively even if

he won. I did not take him seriously. But, you may ask,
is such a consideration proper to our debate? I can only
say that I think it is: it is germane to public opinion,
to the perception of leaders by the governed, it is part
of the interaction process of the power relationship. You
can be as ethical as your nature will permit, you can
speak with the tongues of angels for every pulpit; but unless I can be convinced that what you are saying will issue an effective action, I am not going to vote for you.

That is not the end of the matter, of course. I
repeat that my pragmatism may begin with the words, "please
get yourself elected." If does not end there. What I am
saying is, "if you cannot get elected, will you please try
to figure out what is wrong?" To do that, I think, you
must get in touch with us, the governed. We need you.
Our powers are largely negative. I can, and I do, withdraw our consent of your rule and we make this clear in
a variety of ways—beginning perhaps with letters to the
New York Times and the *Washington Post*. But only through
leaders vested with legitimate authority (and that authority is our's to grant), can we see our purposes effectuated.

Equally, these leaders need us. They need our votes,
of course; but they also need to know what we know that
they do not know. We know what is wrong with things, right
now. We know what is not working well. We know the in-
justices that exacerbate us, the limits that inhibit our
ambitions and hopes and so deny to our society the use of
our talents. We know what it is like to work long hours
for short wages, to be refused a chance at promotion for
not very good reasons which may have to do with skin color
or sex or other standards that are no more relevant to the
job in hand than are skin color and sex. We know the
underside of bureaucracy—"the oppressor's wrong, the

proud man's contumely...the law's delay, the insolence
of office, and the spurns that patient merit of the un-
worthy takes." Our leaders need to share, in some fashion,
our knowledge of these burdens of everyday existence—and
to share also the dreams that arch over it. If they convince us that they do share this experience, are sensitive to its meaning, then we will trust them; and that
too they need, most of all.

Where do we factor into our discussion, as defined
by our title, this sense of community and connection? Is
it part of public ethics? If so, I am willing to give
priority to the public side. But in fact, I think it also
touches on the private self of the individual who has a
choice of how to behave in public office; and I ask that
we incorporate into any ideal of "ethical autonomy" the
ability to listen to others, to learn and to conceive the
idea that one can be wrong. I guess it used to be called
humility.

In closing, let me put before you another view on
the right approach to high policy decision. In 1941 Re-
becca West published a book called *Black Lamb and Grey
Falcon*. It is a bit difficult to classify. It is in part
a discussion of Slav culture, with its then still-living
vernacular epic tradition, flowing through a world of feudal loyalties and dooms, of natural artistic expression,
of life lived at a preindustrial tempo. But it is also a
meditation of history, and on movements of historical
choice; choice which West sees as lying between life and
death; life and death of the spirit at the very least,
but in fact, human life and death of the body, for rulers
and ruled both. This choice is signified by her title:
Must we choose to be the black lamb of sacrifice, if we
refuse to take on the role of hawk, of grey falcon?

Well, just like me, she is fighting with the definitions that are ascribed to the conditions signified by
the title. Is this the only choice? And, if it is, what
is the result of choosing? At the end of her book she
cites the national epic of Serbia, which tells of the defeat of the last Serbian Tsar, Lazar, at the hands of the
Turks on the field of Kossovo in 1389. Following are lines
from this poem which she reproduced:

> There flies a grey bird, a falcon,
> From Jerusalem the Holy,
> And in his beak he bears a swallow.
>
> That is no falcon, no grey bird,
> But it is the Saint Elijah,
> He carries no swallow,
> But a book from the Mother of God,
> He comes to the Tsar at Kossovo,
> He lays the book on the Tsar's knees.
> This book without like told the Tsar:
> "Tsar Lazar, of honorable stock,
> Of what kind will you have your kingdom?
> Do you want a heavenly kingdom?
> Do you want an earthly kingdom?
> If you want an earthly kingdom,
> Saddle your horses, tighten your horses' girths,
> Gird on your swords,
> Then put an end to the Turkish attacks,
> And drive out every Turkish soldier.
> But if you want a heavenly kingdom
> Build you a church on Kossovo;
> Build it not with a floor of marble
> But lay down silk and scarlet on the ground,
> Give the Eucharist *and* battle orders to your soldiers;
> For all your soldiers shall be destroyed,
> And you, prince, you shall be destroyed with them."
>
> When the Tsar read the words,
> The Tsar pondered, and he pondered thus:
> "Dear God, where are these things, and how are they?
> What kingdom shall I choose?
> Shall I choose a heavenly kingdom?
> Shall I choose an earthly kingdom?
> If I choose an earthly kingdom,
> An earthly kingdom lasts only a little time
> But a heavenly kingdom will last for eternity and its
> centuries."

> (So [says West] the Tsar chose a heavenly kingdom and
> the ruin of all his people.)
>
> Then the Turks overwhelmed Lazar,
> And the Serbian Tsar Lazer was destroyed,
> And his army was destroyed with him,
> Of seven and seventy thousand soldiers.
>
> All was holy and honorable,
> And the goodness of God was fulfilled. (pp. 1120-21)

Well, the goodness of God was fulfilled, it might
be held, by the Tsar's choice of personal integrity, the
heavenly kingdom, over the earthly kingdom of victory and
liberty for his people; that is, institutional responsibility. In fact, West makes this interpretation in light of
the times in which she was writing. Let me read on, for
a moment.

"Quite without irony it could be said that in Mr.
Neville Chamberlain's Cabinet...all was holy and honorable.
These men were not actuated by cowardice. When they were
forced by the invasion of Poland to declare war on Germany
they did not flinch.... (But) when Mr. Chamberlain spoke at
Birmingham after the German annexation of Czechoslovakia in
March 1939 his voice carried over the radio a curious double
counterpoint. There was one theme which expressed the anger
of a vain man who finds he has been tricked, and there was
another, the main theme, the profounder theme, which sol-
emnly received the certainty of doom and salvation. 'We
shall fight,' came the sharp and shallow note of resentment
against Hitler; 'we shall fight,' sounded the cavernous
secret thought, 'and no doubt we shall be defeated and the
goodness of God shall be fulfilled.' Again the gray falcon
had flown from Jerusalem, and it was to be with the English
as it was with the Christian Slavs; the nation was to have
its throat cut as if it were a black lamb.... We were back
at the rock...in the power of the abominable fantasy which

pretends that bloodshed is peculiarly pleasing to God and
that an act of cruelty to a helpless victim brings down
favor and happiness on earth. We, like the Slavs at Kossovo, had come to a stage when that fantasy becomes a
compulsion to suicide."

Strong language. We must understand it in the context of the time. But such times have come before and may
come again. West is telling us that they establish the
limits to which we can trust the choice of life and death
to our leaders, on the basis of personal integrity and
private ethics. I cannot dissent from the value that has
been placed on ethical autonomy; but I insist that into
that term there be factored the understanding of the human
existence of the others, the governed, and a sense of
community with them. Yes, decisions must be taken; but
unless they are taken with—not for, with—the consent and
validation of the rest of us, they will go astray. If
power tends to currupt, then the corruption feeds on iso-
lation and its cure or preventive is community.

SELECT BIBLIOGRAPHY

BOOKS

Ahmed, Sheikh. *Ethics in Politics*. Karachi, Pakistan: Institute of Arts and Book Production, 1970.

Anderson, John Bayard. *Between Two Worlds: A Congressman's Choice*. Grand Rapids, Michigan: Zondervan Publishing House, 1970

_____, ed. *Congress and Conscience* (essays). Philadelphia: Lippincott, 1970.

_____. *Vision and Betrayal in America*. Waco, Texas: Word Books, 1975.

Appelby, Paul Henson. *Morality and Administration in Democratic Government*. New York: Greenwood Press, 1969.

Arendt, Hannah. *Eichman in Jerusalem*. New York: Viking Press, 1963.

Bailey, Stephen Kemp. *Ethics and the Politician*. Santa Barbara, California: Center for the Study of Democratic Institutions, 1960.

Beard, Edmund. *Congressional Ethics: The View from the House*. Washington: Brookings Institute, 1975.

Bennett, John C. *Foreign Policy in Christian Perspective*. New York: Charles Scriber's Sons, 1966.

Berger, Peter. *Pyramids of Sacrifice: Ethics and Social Change*. New York: Basic Books, 1975.

Boland, John E. *Deciding How to Act in a Political Society: The Ethics of Political Behavior*.

Bok, Sissela. *Lying: Moral Choice in Public and Private Life*. New York: Pantheon Books, 1978.

Burns, Arthur Lee. *Ethics and Deterrence*. London: Institute for Strategic Studies, 1970.

Cunham, Erwin D. *The Ethics of United States Foreign Relations*. Columbia, Missouri: University of Missouri Press, 1966.

Carritt, Edgar Frederick. *Ethical and Political Thinking*. Westport, Connecticut: Greenwood Press, 1973.

Chapman, John Jay. *Practical Agitation*. New York: Johnson Reprint Corporation, 1970 (original, 1900).

Childress, James F. *Civil Disobedience and Political Obligation*. New Haven: Yale University Press, 1971.

Cranston, Maurice. *Politics and Ethics*. London: Wiedenfeld and Nicholson, 1972.

Davis and Good. *Reinhold Niebuhr on Politics*. New York: Charles Scribner's Sons, 1960.

De George, Richard. *Ethics and Society*. Garden City: Anchor Books, 1966.

Douglas, Paul Howard. *Ethics in Government*. Westport, Connecticut: Greenwood Press, 1972.

_____. *In Our Time*. New York: Harcourt, Brace and World, 1968.

Eccles, David McAdam. *Life and Politics: A Moral Diagnosis*. London: Longmans, 1967.

Frederich, Carl Joachim. *The Pathology of Politics: Violence, Betrayal, Corruption, Secrecy and Propaganda*. New York: Harper and Rowe, 1972.

French, Peter. *Individual and Collective Responsibility: The Massacre at My-Lai*. Cambridge, Mass.: 1972.

Frohock, Fred M. *Normative Political Theory*. Englewood Cliffs, New Jersey: Prentice Hall, 1974.

Gordes, Robert. *Politics and Ethics*. Santa Barbara, California: Center for the Study of Democratic Institutions, 1961.

Goodin, Robert E. *The Politics of Rational Man*. London and New York: Wiley, 1976.

Hadley, Arthur Twining. *Standards of Public Morality*.
    New York: Arno Press, 1973.

Hampshire, Stuart. *Public and Private Morality*. New York:
    Cambridge University Press, 1978.

Hanson, Galen. *Candles in Conscience: Ventures in the
    Statecraft of Rigor and Restraint*. Detroit: Harlo
    Press, 1965.

Harding, Phillip S. *Political Morality: A General Theory
    of Politics*. Cambridge, Mass.: Schenkman Publishing
    Company, 1970.

Harwood, Donald, Jr. *Crisis in Confidence: The Impact
    of Watergate*. Boston: Little, Brown, 1974.

Hatfield, Mark. *Between a Rock and A Hard Place*. Waco,
    Texas: Word Books, 1976.

Herz, John. *Political Realism and Political Idealism*.
    Chicago, Illinois: University of Chicago Press, 1951.

Hilsman, Roger and Robert C. Good. *Foreign Policy in the
    Sixties*. Baltimore, Maryland: The Johns Hopkins
    Press, 1965.

Johnson, George. *The Washington Waste-Makers*. Derby,
    Connecticut: Monarch Books, 1963.

Kaplan, Abraham. *American Ethics and Public Policy*. New
    York: Oxford University Press, 1963.

Kaplan, M. A. *On Freedom and Human Dignity: The Impor-
    tance of the Sacred in Politics*. Morristown: General
    Learning Press, 1973.

Larson, David L. *The Puritan Ethic in United States For-
    eign Policy*. Princeton, New Jersey: D. Van Nostrand
    Company, 1966.

Lauterpact, H. *International Law and Human Rights*. New
    York: Praeger, 1950.

Lefever, Ernest, ed. *Morality and Foreign Policy*. Wash.,
    D.C.: Georgetown University Center of Ethics and
    Public Policy, 1977.

_____. *Ethics and United States Foreign Policy*.
New York: Meridan Books, 1957.

_____. *Ethics and World Politics: Four Perspectives*.
Baltimore: The Johns Hopkins Press, 1972.

Little, David. *American Foreign Policy and Moral Rhetoric*.
Council on Religion and International Affairs, 1969.

Long, Ed LeRoy, Jr. *Conscience and Compromise*.   Philadelphia: Westminister, 1954.

Maguire, Daniel C. *The Moral Choice*.   New York: Doubleday
and Company, 1978.

Manheim, J. B. *The Politics Within: A Primer in Political
Attitudes and Behavior*.   Englewood: Prentice Hall,
1975.

McCloskey, Paul N. *Truth and Untruth: Political Deceit
in America*.   New York: Simon and Schuster, 1972.

McCracken, Daniel D. *Public Policy and the Expert*.   New
York: Council on Religion and International Affairs,
1971.

Mellon Symposium, Marquette University. *Moral Values in
Contemporary Public Life*.   Robert B. Ashmore and Lee
C. Rice, eds.   Milwaukee: Department of Philosophy,
Marquette University, 1975.

Meyer, Donald Harvey. *The Instructed Conscience: The
Shaping of the American National Ethic*.   Philadelphia:
University of Pennsylvania Press, 1972.

Meiklejohn, Donald. *Freedom and the Public: Public and
Private Morality in America*.   Syracuse, New York:
Syracuse University Press, 1965.

Miller, William Lee. *Piety Along the Potomac*.   Boston:
Houghton, Mifflin, 1964.

_____. *Of Thee, Nevertheless, I Sing: An Essay on
American Political Values*.   New York: Harcourt, Brace,
Jovanich, 1975.

Mitchison, Naomi Haldane. *The Moral Basis of Politics*.
Port Washington, New York: Kennikat Press, 1971.

Mintz, Morton. *Power Incorporated: Public and Private*

Rulers and How to Make Them Accountable (with Jerry B. Cohen). New York: Viking Press, 1976.

Money-Kyrle, Roger Ernle. *Psychoanalysis and Politics: A Contribution to the Psychology of Politics and Morals.* Westport, Connecticut: Greenwood Press, 1973.

Morgenthau, Hans, Jr. *Politics Among Nations.* New York: Alfred A. Knopf: 1962.

_____. *Truth and Power.* New York: Praeger, 1970.

Mosse, George Lachmann. *The Holy Pretense: A Study of Christianity and Reason of State from William Perkins to John Winthrop.* New York: H. Ferteg, 1968

Murray, John Courtney. *Morality and Modern War.* The Church Peace Union, 1959.

Niebuhr, Reinhold. *Moral Man and Immoral Society.* New York: Scribner's Sons, 1932.

_____. *The Children of Light and Darkness.* New York: Scribner's Sons, 1944.

_____. Complete bibliography in the *Union Seminary Quarterly Review.* Vol. XXVII, No. 1, Fall 1971.

_____. Ronald H. Stone, ed. *Faith and Politics.* New York: G. Brageller, 1968.

Oppenheim, Felix E. *Moral Principles in Political Philosophy.* New York: Random House, 1976.

Orr, John B. and Robert N. Beck. *Ethical Choice.* New York: The Free Press, 1970.

Osgood, Robert. *Ideals and Self-Interest in America's Foreign Relations.* Chicago: University of Chicago Press, 1963.

Parekh, Bhikhu, ed. *The Morality of Politics.* London: Allen and Unwin, 1972.

Payne, Pierre Stephen. *The Corrupt Society: From Ancient Greece to Present Day America.* New York: Praeger, 1975.

Potter, Ralph. *War and Moral Discourse.* Richmond, Virginia: John Knox Press, 1970.

Proal, Louis Joseph. *Political Crime*. Montclair, New
     Jersey: Patterson Smith, 1973.

Russell, Bertrand. *Human Society in Ethics and Politics*.
     New York: Simon and Schuster, 1955.

Thompson, Kenneth. *Christian Ethics and the Dilemma of
     Foreign Policy*. Durham: Duke University Press, 1959.

_____. *Ethics and National Purpose*. Council on Re-
     ligion and International Affiars: New York, 1957.

_____. *The Moral Issue in Statecraft*. Baton Rouge:
     Louisiana State University Press, 1966.

_____. *Understanding World Politics*. Notre Dame: Uni-
     versity of Notre Dame Press, 1975.

Von Eckhardt, Ursula Maria. *The Pursuit of Happiness in
     the Democratic Creed: An Analysis of Political Ethics*.
     New York: Praeger, 1959.

Wallas, Graham. *Human Nature in Politics*. Lincoln: Uni-
     versity of Nebraska Press, 1962.

Weisband, Edward and Thomas M. Franck. *Resignation in
     Protest*. New York: Penguin Books, 1975.

Winters, Francis X. *Politics and Ethics: Patterns in
     Partnership*. New York: Paulist Press, 1975.

Woods, Perry M. *The Statesman and the Politician*. New
     York, Pageant Press, 1959.

ARTICLES

Acheson, Dean. "Morality, Moralism, and Diplomacy," *The
     Yale Review*, XLVII, No. 4, June 1958.

Ake, Claude. "Political Obligation and Political Dissent,"
     Canadian Journal of Political Science, 2:245-55, June
     1969. Reply BERNARD Wand in same 3:158-59, March 1970.

Anonymous. "The Moral Conscience of Daniel Ellsberg,"
     Humanist, 33:20-22, January-February 1973.

Atkinson, Gary. "Rules and Morality," *Southwestern Journal
     of Philosophy*, 3:97-103, Spring 1972.

Baier, Kurt. "The Justification of Governmental Author-
    ity," *Journal of Philosophy*, 69:700-716, November 9,
    1972.

Beran, Harry. "In Defense of the Consent Theory of Poli-
    tical Obligation and Authority," *Ethics*, 87:260-71,
    April 1977.

Barnhart, Joe Edward. "Democracy as Responsibility,"
    Journal of Value Inquiry, 3:281-90, Winter 1969.

Barraclough, Goeffrey. "History, Morals and Politics,"
    International Affairs, XXXIV, No. 1, January 1958.

Bayles, Michael. "The Justifiability of Civil Disobedi-
    ence," *Review of Metaphysics*, 24:3-20, September
    1970.

Bedrau, Hugo. "Civil Disobedience and Personal Responsi-
    bility for Injustice," *Monist*, 54:517-535, December
    1970.

Ben-Dor, Gabriel. Bibliography, "Corruption, Institu-
    tionalization, and Political Development, the Re-
    visionist Theses Revisited," *Comparative Political
    Studies*, 7:63-83, April, 1975.

Berki, R. N. "Machiavellianism: A Philosophical Defense,"
    Ethics, 81:107-27, January 1971.

Bernstein, Barton J. "Road to Watergate and Beyond: The
    Growth and Abuse of Executive Authority Since 1940,"
    Law and Contemporary Problems, 40:58-86, September
    1976.

Betz, Joseph. "Can Civil Disobedience Be Justified?",
    Social Theory and Practice, 1:13-30, Fall 1970.

Bierman, Arthur. "On the Relation Between Politics and
    Morals," *Journal of Social Philosophy*, 3:8-11, April
    1972.

Bishop, George F. "Resolution and Tolerance of Cognitive
    Inconsistency in a Field Situation: Change in Atti-
    tude and Beliefs Following the Watergate Affair,"
    Psychological Reports, 36:747-53, June 1975.

Blackstone, William T. "Civil Disobedience: Is It Justi-
    fied?", *Journal of Social Philosophy*, 8:233-250,
    Summer-Fall 1970.

_____. "The Definition of Civil Disobedience," *Journal of Social Philosophy,* 2:3-5, Fall 1971.

Branch, Taylor. "Team Spirit," *Harpers,* 247:12, September 1973.

Brandt, Richard. "Comment on Reform, Violence and Personal Integrity," *Inquiry,* 14:314-317, Autumn 1971.

Branson, Roy. "Bioethics as Individual and Social: The Scope of a Consulting Progression and Academic Discipline," *Journal of Religious Ethics,* 3:111-139, Spring, 1975.

Braybraske, David. "The Firm But Untidy Correlativity of Rights and Obligations", *Canadian Journal of Philosophy,* 1:351-363, March, 1972.

Bruce, Douglas. "Gamble on Carter's Piety," *Christianity in Crisis,* XXXVI, October 4, 1976.

Bulmer, Thomas I. "Private Politicians and Public Morals," *Twentieth Century,* 177:20-2, 1969.

Cameron, J. K. "The Nature of Institutional Obligation," *Philosophical Quarterly,* 22:318-332, October, 1972.

Carney, Frederick S. "Public and Professional Accountability," *Perkins School of Theology Journal,* 27:13-25, Summer 1974.

Cashdollar, Stanford. "Aristotle's Politics of Morals," *Journal of the History of Philosophy,* 11:145-160, April, 1973.

Chamberlain, Gary L. "The Concept of Compromise in Ernst Troeltsch," *Encounter,* 37:372-378, August 1976.

Clark, Henry W. "Inviolability, Vision and Possibility: Conscientiousness in Politics," *Andover Newton Quarterly,* 13:227-33, January 1973.

Cleobury, Frank Harold. "Personal Religion and Social Responsibility," *The Modern Churchman,* 16:32-6, October 1972.

Coffey, John W. "Political Realism of George F. Kennan," *Thought,* 47:295-306, Summer 1972.

Congressional Quarterly, "Congressional Ethics."

Washington, D.C., 1977.

Cousins, Norman. "Pentagon Papers, Implications of Deceit by Government," *Saturday Review*, 56:16, July 3, 18, and July 10, 1971.

_____. "Truth in Government," *Today's Education*, 63: 20-2, January 1974.

Cox, Archibald. "Reflections and Firestorm," *Saturday Review World*, 1:12-14, March 9, 1974.

Cranston, Maurice. "Ethics and Politics," *Encounter*, 38: 16-26, June 1972.

Carey, Toni Vogel. "Institutional vs Moral Obligation," *Journal of Philosophy*, 74:587-89, October 1977.

Dagger, Richard D. "What is Political Obligation?", *American Political Science Review*, 71:86-94, March 1977.

Davenhaur, Bernard P. "Politics and Coercion," *Philosophy Today*, 21:103-114, Summer 1977.

Davie, William. "Being Prudent and Acting Prudently," *American Philosophical Quarterly*, 10:57-60, January 1973.

Develin, Robert. "The Good Man and The Good Citizen in Aristotle's 'Politics,'" *Phronesis*, 18:71-79, 1973.

Diggs, Bernard James. "The Common Good as Reason for Political Action," *Ethics*, 83:283-93, July 1973.

Dinan, Stephen. "The Moral Nature of Political Obligation," *Dialogue*, 13:28-36, May 1971.

Di Palma, Giuseppe and Herbert McClosky. "Personality and Conformity: The Learning of Political Attitudes," *American Political Science Review*, 64:1054-73, December 1970.

Doss, S. R. "Comment on Military Service and Moral Obligations," *Inquiry*, 14:266-70, Autumn 1971.

Douglass, R. Bruce. "Watergate and Political Realism," *Christian Century*, 91:929-32, October 9, 1974.

Douglas, Paul Howard. "Three Saints in Politics," *American Scholar*, 40:223-32, Spring 1971.

Durham, Barrows.   "Ethics and Social Struggle," *Nation,*
     209:726-9, December 29, 1969.

"Ethics in Local Government," (Symposium) *Public Manage-
     ment,* 57:2-19, June 1975.

Felkner, Donald.   "Forced Expressions of Loyalty and Cog-
     nitive Dissonance," *Education Theory,* 20:30-38,
     Winter 1970.

Feinberg, Jack.   "The Nature and Value of Rights," *Journal
     of Value Inquiry,* 4:263-67, Winter 1970.

_____.   "Duty and Obligation in the Non-Ideal World,"
     Journal of Philosophy, 70:263-75, May 10, 1973.

Fishkin, James and Kenneth Keniston and Catherine Mac-
     Kinnon.   "Moral Reasoning and Political Ideology,"
     Journal of Personality and Social Psychology, 27:
     109-19, July 1973.

Foulk, Gary J.   "Brandt and the Concept of Human Rights,"
     Southwestern Journal of Philosophy, 4:39-42, Summer
     1973.

Frazier, Clyde.   "Between Obedience and Revolution,"
     Philosophy and Public Affairs, 1:315-34, Spring 1972.

Frohock, Fred M.   "Ethics and Politics," *Polity,* 4:530-
     540, 1972.

Goetz, Ronald.   "Private Lives of Public Figures," *Chris-
     tian Century,* 90:821, August 28, 1973.

Garrett, James B. and Wallace, Benjamin.   "Cognitive Con-
     sistency, Repression, Sensitization, and Level of
     Moral Judgment; Reactions of College Students to the
     Watergate Scandal," *Journal of Social Psychology,* 98:
     69-76, February 1976.

Ginsberg, Robert.   "The Right to Privacy vs. The Govern-
     mental Need to Know," *Journal of Social Philosophy,*
     4:5-8, April 1973.

Getlein, Frank.   "Eccentricities of Ethics," *Commonweal,*
     104:228-9, April 15, 1977.

Grady, Robert C.   "Obligation, Consent, and Locke's Right
     to Revolution, Who is to Judge?", *Canadian Journal*

of Political Science, 9:277-92, June 1976.

Granrose, John.   "The Authority of Conscience," *Southern Journal of Philosophy,* 8:205-214, Summer-Fall 1970.

Hare, William.   "Human Rights, Rhetoric and Idle Uses," *Journal of Thought,* 8:138-46, April 1973.

Harrison, John M.   "Media, Men and Morality," *Review of Politics,* 36:250-264, April 1974.

Harrison, Ross.   "No Paradox in Democracy," *Political Studies,* 18:514-17, December 1970.

Harrod, Howard L.   "The Human Center: Moral Discourse in the Social World," *The Journal of Religious Ethics,* Fall 1977.

Horowitz, Robert.   "Breaking the Rules, Ten Ways to Justify Disobedience," *Personalist,* 52:322-34, Spring 1971.

Howard, W. Kenneth.   "Must Public Hands Be Dirty?", *Journal of Value Inquiry,* 11:29-40, September 1977.

Hurst, James Willard.   "Watergate: Some Basic Issues," *Center Magazine,* 7:11-25, January 1974.

Ionescu, Ghita.   "Responsible Government and Responsible Citizens: Six Variations on a Thesis by Machiavelli," *Political Studies,* 23:255-70, June/September 1975.

James, Gene.   "Socrates on Civil Disobedience and Rebellion," *Southern Journal of Philosophy,* 11:119-27, Spring-Summer 1973.

Jenkins, Peter.   "Portrait of a Presidency," (Nixon). *New Statesman,* 87:688-92, May 17, 1974.

Jewitt, Robert.   "Whispered in Private Rooms, Shouted from the Housetops: Watergate and Luke 12:2-3," *Christian Century,* 90:648-50, June 6, 1973.

Johnson, Karen.   "Perspectives on Political Obligation," *Western Political Quarterly,* 27:520-535, September 1974.

Jonas, Hans.   "Freedom of Scientific Inquiry and the Public Interest," *Hastings Center Reports,* 6:15-17, August 1976.

Jonsen, Albert K. and Lewis H. Butler.   "Public Ethics .
     and Policy-Making: The Role of Ethics in the
     Twilight Zone," *Hastings Center Report,* 5:19-31,
     August, 1975.

Kempton, Murray.   "Senators for Sale," *Progressive,* 39:17,
     November 1975.   "Corruption, Conscience and Govern-
     ment," *Commonweal,* 102:6-7+, March 28,
     1975.

Kennan, George.   "Foreign Policy and Christian Conscience,"
     The Atlantic Monthly, CCIII, No. 5, May 1959.

Khatchadourian, Haig.   "Institutions, Practices and Moral
     Rules," *Mind,* 86:479-496, October 1977.

Kipnis, David.   "Does Power Corrupt?", *Journal of Personal-
     ity and Social Psychology,* 24:33-41, October 1972.

Kirk, Russell.   "Persistence of Political Corruption: The
     Greeks had a Word for It," *Century Magazine,* 7:2-7,
     January 1974.

Kristol, Irving.   "Post Watergate Morality, A Dubious Leg-
     acy," *Reader's Digest,* 110:169-71, May 1977.

Ladenson, Robert.   "Legitimate Authority," *American Philo-
     sophical Quarterly,* 9:335-41, October 1972.

Landesman, Bruce.   "The Obligation to Obey the Law,"
     Social Theory and Practice, 2:67-84, Spring 1972.

Larber, Neil.   "Conformity vs. Non-Conformity to Social
     Ethics," *Monist,* 58:674-82, October 1972.

Le Baron, Bentley.   "Three Components of Political Obli-
     gation," *Canadian Journal of Political Science,* 6:
     478-93, September 1973.

Lee, Orlan. "The Right to Do Anything Which Does Not Inter-
     fere With Another's Rights vs. the Unity of Moral and
     Social Order," *Logique et Analyse,* 14:505-15, March-
     June 1971.

Lefever, Earnest W.   "Moralists and U.S. Foreign Policy,"
     Orbis, 16:396-410, Summer 1972.

Lipset, Seymour Martin.   "Paradox of American Politics,"
     Public Interest, 41:142-65, Fall 1975.

Lloyd-Thomas, D. A.   "Political Decision Procedures,"

Proceedings of the Aristotelian Society, 70:141-60, 1969-1970.

Lucas, George. "World Famine and Lifeboat Ethics: Moral Dilemmas in the Formation of Public Policy," *Soundings,* 59:1-137, Spring 1976.

Lyons, David. "The Correlativity of Rights and Duties," *Nous,* 4:45-57, February, 1970.

Magruder, Jeb Stuart. "Ethics Student Rationalizes Watergate," *Christian Century,* 90:723-4, July 4-11, 1973.

Martin, David. "Ethical Commentary and Political Decision: Duty and Discernment," *Theology,* 76:525-31, October 1973

McCarthy, Eugene Joseph. "Pentagon Papers: Games Presidents and Other People Play," *New Republic,* 165:14-17, July 10, 1971.

McCloskey, Henry John. "The Right to Political Power and the Objectivity of Values," *Southern Journal of Philosophy,* 15:101-11, Spring 1977.

Meyer, William J. "Political Ethics and Political Authority," *Ethics,* 86:61-9, October 1975.

Miller, William Lee. "Political Ethics - Then and Now: An Interview," *Center Magazine,* 8:63-8, July 1975.

Moore, Stanley. "Hobbes on Obligation, Moral and Political," *Journal of the History of Philosophy,* 10:29-42, January 1972.

Morganthau, Hans. "Aborted Nixon Revolution: Watergate and the Future of American Politics," *New Republic,* 169:34, September 8, 1973.

_____. "National Interest and Moral Principle in Foreign Policy," *American Scholar,* Spring 1949.

Murn, Sylvia. "Moral Issues in Civil Disobedience," *Dialogue,* 15:33-36, January 1973.

Nelson, Benjamin. "Consciences, Sciences, Structures of Consciousness," *Main Currents,* 29:50-53, November 1972.

Niebuhr, Reinhold. "Our Moral and Spiritual Resources for International Co-operation," *Social Action,* XXII, February 1956.

_____. "The Cultural Crisis of Our Age," *Harvard Business Review*, XXXII, January-February 1954.

_____. "Politics and Morals," *Messenger*, XXII, January 1, 1957.

Nuttall, P. D. "Ethics and the Professions: The Law, Nursing, and Social Work," *Journal of Medical Ethics*, 1:2-4, April 1975.

Olgetree, Thomas. "Values, Obligations and Virtues," *Journal of Religious Ethics*, 4:105-30, Spring 1976.

O'Neil, Kevin. "Law, Order and Disobedience: Some Reflections on the Relation Between Law and Conscience," *Southwestern Journal of Philosophy*, 1:170-86, Spring-Summer 1970.

Padovano, Anthony T. "Authority and Conscience," *Catholic World*, 213:79-82, May 1971.

Parsons, Howard L. "Human Value, Value Conflicts, and Ways of Dealing with Them," *Revolutionary World*, 4/5, 105-113, 1973.

Petras, James. "President Carter and the New Morality," *Monthly Review*, 29:42-50, June 1977.

Platt, Thomas. "Human Dignity and the Conflict of Rights," *Idealistic Studies*, 2:174-81, May 1972.

_____. "Individual Rights in a Rationalized Society: An Instance of Conflicting Ideals," *Journal of Social Philosophy*, 3:4-7, February 1972.

_____. "Watergate and the Democratic Ideal," *Journal of Social Philosophy*, 4:16-19, September 1973.

Plumb, John Harold. "Private Lives, Public Faces; In the Light of the Past," *Horizon*, 16:56-7, Spring 1974.

Pocklington, Thomas. "Protest, Resistance, and Political Obligation," *Canadian Journal of Political Science*, 3:1-17, March 1970.

Potter, Nelson. "The Social and the Causal Concepts of Responsibility," *Southern Journal of Philosophy*, 10:97-99, Spring 1972.

Pratts, Richard. "Moral Questions in the Context of

Today's Rapidly Changing Society," *Journal of Thought,*
5:254-61.

Price, Thomas J.   "Behavior Modes: Towards a Theory of
Decision-Making," *Journal of Politics,* 37:417-35,
May 1975.

Reynolds, Charles H.   "Elements of a Decision Procedure
for Christian Social Ethics," *Harvard Theological Review,* 65:509-30, October 1972.

Robert, Paul Craig.   "Morality and American Foreign Policy,"
Modern Age, 21:153-60, Spring 1977.

Royster, Vermont.   "The Public Morality: Afterthoughts on
Watergate," *American Scholar,* 43:249-59, September
1974.

Russel, Bruce.   "Social Scientist as Political Activist:
The Ethical Dilemmas," *Worldview,* 18:45-49, November
1975.

Salkever, Stephen G.   "Virtue, Obligation and Politics,"
American Political Science Review, 68:78-92, March
1974.

Sampson, Ronald Victor.   "Morals and Politics: The Truth
is Very Simple," *Nation,* 220:584-9, May 17, 1975.

Sandoz, Ellis.   "Political Obligation and the Brutish
in Man," *Review of Politics,* 33:95-121, January 1971.

Sartorius, Ralph.   "Individual Conduct and Social Norms,"
Ethics, 82:200-18, April 1972.

Schanche, Don A.   "Senator Walter Mondale: There Can Be
Morality in Politics," Interview, *Today's Health,*
50:16-19, September 1972.

Searing, Donald D.   "Measuring Politicians' Values: Administration and Assessment of a Ranking Technique
in the British House of Commons," *American Political
Science Review,* 72:65-79, March 1978.

Shinn, Roger L.   "Morality and the Presidency," *Christianity and Crisis,* 34:122-3, July 10, 1974.

Sibley, Mulford.   "Conscience, Law, and the Obligation to
Obey," *Monist,* 54:556-86, October 1970.

Skemp, Joseph Bright.   "Individual and Civic Virtue in
    the Republic," *Phronesis,* 14:107-10, 1969.

Stack, George.   "Kierkegaard: The Self as Ethical Possi-
    bility," *Ethics,* 83-108-25, January 1973.

Stearns, Brenton J.   "Bentham on Public and Private Eth-
    ics," *Canadian Journal of Philosophy,* 5:583-94,
    December 1975.

Stirn, Axel.   "Two Kinds of Moral Responsibility,"
    Journal of the British Society for Phenomenology,
    3:126-34, May 1972.

Stocker, Michael.   "Moral Duties, Institutions and Natur-
    al Facts," *Monist,* 54:602-24, October 1970.

Thompson, Kenneth.   "Moral Reasoning in American Thought
    on War and Peace," *Review of Politics,* 39:386-99,
    July 1977.

_____.   "Moral Values and International Politics,"
    Political Science Quarterly, 88:368-74, September
    1973.

Van Dyke, Vernon.   "Human Rights and the Rights of Groups,"
    American Journal of Political Science, 18:725-41,
    November 1974.

Vidich, Arthur J.   "Political Legitimacy in Bureaucratic
    Society: An Analysis of Watergate," *Social Research,*
    42:778-811, Winter 1975.

Wall, James M.   "Morality Talk Along the Potomac," *Chris-
    tian Century,* 91:923-4, October 9, 1974.

_____.   "Politics and Morality: A Post-Election Inter-
    view with George McGovern," *Christian Century,* 90:
    119-24, January 31, 1973.

Wakefield, Susan.   "Ethics and the Public Service, a Case
    for Individual Responsibility," *Public Administration
    Review,* 36:661-6, November 1976.

Waldo, Dwight.   "Reflections on Public Morality," *Admini-
    stration and Society,* 6:267-82, November 1974.

Walsh, William Henry.   "Social and Personal Factors in
    Morality," *Idealistic Studies,* 1:183-200, Spring,
    1971.

West, Charles.   "Faith, Ethics and Politics," *Dialog*,
     14:169-80, Summer 1975.

Williamson, George, Jr.   "The Pentagon Papers and the
     Desecration of Pragmatica," *Christianity and Crisis*,
     32:99-109, May 1, 1977.

_____.   "Have We Not All Conspired With the Berrigans?",
     Encounter, 33:272-77, Summer 1972.

Weinstein, Michael A.   "Politics and Moral Consciousness,"
     Midwest Journal of Political Science, 14:183-215,
     May 1970.

Wolin, Sheldon.   "The Politics of Self-Disclosure," *Po-
     litical Theory*, 4, 321-34, August 1976.

Zetterbaum, Marvin.   "Self and Political Order," *Inter-
     pretation*, 2:233-46, Winter 1970.

CONTRIBUTORS

Reinhold Niebuhr, Professor of Christian Ethics at Union Theological Seminary, New York City until retirement in 1960.

Ernest W. Lefever, Director of the Ethics and Public Policy Center of Georgetown University, Washington, D.C.

Charles Frankel, Professor of Philosophy and Public Affairs at Columbia University, New York City.

Michael Walzer, Professor of Philosophy at Harvard University, Cambridge, Massachusetts.

David Little, Professor of Ethics and Public Policy at the University of Virginia, Charlottesville, Virginia.

Edward LeRoy Long, Jr., Professor of Christian Ethics, Drew University, Madison, New Jersey.

Thomas M. Franck, Professof of Law, New York University, New York City.

Edward Weisband, Professor of Political Science and Director of International Studies at the State University of New York, Binghamton, New York.

J. Perry Leavell, Jr., Associate Professor of History at Drew University, Madison, New Jersey.

Richard L. Rubenstein, Distinguished Professor in the Department of Religion at Florida State University.

Frank Wolf, Associate Professor of Political Science at Drew University, Madison, New Jersey.

Karen McCarthy Brown, Assistant Professor of the Sociology of Religion at Drew University, Madison, New Jersey.

Elizabeth Janeway, author and culture critic residing in New York City.

Donald G. Jones, Associate Professor of Ethics and Religious Studies at Drew University, Madison, New Jersey.

DATE DUE
